So What's the Good News?

AF149305

THE CATECHIST'S GUIDE TO

READING THE GOSPELS

STEVE MUELLER

Faith Alive Books

Grand Rapids, MI

www.faithalivebooks.com

Faith Alive Books
491 Prestwick Dr. SE
Grand Rapids MI 49546
tel: 616-956-5044
www.faithalivebooks.com

Cover photo by Steve Mueller, *The Book of Kells* (Trinity College Library, Dublin). The four symbolic figures represent the evangelists: Matthew/a winged angel, Mark/a winged lion, Luke/a winged ox, John/an eagle.

ISBN 978-0-9764221-5-0

Contents

AN EARLY GREEK PAPYRUS MANUSCRIPT, CA. AD 200
(Papyrus Bodmer XIV-XV [𝔭⁷⁵] from the Vatican Library)
The text shows the end of Luke's Gospel (ΕΥΑΓΓΕΛΙΟΝ ΚΑΤΑ ΛΟΥΚΑΝ) and
then the beginning of John's Gospel (ΕΥΑΓΓΕΛΙΟΝ ΚΑΤΑ ΙΩΑΝΗΝ, 1:1-6).

The Catechist & the Gospels

*"Read the Gospel. Read a passage of the Gospel every day
and carry a little Gospel with you, in your pocket, in a purse,
to keep it at hand. And there, reading a passage, you will find Jesus.
Everything takes on meaning when you find your treasure there, in the Gospel.
Jesus calls it 'the kingdom of God,' that is, God who reigns in your life,
who is love, peace and joy in every person and in all persons.
To read the Gospel is to find Jesus and to have Christian joy,
which is a gift of the Holy Spirit."*

—*POPE FRANCIS*
Homily, July 27, 2014

As we know, the first words that the main character in a story speaks often give us clues about his character, thought and what he might be doing in the story. And so it is with Jesus. In the earliest written Gospel, that of Mark, Jesus' first words reveal the key elements of his message and ministry: "The time is fulfilled, and the kingdom of God has come near; repent (be converted or changed, Greek: *metanoeite),* and believe (trust, give your loyalty to, Gk: *pisteuete)* in the good news" (1:14-15).

"Thanks be to the Gospel, by means of which we also, who did not see Christ when he came into this world, seem to be with him when we read his deeds."

—*ST. AMBROSE, BISHOP OF MILAN*
Concerning Widows, #61

In this brief programmatic statement, Mark summarizes not only the announcement of the Good News that God was once again coming to rule over the house of Israel but also identifies the proper responses required in response—changing one's life (conversion) because of this message and being loyal to God, the ruler in the community that God wanted. And it is around these four elements—the fulfillment of God's plan, God's forthcoming kingdom, the need for changing our minds and hearts, and how this constitutes "Good News"—that we can learn to read the Gospels more effectively and discover why Jesus' message is "Good News."

Focusing on these elements also helps us as catechists recognize what the Gospels are all about. As we will discover, although there is much about theology and morality in them, the Gospels are not abstract theological treatises or collections of moral guidelines. Rather, they are narratives that proclaim the Good News of our salvation by recounting the story of Jesus of Nazareth, whose life, death and resurrection are the foundation of our Christian way of relating to God. They are also our chief resources for learning who Jesus was and what his mission was. [For a more detailed consideration of this see my book *Who Do You Say I Am? The Catechist's Guide to Jesus in the Gospels* (Faith Alive Books, 2015)].

Moreover, although the Gospels are often represented as documents that we might use to invite others to become followers of Jesus—*to evangelize* as we say today—a careful reading reveals that the Gospels would be very hard to understand without some familiarity with Jesus' story and his expectations for his followers. In other words, the Gospels were not written to convert outsiders but as catechetical documents to deepen the faith of those who have already committed themselves to Jesus and his community by adopting his vision of the world, his values for living in it, and the vocation to continue his mission of bringing the Good News to others.

"At the heart of catechesis we find, in essence, a person, the person of Jesus of Nazareth. Jesus is 'the way, and the truth, and the life,' and Christian living consists in following Christ. Accordingly, **the definitive aim of catechesis is to put people not only in touch but in communion, in intimacy, with Jesus Christ:** only he can lead us to the love of the Father in the Spirit and make us share in the life of the Holy Trinity."

—*POPE JOHN PAUL II*
Catechesis in Our Time (Catechesi Tradendae) (1979), #5

So as we begin our examination of the Gospels, we must constantly keep in mind that they are the original Christian catechetical tools for the ongoing conversion of disciples who are trying to put on "the mind of Christ," Phil 2:5) by following Jesus' example (Jn 13:15) so they can carry on Jesus mission of "disciplizing all nations" (Mt 28:19). They are the original and highly effective way that we have of fulfilling the task of all catechesis as emphasized by Pope St. John Paul II of putting "people not only in touch but in communion, in intimacy, with Jesus Christ."

Thus the goal of this book is to bring you into a closer and deeper relationship with Jesus through your reading, reflecting and responding to these Gospels and their message of Good News.

Craving for News

We live in a new and different world than ever before. And part of what makes our world so different is our addiction to "news." Unlike any previous time in history, global electronic communication inundates us 24/7 with information about what is happening right now all over the world. But the real news that we as Christians are interested in is the Good News that we find presented in the four texts that we call our Gospels, which comes from the Greek word meaning good news.

Unlike readers today who presume that these Gospels are "objective" news reports (as if they were like video tapes of Jesus' life) relating somehow only the "facts" about Jesus and his message, the ancient audience took for granted that these Gospels, like all speech and communication, had a persuasive agenda. They represent the Christian community's memory and message—*the* Good News—about not only the fact but also the meaning or significance of Jesus' life, death and resurrection as the pivotal events in the relationship of humanity and God.

"The proclamation of the gospel is not an ensemble of dogmas and regulations, but rather God's message, addressed, in Christ, to us."
—*CARDINAL JOSEPH RATZINGER (POPE BENEDICT XVI)*
to the Synod of European Bishops (1991)

As we will discover, the Gospels were created to help Christians understand their Christian identity and learn how to be a Christian in a world that was not particularly Christian. So as we read and study the Gospels and let the power of God's Good News work on us, we will also be challenged and changed as we deepen our Christian identity and renew our commitment to Jesus and the community of his followers.

What Makes Something News & Why It's Good

In previous ages, although "news" was less immediate because it took much longer to arrive and was less extensive because its sources and distribution methods were more restricted, nevertheless the process of "news"

THE CATECHIST & THE GOSPELS

gathering and reporting was similar to today because people hungered to know about what was beyond the limits of their own personal and immediate experience. This desire to know more is the driving force of "news." Perhaps the best way to understand what "news" is and what makes it "good" is to consider the dynamic process by which "news" is generated and thus illustrates what "news" is all about.

"News" is a process that generally consists of five distinct and necessary elements that also interact in a temporal sequence to produce it. Since it is a process, we must be careful not to confuse the distinctive elements or think that concentrating only on one element, such as the reporting alone, is enough to make something "news." The basic elements of the "news" process are:

1. The Event

News always begins when something happens. If we happen to be present and witness the event, then it will not be "news" to us, though it might be "news" to others who were not there.

2. Our Absence

When the originating event occurs, it must be outside our direct experience. This is the real key to what makes something "news" because if I experienced the event itself, then I do not need to have someone report to me about something I witnessed. Since so much that happens is not within my direct experience, there is always a need to enlarge my experience by learning about these events beyond my immediate experience. Hence the need and desire for "news" about these events.

"Just as it takes real people to shape Jesus' message, so it takes a 'realistic' or 'connected narrative' to make his message available to those who come along after the eyewitnesses with a need and a desire to see for themselves who this Jesus was."

—*JAN WOJCIK*
The Road To Emmaus: Reading Luke's Gospel (1989)

---

3. The Witness

For the "news" process to occur, there needs to be someone who did witness the event and so can share that experience with others, who can then in turn share it with even more persons. If something happens and there are no witnesses, as trial lawyers know so well, then only conjectures, possible scenarios and theoretical reconstructions of the event are possible.

4. The Report

"News" occurs when the witness reports what happened in the event. The form of the report can be oral (for example face to face or over the phone or via television) or written (whether by hard copy in a memo or letter or newspaper or digitally in an e-mail, text message or over the Internet).

"We cannot know Jesus by direct observation. The lapse of historical time, if nothing else, makes that impossible. We have nothing written by his hand. We are dependent on the records and reports of others and can see him only through their eyes."
—*STEPHEN NEILL*
in *The Jesus Book,* compiled & edited by Michael F. McCauley (1978)

The essential point is that we get the report in some form so we can learn both the facts of the event (the particulars as they are known and understood, often spelled out in the reporter's handy guide for information: who, what, why, when, where, how?) and their significance to us (the meaning, often indicated by some presumption of its interest related to our needs or values). We must also be clear that the actual event is not the report, which is always secondary, removed from the event by time (after the fact) and distance (no longer at the scene), and thus is always derived from and dependent on the event itself.

5. Our Reception

The final stage in the "news" process is our reception. When we receive the report, we respond to the "news" of the reported event and in some way we are always changed either by its acceptance or rejection based on our evaluation, which is usually guided by our interest or need. When we learn some "news," if it is interesting, helpful for our lives or significant for some reason, we consider it as "good news" and will usually accept the changes that might be required by accepting it. But if it is threatening or perceived as harmful to our lives or of no value then we will label it "bad news" and reject it or even try to prevent others from hearing it.

God's Good News

Jesus' announcement of God's rule over our world and of the kingdom

THE CATECHIST & THE GOSPELS

community that will be open to everyone who accepted it, satisfies all the essential elements that make it "news" for us. The originating event of Jesus' Good News is God's hidden but now-being-revealed presence to rule over us, and so create a kingdom where that rule is effective. But this event, because it was beginning to be realized in Jesus' words and deeds, is beyond our immediate experience and so is something that we yearn to know about but do not yet understand. As Jesus once told the Pharisees: "The kingdom of God is not coming with things that can be observed; nor will they say, 'Look, here it is!' or 'There it is!' For, in fact, the kingdom of God is among you" (Lk 17:21).

"Jesus' acts are the signs that God is on the move, the God of creation and of new creation. What he was doing with them was new. New in the same way that his vision of God's kingdom was new. New because newness was what he was about. New exodus. New creation. New life, new hope. A new sense of the power and love of the one true God. Good news. But newness came at a price. Jesus saw that his good news would be bad news to people who had invested heavily in the old ways. He saw this opposition, this suspicion and hostility, and was confronting the powers that held people captive."

—*N. T. WRIGHT*
Simply Good News: Why the Gospel Is News and What Makes It Good (2015)

The witness, of course, is Jesus who brings the report to us about what is beyond our experience but is now available to us through his mediation. He has experienced God's powerful rule in himself and understands how perceiving and responding to it changed his life and will change others' lives too. Once God's powerful presence, God's rule, has been acknowledged, nothing can ever be the same again.

The report or message that Jesus proclaims includes both the fact and the significance of God's rule. The fact is that it is here already, just beginning to be realized and will continue to develop until everything finally comes under God's rule. Its significance is that it both challenges all the familiar social relationships of domination that constitute our human world and also re-configures them in a new "kingdom" community that must be established, nurtured and maintained by his disciples.

The modern term for this characteristic of being already begun but not yet done is "eschatological" (Gk: *eschatos,* the end time of fulfillment toward which the process is moving). So although God's kingdom rule is not an already fully accomplished reality, persons are invited to respond to it by adopting Jesus' kingdom vision or worldview and then committing themselves to the vocation of realizing it in the kingdom community of those who will accept God's rule and live according to its guidelines.

Our reception is what happens after we hear the "news" of God's rule. If we understand Jesus' message as important and relevant for our lives, then God's rule will be "good news" and we will accept it, give our loyal commitment to it and change our lives accordingly. If, on the other hand, we see it as irrelevant or threatening, as many persons not only in the Gospels but also in today's world do, then it will be "bad news" and we will reject it, refuse our commitment and not change. In fact, we might even become actively hostile to make sure that its dangerous effects can't corrupt others or change the status quo of our comfortable world.

Rightly Understanding God's Good News

St. Paul reminds us that "faith comes from what is heard, and what is heard comes through the word of Christ" (Rom 10:17). So likewise for us, our Christian lives begin with hearing God's Good News that Jesus announces to us. Moreover, since our Christian lives hinge on this Good News, it is crucial that we understand what this Good News is, so that we can shape our lives by it and not some "other gospel" (Gal 1:7). For this reason, we must learn what Jesus' Good news is (**information**) so that we can assimilate it and make it our own (**conformation**) so that it can change ourselves, our communities and our world (**transformation**) into the kind of world that God envisions.

Preparing to Read & Study the Gospels

What kind of conclusions would we draw if we approached the Gospels not simply as containers for God's revelation (thus a "deposit" of theology!) but with the premise that not only the content or message but also the form in which the Gospel is proclaimed is crucial for understanding the meaning that God wants to reveal to us? In other words, the form or way that the message is expressed is an essential part of God's revelation. If we adopt this approach, then we will recognize that:

THE CATECHIST & THE GOSPELS

- The Gospels do not just inform us but challenge us to respond to what we are reading and make its vision and values or own.
- Reading the Gospels directs and molds us as Christians (His story is our story!). We must be participants in what we read and not just interested spectators. When we read the Gospels to discover their meaning for us and our lives, we are confronted with a spiritual urgency that requires our complete involvement.

Contexts of Meaning: The Three Worlds of the Gospel

Because the meaning of any word or a text depends on its context, to read a text for its meaning means paying close attention to the contexts in which the text is read. (For more on this see *The Catechist's Guide to Reading Your Bible,* [Faith Alive Books, 2014] especially pp. 39-50, 135-156.) Since every text has three contexts or worlds of meaning, our strategy for Gospel reading must attend to each of these contexts if we are going to get the most out of our engagement with the Gospel texts.

"Each narrative, fictional or historical, provides an alternative story set in a created 'world' that is itself an fresh alternative to the 'world' or 'worlds' previously serving as the boundaries of the reader's imagination."

—*WAYNE BOOTH*
The Company We Keep: An Ethics of Fiction (1988)

The World Behind The Text: The Author & His Audience

This is the historical, cultural, social and literary situation in which the original authors and audiences lived, c. AD 65-95 in the Roman empire. This "world" controls the Gospel's meaning because it was in this situation and in response to the pressing problems of the original audiences that the authors first composed their Gospel texts. We must first ask what their texts *meant then* to the author and these original audiences.

The World of the Text: Jesus & His Disciples

This is the Gospel's narrative story as a whole, describing the ministry, death and resurrection of Jesus of Nazareth c. AD 27 to 30 in Roman Palestine. Each author shaped his version in a particular way to make the desired impression on his readers and transform their lives as Jesus' disciples. Here we must notice the literary form of the text as a narrative and the various techniques that the author uses to achieve his intended results. In a narrative this includes the choice of the beginning, the dramatic action, the plot, character, settings, images, themes and rhetorical strategies (e.g., irony, ambiguity, repetitions, allusions, gaps, echoes, humor, etc.).

The World in Front of the Text: Readers Then & Now

This is the situation of later readers like ourselves who attempt to apply the meanings to their own lives and the problems of their culture and world. In reading the Gospels, we do not just want information about Jesus and his Good News. We want to use his example and his message to shape our lives as his followers—as Christ-ians.

"What is happening in imaginative literature such as a story and poem is the creation of worlds alternative to our own present reality. If we are fascinated into acknowledging the alternative world as part, at least, of what we want to have as our own real world, two horizons merge; that of our prior world and that of the alternative world. In religious language, this is called 'hearing' Scripture."

—*D. J. A. CLINES*
"Story and Poem: The Old Testament as Literature and as Scripture," *Interpretation* 34 (1980)

The Three Worlds of Gospel Text & the Three Parts of This Book

The goal of my book then is to explore with you the meaning and the implications of Jesus' Good News that the forthcoming kingdom of God is here by reading the four Gospel accounts of this life-changing message. The main goal is to encourage you to read the Gospels themselves and engage with them to begin understanding their message and how that message can change your life and the lives of those around you.

The overall format of the book follows the general pattern of the three worlds of the Gospel text outlined above. In **Part 1, God's Good News, Chapters 1-4** offer some basic information about the **world behind the text,** that is, information about the first-century world of the original authors and their audiences. This information describes their world in general, which was so very different from ours in culture and mentality that a broad grasp of its essentials is important for a better understanding of the Gospels.

Chapter 1 briefly examines the first-century Mediterranean social world of Jesus and the first Christians by noting its agrarian character and its subjugation under the domination system of the Roman empire. We describe the four basic organizational and institutional patterns of their social experience—the realms of kinship (families), politics (nations), economics (goods) and religion (gods). Then we explain their historical situation, in particular the fundamental Yahwist worldview and the competing agendas of five groups—the Priests, Pharisees, Essenes, Zealots and Jesus and his followers—that were seeking to reform first-century Judaism and advocating for the best way to live their covenant obligations.

"The past is not only distant, it is in various ways a different world. The basic experiences are different from ours, yet they seemed to the people who experienced them then to be so normal that they did not record things that we would consider to be strange and particularly interesting."

—*BERNARD BAILYN*
On the Teaching and Writing of History (1994)

Chapter 2 examines the meaning and content of Jesus' message that God's kingdom rule is here. We first explore its biblical roots and then how it embodies Jesus' new vision and alternative worldview that can provide the basis for our Christian identity and the guidelines for a new type of community. Once we grasp the content of his kingdom message, we can recognize how this message challenges those who want to accept it.

Chapter 3 spells out what happens when we adopt Jesus's vision or worldview as our own and commit ourselves to realizing it in his alternative kingdom community. If, as Jesus claims, God indeed rules as our Lord (Lat: *dominus*) then not only our personal lives and loyalties must to be reoriented and changed, but the social and cultural institutions of the four social realms must also be reordered. Thus, if God rules, then the father of the family (household) doesn't (the kinship realm); if God rules, then Caesar doesn't (the political realm); if God rules, then the rich don't (the economic realm); if God rules, then the Judean priests and Temple authorities don't (the religious realm); and finally if God rules, then Satan and other gods don't (the cosmic realm).

Chapter 4 explores the reasons why the four different versions of the Gospel were composed and written down, revised, added to and taken in a different direction by each of the evangelists in the last third of the first century. This allows some brief considerations about why the Gospels are similar and yet also why they are quite different from one another.

After these preliminary chapters with background about the New Testament world, **Part 2, The Good News in Four Versions, Chapters 5-8** examines **the world of the text** for each Gospel, i.e., the particular way that each Gospel proclaims the Good News of our salvation as it is realized in Jesus and his ministry. Guided by the six necessary questions that ground the historical-critical method of modern biblical scholarship (author, audience, situation, form, content, function), each chapter considers the particular historical background information about the author, his audience and the situation that gave rise to the need for that Gospel, followed by a critical analysis of the Gospel's structure, style and relation to the other Gospels, together with a brief summary of each author's distinctive portrait of Jesus and of the disciples. Then I offer a brief *Reading Guide* to help you through your initial reading of each Gospel as a complete story and conclude with a final reflection on why it remains important for us to read that Gospel today. Reading the Gospels themselves and engaging with them directly is the only sure way to begin to understand their life-changing message and how that message can change your life.

"Evangelization should not be seen primarily as the communication of doctrine or even a 'message.' It means introducing people to a blessed and liberating union with the Lord Jesus, who lives in the community that cherishes his memory and invokes his spirit. To evangelize, in the catholic understanding of the terms, is never a matter of mere words. It is an invitation to others to enter the community of disciples and to participate in the new consciousness that discipleship alone can bring."
—*AVERY DULLES, SJ*
A Church to Believe In (1982)

Part 3, Good News that Stays News, chapters 9-12 focus on **the world in front of the text,** that is, our response to each Gospel and how we might apply what we have learned to our own lives today.

Chapter 9 considers how Jesus' Good News and the kingdom worldview it embodies serve as the basic Christian vision and the foundation of our Christian vocation as disciples. We explore in greater detail the essential aspects of a discipleship spirituality which demands adopting

Jesus' worldview as our own (the challenge of conversion) and then sharing that worldview with others (the challenge of evangelization). Since our Christian conversion requires re-imagining and reordering our lives, our relationships and our communities according to God's rule by shaping our own discipleship spirituality, we must rely on what we learn from the Gospels as the primary source for this discipleship spirituality. And since our vocation to evangelization moves us to share Jesus' Good News, we must use the Gospels to make sure that we have understood his message so we can communicate it to others. The chapter ends with practical suggestions about how to shape your own gospel spirituality.

Chapter 10 offers information and suggestions about various scholarly resources that can help you continue your exploration of the Gospels through both reading and study. This includes information about various Bible translations, methods and approaches for biblical interpretation, including a basic method for doing comparisons of the synoptic Gospels, and finally suggestions for how to create your own version of "the gospel according to you!"

"The best incentive for sharing the Gospel comes from contemplating it with love, lingering over its pages and reading it with the heart. If we approach it in this way, its beauty will amaze and constantly excite us. But if this is to come about, we need to recover a contemplative spirit which can help us to realize ever anew that we have been entrusted with a treasure which makes us more human and helps us to lead a new life. There is nothing more precious which we can give to others."

—*POPE FRANCIS*
The Joy of the Gospel (2013), #264

Chapter 11 offers suggestions for using a eucharistic format to share the Good News through your personal reflection, with members of your household or with a faith sharing or Bible study group. Questions for your personal reflection and/or for small group discussion are also provided for each chapter of this book.

Finally, **Chapter 12** offers a brief glossary of several important terms related to our Gospel reading and study.

This book, then, is a chance to engage with the Gospels and to think about your own spirituality by seeing it against the spiritualities offered by the evangelists and to take from the Gospels what you need to become a more faithful follower of Jesus. The goal is nicely expressed by St. Paul: "Do not be conformed to this world, but be transformed by the renewing of your minds, so that you may discern what is the will of God—what is good and acceptable and perfect" (Rom 12:2).

By engaging with the Gospels through your reading, reflection, study and prayer, you are invited to use your imagination to enter into Jesus' story, to make that story your own, to enter into a world that is very different from our own and ask: What if that vision of the world described by Jesus in the Gospel is true? What if his story as the Christ becomes the pattern for my story as a Christ-ian? What if, as Jesus proclaims, "The kingdom of God is here?"

"What the gospel writers wrote could only be grasped through imagination. Their message was a source of vision rather than a deposit of doctrine. When we move beyond the confines of 'either/or,' 'is/is not,' and cross the threshold into the world of 'both/and,' 'what if?,' the message of the gospel can indeed become good news to our weary hearts."

—*NORTHROP FRYE*
Educating the Imagination: the Double Vision (1991)

What happens when we discover God's awesome, mysterious, powerful transforming presence? What happens when that powerful presence is found in our own lives and hearts? If we do, then we know that the time of decision is at hand and to shape and reshape our whole lives will be our way of responding to this Good News.

So let us now begin our consideration of God's Good News, always remembering Jesus' advice to his disciples as they tried to unravel his teaching in parables about the mystery of God's kingdom:

"Let anyone with ears to hear listen!"

"Pay attention to what you hear." (Mk 4:23-24)

The Good News in AD 51

Suppose that about AD 51 you were a sufficiently wealthy young man living in the mountains of Lydia in the western central area of the Roman Province of Asia (Turkey today). Ever since boyhood, you had yearned to travel to Corinth for the famous Isthmian Games held every two years—one of the four major panhellenic (all-Greek) competitions drawing athletes from all over their world and second in importance only to the Olympian Games.

So, seizing the opportunity (which only a male in their society could realistically do), with your father's support and blessing you venture forth from your tiny village of a few hundred or so persons, make your way on foot (perhaps with a trusted older slave as companion) with other travellers to the port city of Smyrna and there embark by boat across the Aegean Sea to the booming bustling city of your dreams: Corinth.

Rebuilt by the Romans about a hundred years before, it was now Greece's largest city (population about 200,000) and the crossroads port of the Mediterranean world. Like Los Angeles or New York today, its was socially, ethnically and economically diverse. The fabulously rich, merchants of all kinds, wandering philosophers, sailors, slaves and prostitutes all vied for the attention of its many visitors.

After disembarking at the port, you make your way on foot the last few miles to the city center, where you are overwhelmed by the noise, the number of people bustling about on the streets and the great variety of goods on display in the market. There you remember that you need to purchase a tent in which to stay during the games. So you inquire and finally discover the street of the leatherworkers.

After a brief survey of the shops, you enter into one tiny crowded shop and meet a leatherworker named Paul who has also recently come to Corinth from his city of Tarsus in Cilicia, in the southeastern end of the province. As you talk over the possible tents that might suit your needs, he asks you, "Have you heard the good news?" (Gk: *euangelion*, Lat: *evangelium*). Wary in this strange new atmosphere and not sure what he is talking about, you hesitantly reply, "No. So what is the good news?" Then he says, "The good news is this:

Our Lord	(Gk: *kyrios*/ Lat: *dominus*)
and Savior	(Gk: *sōtēr*/ Lat: *liberator/salvator*)
this son of God	(Gk: *huios theou*/ Lat. *filius divi* or *dei*)
has ushered	
in the new age.	(Gk: *neon aiōn*/ Lat: *novus ordo saeculorum*)
His coming	(Gk: *parousia*/ Lat: *adventus*)
has established	
his kingdom	(Gk: *basilea*/ Lat: *regnum* or *imperium*)
brought justice	(Gk: *dikaiosynē*/ Lat: *justitia*)
and prosperity	(Gk: *eutuxia*/ Lat: *prosperitas*)
peace and security	(Gk: *eirenē kai asphaleia*/ Lat: *pax et securitas*)
to all nations	(Gk: *ta ethnē*/ Lat: *gentes*)
so let us offer	
our obedience	(Gk: *hypakoē*/ Lat: *obedientia*)
and loyalty.	(Gk: *pistis*/ Lat: *fides*)
And to this	
great gift-giver	(Gk: *euergetes*/ Lat: *benefactor*)
who in his mercy	(Gk: *eleos*/ Lat: *clementia*)
has bestowed on us	
all these gifts	(Gk: *charis*/ Lat: *gratia*)
let us give thanks	(Gk: *eucharistein*/ Lat: *gratias agere*)
in the assembly	(Gk: *ekklēsia*/ Lat: *ecclesia*)
and bow down	
in worship	(Gk: *proskynein*/ Lat: *venerare*)
and serve him.	(Gk: *latreuein*/ Lat: *ministrare*)

Surprised, you wonder, who is he talking about? Who is this "lord and savior"? Certainly this "good news" must surely be about the Roman emperor Claudius Caesar, who alone could do such wonderful deeds to benefit all humanity and for whom at one time or another all these terms have been used to describe his highest honor and majesty. Then Paul explains it is not the Roman emperor whom he describes, but rather an obscure Jewish prophet and teacher name Jesus, who is also called the Christ or anointed one. Intrigued by his words, you decide that you might just come back later to discuss this further with him after the games are over.

First Century Yahwisms
A Note on Terminology

The more recent scholarly insight that religion in the first century was not an independent reality as we usually think of it today but always subordinated to the social organizations of family and of politics means that there was no such thing as "Judaism" or "Christianity" as independently organized religions as we think of them today. This creates several problems, e.g., thinking that conversion then meant transferring from one "religion" to another or applying the anachronistic (and therefore misleading) label "Judaism" (which describes later forms of Judaism developed after the destruction of the Jerusalem Temple in AD 70) to describe the complexity of the Israelite covenant people in the first century.

I realize that a change of terminology might be somewhat confusing because it differs from our familiar way of describing the first century religious situation, but it is helpful to make more precise distinctions to understand the diversity Israelite believers or **Yahwists.**

Thus instead using "Judaism" as a general label for all groups, I will distinguish three forms: **Yahwism** (the general belief in Yahweh), **Judahism** (Judean Yahwism) and **Judaism** (Pharisaic Yahwism after AD 70). All these share a common Yahwist belief and covenant, but they advocate distinctive forms of community life and worship. The new labels also reflect the developing nature of Yahwism as it adapted to three major historical phases commonly identified by scholars as: First Temple Judaism (c. 1800–587 BC, from the original ancestors and the exodus from Egypt to the exile), Second Temple Judaism (post-exilic 537 BC–AD 70) and Judaism without a Temple or Pharisaic Judaism (AD 70 to today).

Yahwism (**common Yahwist beliefs and practices**) describes the shared religious orientation of all the groups who give exclusive loyalty to the one God named *Yahweh* (Ex 3:14), the creator of the world and the covenant maker with Israel. Similarly, in our modern world we can identify a religion under one generic label without listing any of its specific traditions or their subsets—thus *Christian* includes Roman Catholics, Protestants, Orthodox Churches; *Muslim* includes Sunni and Shiite branches; *Buddhist* includes Theravada and Mahayana types. So **Yahwism** identifies the shared covenant belief and community guidelines described in the Old Testament books Genesis–Kings, which narrated its ancestral roots and its introduction by Moses (c. 1250 BC), its adoption by the 12 tribes who entered, conquered and ruled the holy land first as a tribal confederation, then as a united kingdom under David and Solomon (c. 1000–922 BC), then as a divided kingdom of Israel in the north and Judah in the south until the conquest of Israel by Assyria (722 BC) and finally the conquest of Judah and the destruction of the first (Solomon's) Temple by the Babylonians in 587 BC. Throughout the centuries, then, many Yahwists resided not just in the holy land but (as is true today) were dispersed (Gk: *diaspora*) throughout Egypt, Mesopotamia and the whole Roman Mediterranean world.

Judahism (**Judean 2nd Temple Yahwism**) identifies the refocused way of being a Yahwist that originated in the Babylonian captivity by the exiled Judahites and was formulated in their Bible (now our Old Testament) and then adopted for community life in the post-exilic, Second Temple era in the territory of Judah (Judea). It emphasized distinctive practices that not only focused on exclusive loyalty to Yahweh but also on exclusive worship of Yahweh only in the Jerusalem Temple (and not in other Yahwist temples in Samaria or Elephantine island in the upper Nile River), together with the zealous keeping of the *Torah* and the enforcing of stringent boundaries to set apart the covenant community in their sacred territory.

Judaism (**Pharisaic Yahwism**) identifies the way of being a Yahwist developed by the Pharisees after the Romans destroyed the Jerusalem temple in AD 70. This form of Judaism adapted to a religious life without the Temple and its sacrifices and without a specific territory. This is the form that developed historically into the Judaisms we find today.

Israelites is an insider's self designation for all those who belong to the Yahwist covenant group (the house of Israel, the people of God as descendants of Abraham) regardless of blood heritage in the twelve tribes or other internal distinctions into different groups like Judeans, Samaritans or Egyptians who had competing beliefs, practices and temples (see the exchange of Jesus and the Samaritan woman in John 4).

THE CATECHIST & THE GOSPELS

"Jews" (derived from "Judah," the tribe and territory where the Judahist Temple was in Jerusalmem) is an outsider or non-Israelite (Gentile) label for all Israelites or Yahwists, even though some of these Israelites might not be Judean Yahwists (Judahists) because they live outside Judea and might not follow some of its specific customs and practices. Thus *from a Gentile outsider's point of view*, the distinction can be made between "Jews" (meaning all Israelite Yahwists) and "Gentiles" (meaning "the other nations" or everyone else who is not an Israelites).

Hebrew identifies the original descendants of Abraham who were liberated from Egypt in the Exodus, but by Jesus' time the term identified not so much a people (an ethnic identity better expressed by *Israelite)* but rather the scholarly language of their holy books (Gk: *biblia),* which was no longer the commonly spoken language (Aramaic) of Palestine, and the adoption of customs arising from these scriptural texts.

Hellenists describes anyone who adopted the Greek language and many cultural, civic and moral customs. Note that Greece was not a single nation but a collection of separate city-states connected by a shared cultural heritage and administrative relations. After the Greeks conquered the Mediterranean world, Yahwists differed about their acceptance of the Greek culture and morality. Hellenism was especially popular with Yahwists in the cities of the Greco-Roman *diaspora* and also in the Judean city of Jerusalem. Thus **Hebrews/Hellenists** (see Acts 6) describes the conflict between two types of Yahwists in the early Jerusalem Christian community and not a conflict between Israelites and Gentiles. This latter form of conflict, **Jew/Greek (Judean/Hellenist)** arose when missionaries like Paul and others began forming communities of both Yahwist (Israelite) and Gentile (non-Israelite) converts in Greek cities, some who wanted the more traditional practices of Judahism (Judean Yahwism) and others who wanted the new Hellenist practices (the Greeks) to be adopted as the dominant practices of the new Christian groups. The Gospels also reflect the mixed character of their audiences resulting from the incorporation of these different backgrounds in one community. This conflict was eventually resolved as Christianity distinguished itself from Pharisaic Judaism in belief, worship and practice over the next century.

The Catechist & the Gospels

Part 1
God's Good News

"The Kingdom of God was what all Israel had been waiting for. It wasn't a new piece of good advice. It wasn't a new political agenda. It wasn't a new type of spirituality. It might eventually lead to advice, agendas and certainly to prayer, but it was itself something more than all of these. It was the good (and extremely dangerous) news that the living God was on the move, and was indeed now coming into his kingdom. And it demanded a definite response. It was God's good news."

—TOM WRIGHT
Mark for Everyone (2008)

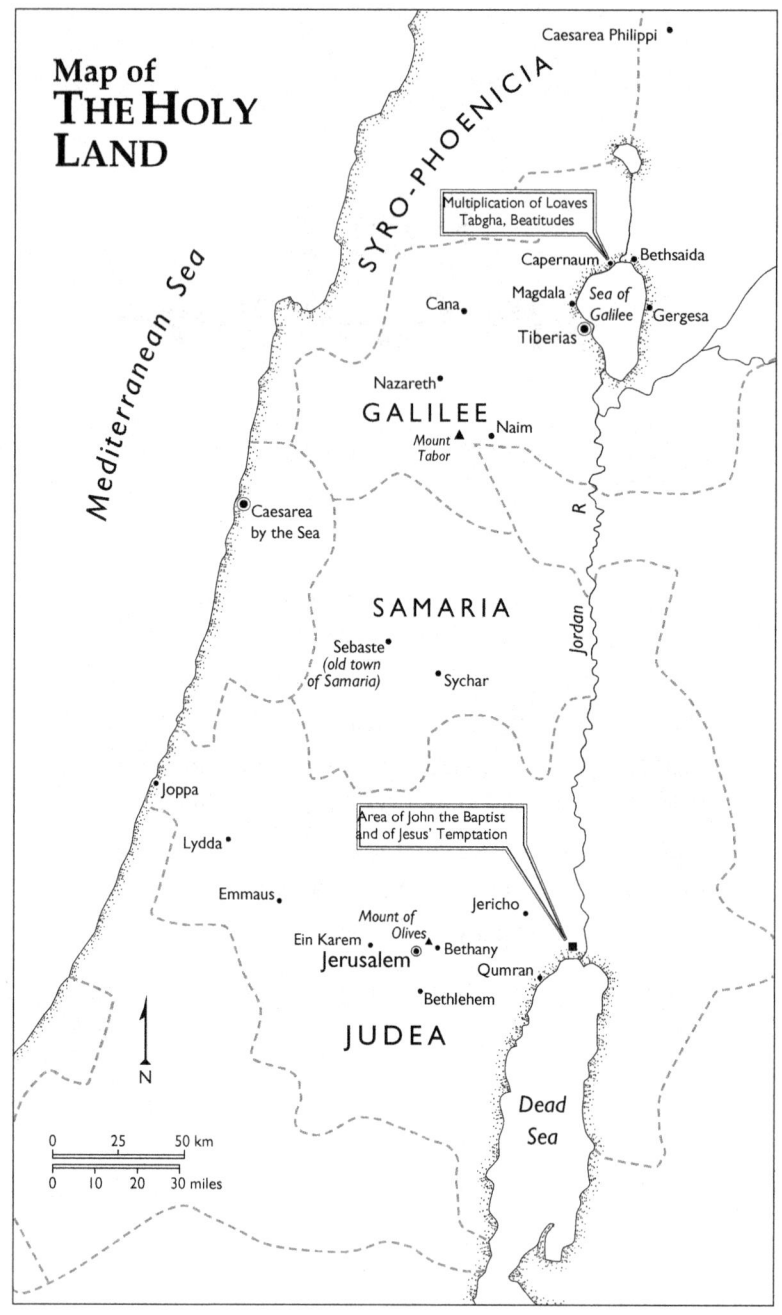

Map of
THE HOLY LAND

Mediterranean Sea

SYRO-PHOENICIA

Caesarea Philippi •

Multiplication of Loaves
Tabgha, Beatitudes

Capernaum • Bethsaida

Magdala

Cana •

Sea of
Galilee

Gergesa

Tiberias

Nazareth •

GALILEE

Mount
Tabor

Naim

Caesarea
by the Sea

SAMARIA

Sebaste •
(old town
of Samaria)

• Sychar

Jordan R.

• Joppa

Lydda •

Area of John the Baptist
and of Jesus' Temptation

Emmaus •

Jericho •

Mount of
Olives

Ein Karem •

Jerusalem

• Bethany

Qumran •

• Bethlehem

JUDEA

N

0   25   50 km

0   10   20   30 miles

Dead
Sea

"The landscape is like a fifth gospel. Torn but still legible."

— *ERNST RENAN*
The Life of Jesus (1864)

CHAPTER ONE

The New Testament Social World
Families, Nations, Goods & Gods

In the first-century world, "good news" referred to the report of something important for the community like a military triumph, the birth or enthronement of a new ruler, or something that had life-changing implications. It occurs a few times in the Old Testament but always refers to the report of an event that the recipients can profit by. Only with the New Testament writers does good news becomes the Good News.

The Good News Then & Now

In the New Testament, "good news" (almost always connected with the words proclaim or bring) is most often identified as the Good News of God's kingdom rule. In the earliest New Testament writings of Paul to his missionary communities starting about AD 50 (some twenty years after Jesus' death and resurrection), he describes himself as the servant of "God's Good News" (Rom 1:1) and his message as the Good News or with variations such as the Good News of God (Rom 15:16), of Christ (Rom 15:19; 1 Cor 9:12), or of God's grace (Acts 20:24).

So by the time of the second generation of Christians (like the four Gospel writers and their communities) some twenty to thirty years later, the "Good News" (gospel) was already a Christian code-word for their message "about Jesus and his resurrection" (Acts 17:18). But because the Gospel writers focused on the story of Jesus, they described Jesus' Good News as not about himself and his resurrection but rather about God's kingdom (or as Matthew likes to say, because he is probably influenced by the Judahist practice not to pronounce God's name directly, *the kingdom of heaven*). So if we want to discover what Jesus' message about God's kingdom meant, then we will have to understand a little more about the first-century context in which it was first proclaimed.

While first-century readers had a lot of first-hand knowledge of kings and empires from their daily lives to understand what Jesus meant by God's kingdom, unfortunately we don't. So we must become more aware of the historical and social context in which Jesus and the evangelists were living and writing because the meaning of what they were trying to communicate depends upon this context. In other words, we must try hard to avoid anachronism and not to project our social world back into theirs, which would make them into twenty-first century persons with our values and experiences instead of their own.

> "It is very difficult to work your way back into another way of thinking, into the mentality of a lost world. So, the first thing about trying to avoid anachronism is to recognize that the past is not only distant, but different, and that it takes a great effort of imagination and substantial knowledge to get back into such remote experiences."
> —*BERNARD BAILYN*
> *On the Teaching and Writing of History* (1994)

Perhaps we might approach this challenge in a slightly different way. Anticipating much of what we will explain in more detail in chapter 2, we might summarize Jesus' message in this way. His proclamation of God's kingdom, which almost all scripture scholars recognize as the core of his message, essentially imagines and describes a new vision of the world under God's rule and a vocation to realize this vision in the nascent community of his followers. Thus, as we will consider further in chapter 3, for those who adopted Jesus' worldview and then lived according to its guidelines, both they and their present world would be transformed into a "new creation" (2 Cor 5:17).

In order to get a sense of how God's kingdom message would affect the basic orientation and social organization of their lives, which is both the main task of this book and also the challenge of Christian conversion, let us examine briefly how their society was structured and how it worked, and then review the historical experience of the early Christians in the first century. This will then allow us to understand why this Good News about God's new rule meant turning their world upside down (Acts 17:6).

The Social World of First-Century Christians
Christians did not create the world they lived in but shared a common social world with many other first-century Mediterranean peoples living

in agrarian societies under the overall domination of the Roman empire. This shared public world was a complicated system of meaning embodied in social institutions. It was organized around certain fixed common concerns established in the past and experienced in complex systems of action and communication, observable practices, common values and structured institutions that together constituted its worldview. Thus their social world and their worldview went together.

Their public social world was most often spatially centered around a common object like a city or a temple and its common life was governed by laws, rules and customs. In particular, the earliest Christians lived under the influence of the Roman-dominated Judean society that was focused on the Jerusalem Temple, administered by the wealthy families of the priestly class and their retainers and servants, and governed by the religious guidelines of the *Torah* or Mosaic Law.

Every society has its distinctive cultural elements that together form its particular worldview, which is the customary way that those who adopt it understand the world, evaluate it and act in it. A group's worldview provides the coherent and ordered understanding of the way things are and how they work by integrating the complex, interlocking network of ideas, values, symbols, aspirations, attitudes and beliefs of those who share it. It has social, political and religious consequences for the group because it supplies the crucial context that determines the meaning, meaningfulness and truth of their shared existence as expressed in and legitimated through its institutions, language and whatever it produces.

As a world of meaning, a cultural worldview is not automatically inherited at birth but must be handed on from generation to generation. It must be learned and assimilated by each individual through education and personal appropriation. Moreover, in addition to its worldview, every society requires larger patterns of organization to facilitate life together as a group. Thus all societies devise particular ways to deal with four general interlocking realms of experience—kinship, politics, economics and religion—with their differentiated categories of understanding, values and patterns of relationship. Together they provide the group with an ordered universe held together by systems of relationships and shared values. So to understand briefly the way the first-century Mediterranean world worked, let us consider first the "logic" that held their agrarian society together and then its distinctive social organization as manifested in these four realms.

Survival and Success in an Agrarian Society

First of all, theirs was an agrarian society based on food production and storage, with a relatively stable technology—not an industrialized society like ours with its highly complex institutions and ever-developing technology. This general agrarian social organization lasted from about 3500 BC to about AD 1700 when new technologies created industrialization. To understand how this ancient agrarian society was structured, and also to recognize how different this social organization was from our present one, let us consider briefly how their agrarian society was organized.

"The agrarian age witnessed an enormous expansion of human populations, made possible by food production and storage. This in turn made possible an enormous increase in the complexity of the division of labor and of social organization: extensive strata of specialists in coercion and violence, on the one hand, and in ritual, doctrine, salvation, therapy and mediation with the transcendent, on the other."

—*ERNST GELLNER*
Nationalism (1997)

The agrarian revolution was triggered by increases in the ability to cultivate land and especially to produce modest surpluses of food for the first time in human history. Controlling and managing these surpluses led to the development of a domination system of power and privilege that exhibited the distinctive and enduring characteristics of patriarchal, hierarchical agrarian societies: fortified cities, nation states ruled by monarchs, state exploitation of farmers, large scale warfare to acquire land and wealth, massive inequalities between elites and peasants, the subordination of women and slavery—all legitimated by various religious belief systems and the raw use of power to dominate and control resources.

In the first century Mediterranean Roman world, more than 95 per cent of all people were peasants living in rural areas who supported themselves by subsistence farming primarily for their household. Survival depended directly on their food production. But since their technology was basic and relatively stable rather than innovative and developing, it imposed severe limits on the production of food and tools. Increases in food production came only by acquiring more land (either by conquest or commerce), which in turn meant getting more laborers to produce food (by enslavement or servitude). Since technology could do little to produce more food, more goods, more security or more wealth, everything was perceived to be in limited supply and life was experienced as a struggle.

Since food production depended on land and labor, owning land was the primary source of wealth. Labor meant that all household members contributed, with occasional help from hired laborers if necessary. In larger groups like villages, cities and nations, a more complex organizing structure arose to create and control surplus food. Thus the "government" or "state" was conceived and dedicated to survival by using its power to control the food surplus and other wealth and then to distribute it—first to the ruler and then the higher ranking "elite" families or households, and then to others down the ladder of social status, always ensuring that the elites got more than the others and that the poorest peasants usually got only enough to survive.

"Agrarian society tends to be organized hierarchically, with each stratum, and its members, jealously guarding its standing and its privileges, and eager to differentiate itself from lower strata which would, given the chance, usurp some of its perks."
—*ERNST GELLNER*
Nationalism (1997)

Because of the limits imposed on production by their technology and by the amount of cultivated land they controlled, both households and governments (which, through taxation, usually controlled the largest surpluses) were never one or two failed harvests away from starvation. Moreover, when famine threatened, people starved according to their rank or status in society, that is, their relationships to those with governing power who controlled surplus food and goods and distributed them according the group's determination of each member's entitlement.

Their sense that everything was limited, like a giant pie, meant that, in order to survive, every household and its members had to be intensely concerned with its rank or social status in the group (called honor) in order to receive its portion of the distribution of benefits and privileges.

THE NEW TESTAMENT WORLD

Thus everyone always had to "know their place" in the complex hierarchy of social relationships and also constantly strive to increase their honor status or rank by working the system of relationships to acquire more honor which in turn led to more wealth and more benefits.

"The correct strategy for any individual or group within this society is to be intensely concerned with its own position or rank, within the social order, and not with the enhancement of output. It is your social standing, your station and its entitlements, which will determine your fate. Extra output is only likely to attract pillage or taxation. It is pointless. Occasionally, extra output may be hidden and used to enhance its owners' security and prospects. But that is rare. More often, the path leads from power to wealth, rather than from wealth to power."

—*ERNST GELLNER*
Nationalism (1997)

The strategy for survival and success meant that each household, through its males, first tried desperately to cling to what they had and then to scramble and claw for a greater share of the limited goods that were distributed by status ranking or "honor." But since all goods were perceived as limited, to get more for oneself or one's household meant others then had less—hence greed (the desire always for "more") and envy (the desire for what others have) were constant sources of much evil (see 1 Tim 6:10) and the cause of much anti-neighborly behavior that jeopardized Israelite community life. This situation of intense public competition (Gk: *agon* or contest) created a strongly *agonistic* society with competition, rivalry and challenges as the essential condition of social existence and survival.

Since households were the primary production unit for food and goods rather than as factories are today, in order for households to get what they needed and could not produce themselves, they had to exchange goods and services with other households, which created the economic substructures of the kinship and political institutions. Economic exchanges were mostly limited to those between local households and then between others in a village market. But as needs arose that could not be filled locally, one ventured to the markets of the larger towns or the big cities where a greater variety and quantity of goods and services, especially those from foreign lands, were exchanged.

A second way that needs were filled was through the relationship pattern of patron and client (patronage), which permeated all the various agrarian cultures of the ancient Mediterranean world (and which we will see in chapter 2 is also the fundamental analogy of the relationship of God and Jesus to humanity). In their highly stratified society, the patron/client system of relationships provided a way for those patrons or heads of households who controlled the necessary and important resources like land, surplus food and other wealth, to enter into a relationship with those in need (clients, dependents). Thus the patron/client system of voluntary relationships based on mutual reciprocity of giving and receiving created intricate social networks of loyalty and dependence between those who controlled resources and those who needed what they had.

"Patrons were powerful individuals who controlled resources and were expected to use their positions to hand out favors to inferiors based on friendship, personal knowledge, and favoritism. Brokers mediated between patrons above and clients below. First-order resources—land, jobs, goods, funds, power—were all controlled by patrons. Second-order resources—strategic contact with or access to patrons—were controlled by brokers who mediated the goods and services a patron had to offer. Clients were those dependent on the largesse of patrons or brokers to survive well in the system. They owed loyalty and public acknowledgment of honor in return. Patronage was voluntary but ideally lifelong."

—*BRUCE J. MALINA & RICHARD L. ROHRBAUGH*
Social Science Commentary on the Synoptic Gospels (1992)

Permeating this social sense of limited good and the networks of dependency established by the patron/client relationship was the extremely high concern regarding male honor and the abhorrence of shame (disregard of honor). Honor described the social recognition publicly acknowledged by the community of a man's self worth and reputation, which established his social status, rank and authority in the community. Honor consisted both of the status of one's household or family (inherited honor) and the status won through one's competitive efforts with others (acquired honor) whether in politics, business, education or especially war. Thus honor, the touchy sensitivity to one's rank and the various strategies of competition and intimidation used to preserve and increase it, became the central value in all agrarian societies because one's survival and privilege (distribution of benefits) depended on one's social rank.

THE NEW TESTAMENT WORLD

But since honor could belong only to males, the main threats to a man's honor came from direct competition with other men who were always trying to increase their honor at his expense. Since everything was in limited supply, when one man's honor increased, another man's honor decreased. But a man's honor also had to be the concern of his household. Since wives were the primary source of legitimate children for family survival and daughters were a primary way to establish and maintain peaceful relations with other households through marriage, women had a serious potential for a man's loss of honor. Women had to be guarded lest they bring dishonor *(shame)* on the man of the household by not being sufficiently attentive to protecting the family's honor status or social ranking. Thus a social system of gendered space, the public realm for males and a private realm for females, was established and maintained.

"Honor can be understood as the status one claims in the community together with the all-important recognition of that claim by others. It thus serves as an indicator of social standing, enabling persons to interact with their social superiors, equals, and inferiors in certain ways prescribed by society."

—*BRUCE J. MALINA & RICHARD L. ROHRBAUGH*
Social-Science Commentary on the Synoptic Gospels (1992)

Males were outwardly oriented toward the public life of the village. Their world concerned the family fields, the marketplace, law courts and assemblies where political, social and economic issues were debated and policies enacted. Females were inwardly oriented toward the household, where family life, with its childbearing and nurturing, food production and preparation consumed their energy. Thus men and women lived for all practical purposes in two independently organized worlds that, like two circles, touched only tangentially and seldom overlapped.

The constant competition for limited goods, especially for honor, created a society in which every public interaction between men carried with it the potential for gaining or losing honor for the man and for his household. Thus every male learned early in life how to participate in this ritualized social combat for the limited quantity of honor, power, wealth and status available in the village. This competitive, contentious, agonistic attitude was the reason Jesus' opponents constantly tried to bait and trap him into saying something foolish or not being able to answer at all. The Gospels portray Jesus as a teacher with a razor-sharp wit, whose clever answers and memorable one-liners contributed to his honor status and certainly delighted his first-century audience as much as they do us today.

"Just as concern for money is perpetual and pervasive in American society, so was the concern about honor in the world of the Gospels. In this competition for honor the game of challenge-riposte is a central phenomenon that must always be played out in public. It consists of a challenge (almost any word, gesture, or action) that seeks to undermine the honor of another person and a response that answers in equal measure or ups the ante (and thereby challenges in return). Both positive (gifts, compliments) and negative (insults, dares) challenges must be answered to avoid a serious loss of face."

—BRUCE J. MALINA & RICHARD L. ROHRBAUGH
Social-Science Commentary on the Synoptic Gospels (1992)

The Four Organizational Patterns of Agrarian Society

As noted earlier, every society develops institutions to organize the four major realms of social experience by using its power to ensure the community's survival and success: the reproduction and nurturing of life (kinship/household), the maintenance of life together (politics/nation or city), the distribution of food and exchange of goods (economics/markets), and the effective contact with the divine (religion/coherent ideology).

In the first-century world, kinship, which focused on the household or family, and politics, which focused on the larger group (villages, cities, nations), were the only formally developed and thus somewhat independent institutions, with economics and religion always dependent and subordinate to them. This meant that there was no such thing as "religion" in general but only family religion (related to the kinship group and its well-being) or civic religion (related to the political group and its well-being).

Likewise, there was no general "economics" but rather only a family economics for the household and a civic economics for the political group. This is very different from our society in which after the 18th century all four realms developed into complex, distinct and highly differentiated realms—thus creating capitalism and market economies and the separation of church and state, all of which would have been impossible to imagine in the first-century world.

THE NEW TESTAMENT WORLD

If we consider the characteristics, concerns and roles of each of these four realms that delineate their social world, we will better appreciate how Jesus' message of an alternative society would confront, challenge and contrast with the dominant social world into which he was thrust.

Kinship was the realm of the household (whether nuclear or extended), which included the head (lord or master) of the household (Gk: *kyrios,* Lat: *paterfamilas)* who had the legal controlling power (Lat: *patria potestas)* over all the members of the household (wife, children, freedmen, servants, slaves and visitors together with all family land, possessions and businesses). The patron used his power to provide and protect the family members and ensure the family's survival through the begetting and nurturing of children. The primary value that kinship fostered was belonging, which was expressed through the mutual loyalty, commitment, care and trust of the family members. Kinship or "blood" bonds were the strongest and most emotionally charged relationships of all.

Politics was the realm of the larger group (village, town, city, tribal confederacy, nation or empire) whose purpose was to use power to coordinate the efforts of the group in the most effective ways to secure the well-being of the group. Normally this meant finding the best way to protect themselves (armies) and secure the goods they needed (economics of surplus and trade) to survive. Various forms of political organization existed for governing with authority and power: by a king (monarchy), a group (oligarchy) such as priests (hierocracy), the best families (aristocracy) or the male group members (democracy). Politics offered the primary value of a stable (and often enduring) social structure that was normally articulated in the system of law that characterized group life.

Economics was not an independent realm but either familial when embedded in the household or civic when related to political institutions and goals. The concern of economics was to have the goods (wealth) and services necessary for the general well-being and survival of either the household or the group. When those goods were not available, then exchange (trade, barter) was necessary. Groups often provided specific places (markets) where the exchanges could be made and found ways to facilitate the exchanges (coinage, bills of sale, loans). The primary value that economics offered was the ability to acquire through exchange the things that were needed for one's well-being and survival.

Religion was the realm that described and facilitated the relationship with the gods and the divine order of creation (piety, worship, sacrifice). Like economics, it was carried on either in the household (family religion) and in the political group (civic religion). Since the ultimate meaning of human life and its institutions could only be grasped in relation to a larger context, religion provided a coherent picture of how our world was related to the divine order. The primary value that religion provided was the rational structure or ideology that guided people in relation to the divine and legitimated the existence of institutions that coincided with the divinely established order. Thus it could also be used to legitimate the inequalities and suffering institutionalized in a domination system.

Power, Privilege & Domination Systems

Beyond just describing these important social realms, it is important to notice that their existence also creates something that will be crucial in understanding Jesus' proposal of an alternative social organization: the structured inequality of power and privilege called a domination system. This is a modern term that identifies a social system that is based on the dominance of one group over another. The word *domination* comes from the Latin word for a master or lord *(dominus)*. (We must distinguish here between simple hierarchies, which every society will have, and domination systems which are inherently unjust and legitimated by violence.)

"Imperial power actually rested upon patronage. The emperor was the patron, the benefactor, of his every subject. The subjects, in turn, paid him back for his bene-factions with their loyalty; this was the basis of his power. Thus, the empire was a single enormous spider's web of reciprocal favors."

—J. E. LENDON
Empire of Honour: The Art of Government in the Roman World (1997)

In order to know who is to dominate whom, a domination system is rooted in the initial categorization of dyadic groups (us/them, male/female, strong/weak, rich/poor, citizens/non-citizens, haves/have nots) that generates a related dyadic valuing system (one group is better and more valuable than the other) and a hierarchical ranking system (one group should rule over the other) as the basis for privileges (one group is entitled to get food and additional goods that others don't). Since a domination system establishes essentially unjust social relationships that assume that one group is entitled to rule or dominate another, it requires that power (whether in actual violence or the threat of violence) must be continually applied to hold the essentially unjust system together. Thus domination systems rule by power and privilege, favor and fear.

Historically, domination systems proliferated and intensified about 3500 BC when social organization changed from nomadic forms to more complex agrarian forms. When the non-farming warriors use their military power to control farmers and their surplus food supply, this dominance was concretized in a social system in which their minority group can continue to control the conquered majority and distribute food and goods according to hierarchical ranking, that is by social status or honor.

"The world into which Jesus was born was a world of domination. The rich dominated the poor; men, women; Romans, their subjects. Power was patriarchal, hierarchical, autocratic, and androcratic, and was exerted through conquest, deception, competition, and force. Violence and war were regarded as inevitable and redemptive. Ethnic barriers separated Jew from Gentile. Status distinctions were jealously preserved; a man's place at a banquet was a delicate matter of relative ranking. The more powerful surrounded themselves with clients; patrons exercised control through honor and shaming, gifts and obligations. Slavery was ubiquitous. Women's reproductive capacities and sexual expression were subject to male control, and their freedom in relationships and movement were sharply circumscribed. Divine beings were scarcely distinguishable from human tyrants, demanding propitiation by means of bloody sacrifices. A coterie of priests held a monopoly on temple wealth and power. Nature itself existed to be exploited by a single one of its species."

—*WALTER WINK*
"Jesus and the Domination System" in *SBL 1991 Seminar Papers* (1991)

Thus, although power (the ability to get done what is necessary for survival and success) is essential in each of the four realms, the important question is not simply about the use of power but about the goal to which the power is directed or for which the power is used. Unfortunately for many societies, this goal—although seldom will it be admitted or even recognized as such—is nothing more than the continuation of the domination systems that are embedded in the fabric of its life.

Since domination systems are often crucial for the way a society is organized, societies have devised many ways to legitimate and explain why those domination systems are "natural" or the way the society "ought to be." Another way of saying this is that most often domination systems are not consciously perceived by the system's members, especially those who benefit most from society's privileges. Thus nothing drives the system to change unless those who are privileged by their membership in the hierarchy perceive their privileges as a source of dis-ease that must be changed.

Another aspect of domination systems is that they become embedded in the particular worldview of the social group. Consequently, when that worldview is challenged by a new worldview, the two worldviews cannot exist in harmony. Thus one must be rejected and the other embraced.

Although we will examine this in more detail in chapter 3, we can note here that, because domination systems permeate all realms of the social system, when Jesus announces his new kind of kingdom community it will challenge the legitimacy and power of the domination systems that already control each social realm. Jesus proclaims an alternative kingdom community with new types of social organizations that challenge the current domination system assumptions—dualistic categories and values, one-up one down ranking, and social roles institutionalizing dominance.

"The gospel has a very specific context, even if it has been essentially the same context for five thousand years: the Domination System. And the gospel has a specific purpose to that system: the liberating message of Jesus. *The gospel is a context-specific remedy for the evils of the Domination System.* This means that the overthrow of any particular manifestation of oppression can never satisfy the demands of the gospels if what replaces one form of domination is simply another. The gospel is thus permanently critical of every political program, reform and revolution."

—*WALTER WINK*
Engaging the Powers: Discernment and Resistance in a World of Domination (1992)

While all social realms rely on power, the key question is *power for what*—the desired goal directs how power is used. In Jesus' proclamation of God's rule, God uses power to create and maintain right/just relationships —God's plan is to restore the originally ordered creation, distorted by evil and human sinfulness, through God's agent (Jesus the messiah) with the cooperation of those who will join with him.

33

Assumptions of the Domination System

The need to control society, the church, the group and prevent chaos requires some persons to dominate others.

Those who dominate may use other people as a means to achieve their goals.

Men are better equipped by nature to be dominant than women, and some races are naturally suited to dominate others.

A valued end justifies the use of any means.

Violence is redemptive, the only language enemies understand.

Ruling or managing is the most important of all social functions.

Therefore rulers and managers should be rewarded by extra privileges and greater wealth of all kinds.

Those who have military strength, who control the most advanced technology, the greatest wealth, or the largest markets, are the ones who will and should survive.

Money is the most important value.

The possession of money is a sign and proof of political and social worth.

The production of material goods is more important than the production of healthy and normal people and of sound human relationships (or the former automatically produces the latter).

Property is sacred, and property ownership is an absolute right.

In an organization or nation, great size is proof of its power and value.

Institutions are more important than people.

There is no higher value or being or power than the state, church, group. If there is a God, God is the protector and patron of the state.

God, if there is one, is not revealed to all, but only to select individuals or nations and their rulers and priesthood.

[This page and the page opposite are adapted from Walter Wink, *Engaging the Powers: Discernment and Resistance in a World of Domination* (Fortress Press, 1992), pp. 46-47, 95-96.]

Comparison of Domination and Non-Domination Ways

Gender differences	Patriarchal; difference implies superior/inferior	Equality of sexes; differences may lead to specialization but not to ranking
Power	Power over; power to take life, control, destroy Win-lose Domination Competition	Power with; power to give, support, nurture life Win-Win Partnership Completion/cooperation
Politics	Conquest Autocracy Authoritarian Bureaucratic	Diplomacy Democracy Enabling Decentralized
Economics	Exploitation, greed, privilege, inequality	Sharing, sufficiency, responsibility, equality
Religion	Male God images— jealous, wrathful, punishing, lawgiving	Inclusive God-images— mother/father, loving/judging compassionate/severe, merciful/demanding
Relationships	Ranking Domination hierarchies Slavery, classism, racism We/they Rigidity	Linking Actualization hierarchies Equal opportunity We/we Flexibility
Change mode	Violence, force, war exclusiveness violent conflict resolution	Non-violence, negotiation inclusiveness non-violent conflict resolution
Ecological stance	Exploitation, control, contempt	Harmony, cooperation, respect
Logic	Either/or, analytic	Both/and, analytic/synthetic
Role of Ego	Self-centered	Affiliation-oriented
Education	Indoctrinating	Enabling
Sexual Responsibility	Subordination of women's reproductive capacities and sexual expression to male control	Control of sexuality by individuals in the light of community values
Eschatology	Status quo, holding and keeping power; "this world," "this evil age"	Cultural transformation, sharing power, the reign of God, the coming age, "new creation"
	Eternity in the future, injustice in the present	Eternity in the present, justice in the future

The Domination System of the Roman Empire: Fewer Have More

In Jesus' time, the Roman empire extended over the whole Mediterranean area and ruled about 45 million people (of whom 4 million or so were actual Roman citizens). Its primary concern was with a general system of economic exploitation laid over the local governing authority, which Rome allowed to continue as long as the Roman demand for taxation in the form of tribute (especially food) and various taxes were paid.

"It is best not to overstate the responsibilities and abilities of Roman government. Its aims were limited: the gathering of taxes, the fielding of an army, and the maintenance of civil peace—that is, the prevention of civil war and major riot. Justice also was administered, at least to those whose wealth, influence, or misdeeds secured them a place on the governors' overloaded court schedule. The Roman government did not undertake to provide food, housing, mass education, or any of the manifold social services taken for granted from modern governments, the supply of grain, water, and amusements to a few great cities notwithstanding. It is, then, unsurprising that the Roman government did not bulk very large in the consciousness of a majority of its subjects, who had, from week to week and month to month, few, if any, dealings with it at all."

—*J. E. LENDON*
Empire of Honour: The Art of Government in the Roman World (1997)

The Roman empire, like every other political system in the agrarian world, was predicated on the feeding (survival) and well-being (wealth, goods, etc.) of its citizens—note that Rome was a city and not a "nation." Thus it had to feed its citizens, and to do this it needed land—which explains its constant expansion by conquest, which was the foundation of its imperial system—using its growing power to benefit its citizens by acquiring more territory and then controlling and exploiting its resources by forced taxation (the goal was the plunder of land not its development).

The function of the Roman imperial political-economic system, as the eminent classical scholar Ramsay Macmullen described it in his book on *Roman Social Relations: 50 BC to AD 284,* was to funnel the food and wealth from all over their vast empire back to Rome in a process whereby "fewer had more." Then this plunder, which technically belonged to the emperor (the father/patron of the Romans), was bestowed as benefits first to the wealthy senatorial families who composed the ruling class and then trickling down through the other various ranks of citizens.

The result was three general social categories: the **"have nots"** (the rural peasants who produced the food but whose surplus was taken from them—by force if necessary—through taxes); the **"haves"** (especially the wealthy land owners who profited from their relationship to the emperor through patronage relationships); and finally the **"have mores"** (the very special class—the top .01%—that included the super rich senatorial families of Rome who received the greatest benefits of imperial patronage). There is a biblical description of this Roman exploitation of the world's goods in the book of Revelation where the merchants mourn the swift and surprising fall of Babylon (i.e., Rome) with all its immense wealth and luxury (Rev 18:11-17).

> "The Roman elite assumed that since they possessed the power, they could use it to subject other peoples of the world and to extract resources from them. Peoples who dared oppose the Roman imperial order were simply terrorized with intimidating military violence. Imperial conquests left villages devastated, families disrupted, and survivors traumatized. Intensification of economic exploitation under multiple layers of rulers brought subject peoples under the sort of economic pressures that disintegrated their traditional way of life, especially the fundamental social forms of family and village community. The imposition of Roman imperial order in areas such as the ancient Middle East thus entailed not only military devastation and economic oppression, but also the relentless undermining of the subject peoples' traditional culture and social structure."
>
> —*RICHARD A. HORSELY*
> *Jesus and Empire* (2003)

In everyday life under the umbrella of Roman imperialism, the conquered Israelites of Palestine felt the impact of the Roman empire more economically than culturally (because the Romans had little interest in changing the customs of conquered peoples but let these continue on as before as long as they did not conflict with Roman interests). The economic impact was primarily experienced through tributes and taxes, which were a sign of submission to Roman authority and of non-citizenship (Mt 17:24-5). Tribute was a form of tax levied on a whole community. Individuals paid other taxes such as a head tax, land tax, requisitions, i.e., billeting soldiers, surrendering food and animals for military use (Lk 3:14), impressed labor (Mt 5:41), tolls on all produce and manufactured goods brought to market, and religious tithes (10%) on various things.

In Jesus' time, taxes were collected differently than they are today. Rome set the amount of revenue to be raised by a district and then sold the right to collect taxes to the highest bidder. The man who won the bid could charge whatever he wished in order to make a profit (Lk 3:13). Thus the entire cost of collecting taxes was borne by the taxpayers.

> "The political world served as a vacuum cleaner which sucked up by means of taxes as much surplus as a peasant produced and more. It was impossible, then, to 'better oneself.' With heavy taxation came crushing debt and eventual loss of land and assets."
>
> —*JEROME H. NEYREY*
> "Who Is Poor in the New Testament?," *Scripture from Scratch* (October 2002)

Many tax collectors (also called *publicans*) became very wealthy by demanding excessive taxes and by taking bribes. Tax collectors were extremely unpopular. The tax collection of import-export taxes, customs fees, and tolls for using roads, markets, and harbors were let out on bid to Judean nationals. These tax collectors were thus considered to be traitors to their people as well as crooks because they extorted more than what they needed to pay the Romans. These men and their families were barred from the synagogues and forbidden to give testimony in court.

The right to collect the so-called poll tax, which was actually a combination income tax and head tax, was also sold to the highest bidder. Only Roman citizens were allowed to collect these more direct and lucrative taxes. The income tax was one-tenth of all grain and one-fifth of all wine and fruit produced. The head tax was levied on all persons up to the age of sixty-five. Females were taxed from the age of twelve; males from the age of fourteen. Taxes were a heavy burden (scholars estimate as much as 20-35% or even 40%) on the people and, because of the collection system, a burden that fell unjustly on those who were least able to argue their case or bribe the tax collector.

Besides these Roman taxes, there were various additional Judean taxes, including the annual Temple tax (a "head" tax on each adult male to support the Temple, Mt 17:4) and various other taxes on goods and foods (Mt 23:23; Lk 11:42), and charges that might arise from transporting produce (customs, collected at toll booths, Mk 2:14; Mt 9:9; Lk 5:27).

The Historical Experience of First-Century Christians

Unlike our society that emphasizes that we are individuals first who seek out communities to join, in the ancient world the emphasis was on first belonging to communities, and only secondarily on being individuals. This is important because it reminds us that for them their covenant with their God Yahweh was first and foremost a social experience—God made covenants with the Israelite community not just with an individual (Abraham *and his descendants,* Moses *and the Hebrews in the exodus community).* Salvation or being in the right relationship with God was first and foremost a community affair. Thus to understand what Jesus is doing, we must recognize that he is involved in an internal Yahwist debate over how best to live out their covenant obligations.

Not all Israelites practiced their Yahwism in the same way and so their were different ways of religious life advocated by the Judeans, Samaritans, Galileans, Egyptians and other Yahwists spread throughout the Mediterranean non-Judean world called the *diaspora* (Gk: spread out or dispersed). So when Jesus proposes the Good News about God's new kingdom, he is talking about a new vision for organizing the covenant life of their community that would be an alternative to the present social organization and practices for members of the house of Israel, in particular as an alternative to the dominant Judean form of Yahwism, *Judahism,* and its customs and practices related to its control of the Jerusalem Temple.

The Common Judean Worldview

In first-century Roman Palestine which included the Yahwist areas of Judea, Galilee and Samaria, there were competing agendas for how to live out one's Yahwism. A major division had effectively split Judea and Samaria, which claimed lineage from the ancient northern kingdom of Israel destroyed by the Assyrians in 722 BC. So they resisted when the returning Judean exiles in 537 tried to impose their form of Yahwism (Judahism) on them (see the conversation between Jesus and the Samaritan woman in John 4 or the several references in the Gospels reflecting the enduring religious hostility of the two groups in Mt 10:5; Lk 10:33; 17:6; Jn 8:48). Our concern will focus on the main Yahwist religious groups in Jesus' time and their competing agendas (Lat: *what is to be done)* for the best way to live their covenant obligations with Yahweh.

As historical scholars have discovered, there were easily as many as two dozen Yahwist groups flourishing prior to AD 70 both in Judah and in the diaspora that were each related to the common core of Yahwism but characterized by many different practical variations and emphases. Despite passionate debates over what was wrong with their society and how the ills could be remedied, these different groups all shared the same basic Yahwist belief system with its focus on the covenant, the role of the Jerusalem Temple as the place where Yahweh was worshiped and the covenant was continually ratified, and the many traditional values and practices derived from their sacred writings (the Judahist scriptures, many of which compose our Old Testament).

These competing agendas about the religious definition of their society produced a conflict of standards, a sense of "two ways" (good and evil, light and dark, us and them) and thus different ideas about what ought be done to make their society live up to its covenant obligations. Each group thought that their faith, piety and proper observance were invariable markers of the true "way of God" over against the "way of the world."

From their shared sacred scriptures, all the competing Yahwist groups believed that Yahweh's presence and activity in our world was always for the sake of creating and sustaining relationships that culminated in their unique covenant. God's purpose and plan were revealed in the historical drama of God entering into covenants first with humanity in general (through Adam and Noah) and then with the house of Israel (through Abraham and Moses). Thus human history at its core was really a salvation history—the story of God in search of a people who would become the kind of covenant community that God envisioned and thus help God overcome the evil that now disfigures our world.

Yahweh's plan for creation and humanity illustrates how God's power is used to realize the right kind of relationships. As the familiar salvation story unfolds, Yahweh's roles as life-giver (creator), rescuer and liberator (savior), covenant maker (master), lawgiver and judge (lord) are played out in relation to the communities chosen to become God's covenant partners. God's presence to judge (demonstrating God's ethical seriousness about sanctions for behavior that does not meet the covenant obligations) and to save or liberate (demonstrating God's gracious compassion or mercy) transforms all creation into what God wants it to be.

But Jesus' offer of an alternative worldview suggests that, despite all efforts to implement God's agenda, the people of Israel had failed to fulfill God's dream for a community in right relationship with God and with one another. Thus a new community must be formed. Jesus' kingdom community is to be the fulfillment of God's search for a community in which dominion or lordship would be held by God alone and in response the people would live in right relationships based on justice, held together by love, to provide the fullness of life and well-being for all.

If we look more closely at the historical experience of the early Christian communities, we discover that in the first several decades of their existence, the Christian communities that emerged from Judahism enjoyed relative peace. This was beneficial because it took several decades for a distinctive Christian identity to emerge. This developing awareness took both a negative and a positive form. The easier form was negative definition—we identify who we are by saying what we are not. So Christians identified themselves first as *not* pagans but believers in the one and only God Yahweh now identified as the Father of Jesus of Nazareth, the Son of God, then as *not* Pharisaic Judahists but believers who held that Jesus was Yahweh's promised messiah and thus their new community was indeed the true covenant community of Israel.

Circumstances demanded that Christianity first distinguish itself over against the Judean way of being God's covenant people (first the Judahism before AD 70 and then the post Temple Judaism) from which it sprang. Originating as one of several reform movements within the dominant Temple/holiness emphasis of the Judahists, Christianity offered to all first century Israelites one of several alternatives for revitalizing or reforming their relation to God and their covenant life together.

Besides the Christian agenda articulated by Jesus, there were several other alternative agendas advocated by the Priests, the Pharisees, the Essenes and the Zealots. Despite their differences, all of these non-Christian alternatives were based on an acceptance of a fundamental sense that

God's ideal for the Yahwist community was holiness—which for them meant being set apart. God had said to Moses: "Speak to all the congregation of the people of Israel and say to them: You shall be holy, for I the LORD your God am holy" (Lev 19:2).

After God's judgment on the Judean Israelite community's sin that resulted in their disastrous exile (597 BC) and then God's surprising restoration of their land (539 BC), they concluded and then acted on the premise that their survival and success as Yahweh's covenant people would depend on their attention to holiness. If they could become a holy people in a holy land, they would ensure their survival and well-being as God's covenant people. Hence Judahism was born.

The groups could justify this holiness emphasis because holiness was God's most important characteristic. Moreover, it has no human analogue. In the normal way of understanding God, we begin with something from our human experience, e.g., a shepherd or king or warrior, and by analogy we elevate this idea to its highest degree and apply it to God, who is somehow "like" this but in a superlative way. But holiness is not something that begins from our experience but instead points to what makes God to be divine and not something created. Thus holiness separates the divine from the human as God's essential characteristic and not ours.

Since holiness is not intrinsic to any created reality, it must be communicated to humans by contact with God, which demands that what is holy (sacred, clean, pure) be separated from what is not holy (profane, unclean, impure). This led to a social organization that stressed this separation, which scholars call a "purity system" that sets up clear boundaries that must be scrupulously maintained and defended for right living. This holiness or purity system (which also created a purity politics for the community) was articulated in the **Torah** (God's instruction or law for how to live a holy life), embodied in the Jerusalem **Temple** (the connecting point of divine and human reality where holiness originates) and realized in their ancestral **territory** (a holy land separated and consecrated by God's holy presence in the Temple and the purity system kept by the people).

Thus Judaism's focus on holiness, with its characteristic insistence on separation as the primary organizational principle of their covenant life together, created several important post-exilic attitudes and practices.

Since they were God's chosen holy people, they needed to separate from other peoples to cleanse their land of pollution and keep it holy. This separatist attitude was expressed in an extreme concern for boundaries, rigid classifications of what was acceptable ("clean") and unacceptable ("unclean"), and strict obedience to God's law. Consequently, life in this post-exilic Judahist community was distinguished by

- separation from non-Yahwists
- no intermarriage with foreigners
- strictly enforced Sabbath observance
- emphasis on circumcision as sign of difference
- careful attention to "clean/unclean" categories for all of life
- emphasis on "kosher" food regulations
- careful and complete obedience to the whole *Torah* (God's 10 Words or Commandments and the 603 Mosaic statutes and decrees)

It's not hard to imagine how the people could develop these attitudes after the destruction of their first Temple perceived as punishment for their sins and then fifty years of being in exile without a Temple, which was not only the center of worship but also the center of their covenant identity. Their experience of exile and God's surprising restoration of the people to their homeland, which included rebuilding the second Jerusalem Temple, created a mentality that focused the people much more on their own survival. Just as people suffering pain focus more on themselves for healing, so the Judean community focused more on itself and on the massive task of restoring itself to health. The result, however, created an inward-directed orientation that lingered for centuries.

Five Different First-Century Ways to Practice Yahwism

As we have noted, in the first century although several groups shared a core Yahwist worldview, nevertheless our Gospels reflect how these competing voices advocated different ways for how that worldview ought to be put into practice to shape their everyday community life.

The Priestly Way advocated a Yahwism that focused on the awareness of Yahweh holiness, which identified God's transcendent otherness that set God apart from all creation. God's holiness in turn demanded a consequent holiness of the people that would set them apart from all other nations. This holiness agenda—to be a holy people in a holy land apart from all the nations—could only be achieved by strictly keeping the instructions of the *Torah*. This priestly way of holiness, which had been dominant since the Judahists return from the Babylonian exile in 537 BC, depended on the Jerusalem Temple, its priesthood, and its feasts as the outward signs and the means of fulfilling this holiness agenda.

The Pharisee Way also advocated a holiness agenda, however they wanted not only the priests but also laymen like themselves to observe all of the *Torah* commands. Their interpretation of the law included not only the written form found in the first five books of the Bible (called the *Pentateuch*, Gk: five books), but also oral traditions handed down through the centuries by other teachers providing commentary and interpretations for applying the Torah to the complexities and changing conditions of daily life. Since the Pharisees did not depend on the Temple and priestly status, their movement was not focused in Jerusalem but spread wherever there were Judahist meeting places (Gk: *synagōgē*).

The Essene Way also embraced a holiness agenda but in the most austere form of all. Appalled at what they considered the profanation of the Jerusalem Temple's holiness after the Hasmonean family took over the high priestly office in the first century before Christ, the Essenes separated themselves from contact with the profaned Temple and its priesthood to take up residence in remote regions such as the Qumran community near the Dead Sea. They tried to recapture what they considered the original demands of holy living. They apparently used their own liturgical calendar and rituals (especially various ritual washings) and developed their own interpretations of many of the Judahist sacred texts.

The Zealot Way was shaped by an idea of holiness that advocated not merely religious but also political separation. For over five hundred years, Judah had not been its own political state but rather a colonial people always subjected to other more powerful empires—Assyria, Egypt, Babylon, Greece and now Rome, which in 40 BC had made Herod the Great (who was an Idumean and not even a Judean!) their king. Except for a little over a century under the Maccabees and the subsequent Hasmonean dynasty (164–46 BC), Judah had never been a free nation. Thus the Zealots pushed to start a war of nationalist independence with the Romans. They fervently hoped that once the war began, God would once again come down to free the people from their oppressors—as God did long ago in the exodus from Egypt—and establish a political kingdom as had been promised to their ancestors and had been achieved two centuries before by the Hasmonean dynasty.

The Jesus Way, in contrast to these four variations on the holiness agenda, embraced Jesus' alternative vision for life in the covenant community. Instead of emphasizing God's holiness and separation, he stressed God's mercy and inclusiveness as the foundation of God's covenant reliability. Although he no doubt believed in God's holiness, Jesus did not seem to think that human sin could profane God and make God unholy. Rather, for Jesus God's holiness would go out to touch those in need of divine healing and change their lives for the better. So Jesus proclaimed that God was the king and ruler of this world: the generous heavenly patron or benefactor who has mercy and gives us what we need for our survival and well-being. Because of our needs, our lives are at the mercy of God, who alone can satisfy them. From this perspective, Jesus offers an agenda that is focused on God's mercy or compassion and expects us to trust fully in God's gracious mercy, to receive the gifts that God wants to bestow on us and then to share those gifts with others in imitation of God's generosity.

Jesus' also stressed that God's kingdom community was open to everyone because "God shows no partiality, but in every nation anyone who fears him and does what is right is acceptable to him" (Acts 10:34–5). Since God is impartial, God does not restrict the divine generosity of salvation only to the Judahists and Yahwists. Like a human benefactor or patron, God freely bestows gifts and graces on each and every person as God wishes. God's generosity is free, unaffected by our desires and uncontrolled by our rules and unlimited in its benefits. Moreover, God cannot be bribed or manipulated by us to conform to our interests or plans.

The clash of these two agendas—holiness or mercy, separation or inclusiveness—was evident when some Pharisees challenged Jesus about eating with tax collectors and sinners, who were considered ritually unclean and thus liable to make others unclean and so unable to participate in community worship. Jesus countered with a challenge of his own. "Those who are well have no need of a physician, but those who are sick. Go and learn what this means, 'I desire mercy, not sacrifice' (quoting Hosea 6:6). For I have come not to call the righteous but sinners" (Mt 9:12-13).

If mercy or compassionate and reliable steadfast love, that is, the kind of love that characterizes God's fidelity in covenant relationship with us, was superior to the Temple sacrifices, then how much more to the laws of ritual impurity and the regulations for keeping the Sabbath (Mt 12:7). Jesus' new imperative for those wanting to live according to the mercy agenda was: "Be merciful (compassionate), just as your Father is merciful" (Lk 6:36). This captured the essence of Jesus' proclamation that God was the heavenly father/patron who bestowed all good gifts on humanity.

"Not only did he and his followers repudiate the autocratic values of power and wealth, but the institutions and systems that authorized and supported these values: the family, the Law, the sacrificial system, the Temple, kosher food regulations, the distinction between clean and unclean, patriarchy, role expectations for women and children, the class system, the use of violence, racial and ethnic divisions, the distinction between insider and outsider—indeed, every conceivable prop of domination, division, and supremacy. The gospel is a context-specific remedy for the evils of the Domination System."

—WALTER WINK
Engaging the Powers: Discernment and Resistance in a World of Domination (1992)

The Parting of the Ways of Judaism & Christianity

During the missionary journeys of Paul, many of the conflicts of these competing agendas and their impact on the newly-forming Christian communities were thrashed out in local skirmishes between the Judahist holiness way advocated by Judahizing converts (adopting circumcision as the entry way into the community—it was a man's religion in which women belonged through their man—obedience to the Law or *Torah* as the normative guideline through which holiness was achieved in relationship with God and one another, and using Temple rituals and keeping kosher food restrictions to ensure proper worship of God) and the new Christian way (baptism for men and women as the entry rite, obedience to God's ten direct commandments and Jesus' revised version of the Law's obligations, elimination of kosher food restrictions and using Christian rituals, especially the eucharistic supper).

Things began to change radically for Christians beginning in AD 68, a chaotic year in which the emperor Nero committed suicide, civil war broke out, and there were three Roman emperors (Galba, Otho and Vitellius) in quick succession. Peace was restored only a year later with a fourth emperor, Vespasian. Changing emperors, who held their power by force not law, was always a dangerous time throughout the empire because those at the edges of the empire often took advantage of the weakening at the imperial center to assert independence from imperial rule.

Thus several revolts erupted at this time as subservient Roman client states like Judea attempted to take advantage of the chaos and free themselves from submission to Rome. The Zealots started their longed-for war with Rome. But Rome, under the direction of the new emperor Vespasian, and later under his son Titus, put down the rebellion in its usual brutal way. The cost was the devastation of Judea and the destruction of the Jerusalem Temple in AD 70.

Once the Temple had been destroyed, the critical spiritual center of Judaism was also destroyed. Judaism had to rethink both its theology and its lifestyle. But more to the point, this destruction eliminated three of the five competing agendas that we noted for living out Yahwism. The Zealots, who started the war, were discredited. The Essenes were eliminated when the Romans destroyed their monasteries (like Qumran). The priests, whose theology and role, privileges and livelihood all depended on the Temple, were no longer able to function because without a Temple there was nothing for them to do.

Without a Temple, only the agendas of the Pharisees and the Jesus group remained as viable alternatives for the social reorganization of Yahwism/Judahism. These options were different both because of their theological emphasis on who God was and whether Jesus was the promised messiah and the consequent behavior that this demanded. Simply put, the Pharisees denied Jesus' messianic claim and opted for an emphasis on God's holiness and a life of obedience to the *Torah* to insure holi-

47

ness for the community. The Jesus group opted to emphasize God's mercy or goodness and a life of thanksgiving (Gk: *eucharistein)* and service.

After the destruction of the Jerusalem Temple, the Pharisees became the leaders for a new form of religious identity—Pharisaic Judaism—that did not depend on the Temple but on the synagogue and the study of *Torah*. By the mid-eighties of the first century, their guidelines for Jewish belief and community life prevailed. When this happened, Pharisaic Judaism and Christianity were already drifting apart, as is evident from the tensions and antagonisms disclosed in the Gospels of Matthew and John. Pharisaic Judaism recognized clearly that its way of being a Yahwist and the Christian way were incompatible because they each had different answers to the basic questions that would define their separate and distinctive worldviews and their differing religious beliefs and practices.

Besides distinguishing itself from Pharisaic Judaism, the Christian community also had to discover its place in the Hellenistic culture of the wider world of the Roman empire. Through the leadership of Paul and other Christian missionaries, the Christian community spread rapidly throughout the Roman empire, in particular into the major cities where the language barrier was not so problematic because many immigrants to the cities would speak Greek. So successful was this initial mission to include Gentiles that by the close of the first century they were the dominant group in most Christian communities.

Early Christianity had to identify itself publicly as a religious way of life in this Hellenistic social and cultural situation. This was very difficult because at this time Christians lacked most of what was associated with any religion—ancient origins, temples, priests, sacrifices, public rituals and community approval. Instead, they met in households, celebrated their religious ritual meal, and let their example of caring for one another, solidarity despite deep-seated ethnic differences and a willingness to face persecution because of their beliefs invite public approval.

As followers of Christ, Christians based their lives on Jesus' example. During the sixties of the first century, when for the first time Christians were differentiated from Jews by Nero and singled out for persecution when he made them the scapegoats for the terrible fire that destroyed much of Rome in AD 64, both Romans and Christians had to answer the basic question of what it meant to be a Christian.

As we will see in chapter 4, Christians responded to this challenge by presenting their basic message (their "Good News" or gospel) in the form of Jesus' gospel life. This narrative of the events in Jesus' life, from his baptism through his public ministry of building a new kingdom community in Galilee to his final days in Jerusalem, not only shaped his identity, but it also offered the pattern for his Christian followers to imitate. His story as the Christ was the model for their story as *Christ-ians*.

When Christians heard this gospel, they found the clues they needed to live as a new alternative community according to Jesus' guidelines. Its narrative provided the pattern for life as his disciples, beginning with the call into earthly life at birth and into the faith community at baptism, moving through a faith commitment to the covenant relationship, then to a co-mission to share in building God's kingdom community here on earth, to continual conversion in living out the relationship and finally to the cost that opens the door to a new life with God.

Reading the Texts through First-Century Eyes

With this brief summary of the historical and social situations of the first century New Testament world, we might draw a few conclusions that will help us understand Jesus' message of God's Good News more the way his first-century audience might have heard it. We must always keep in mind the relationships and interconnections of the four basic realms that organized Jesus' social world because this will have consequences for the way that we must read and interpret his message of the kingdom. We must try to understand their world not through the familiar social world of our twenty-first century but through the eyes of his first-century audience.

1. We Can't Christianize Jesus

Since in the first century there was no religion called "Judaism" as we like to think of it as a distinct and developed religion, thus our terminology is often confusing. The most global term for the covenant people was the "house of Israel" or Israelites (Nathaniel calls Jesus "an Israelite in whom there is no guile" Jn 1:47; and boasting about his honor status, Paul claims in descending order of rank, to be "an Israelite, a descendant of Abraham, a member of the tribe of Benjamin," Rom 11:1).

And among the Israelites as we have seen, there were various groups with competing ways of living, the most influential were the "Judeans" since the Temple in Jerusalem was in their capital city. Thus for outsiders, all these Israelites were lumped together as "Judeans" or as we often translate it, "Jews." Their civic religion focused on the Temple and ruled by the priestly political group was "Judean." Thus to outsiders like Pilate, Jesus was a "Jew," a member of the house of Israel.

"Jesus' origins were Jewish: he was born a Jew, socialized as a Jew, and remained Jewish all his life. To be sure, he was not unaffected by other traditions. He lived in a cosmopolitan time and place. Hellenistic culture was present throughout Palestine (perhaps especially in Galilee), and Jesus almost certainly knew Greek as well as Aramaic."

—*MARCUS J. BORG*
"The Teaching of Jesus" in *The Anchor Bible Dictionary* (1992)

In his public ministry, Jesus was involved in public arguments with the other competing groups we described over the best way to live one's Israelite covenant obligations—the "Judean" way or his new way emphasizing mercy and compassion. He did not set out to found a new religion (since there was no such thing as religion in this sense) but he recruited followers who would join him in the controversy over his reform agenda.

2. We Can't De-politicize Jesus & His Kingdom Message

Because it was impossible to separate the first-century religious realm from the other social realms, Jesus' message was not just about "religion" as we think of it as separate from politics, economics and kinship issues. This can be recognized if we think about who killed Jesus. The parties responsible for his crucifixion, a state-sanctioned form of political murder (the state reserves to itself the power to use of violence, and we note that the Romans would not delegate this ability to execute criminals to the Judeans, Jn 18:31), represent the highest ranks of those in the four social realms. At the highest level of direct Roman rule in Judea (political) is Pontius Pilate, the procurator or governor of the Roman Province of Palestine. The other realms contributing to his identity are not really prominent in this trial although Pilate got this job as a result of imperial patronage that depended on his family connections (kinship), his wealth (economic) and civic piety (religious—note his question, "Am I a Judean" in John 18:35, shows he has no relation to their religion and god).

On the next level down, Luke reports that during Jesus' trial, Pilate sends him to Herod Antipas, the Roman subordinate official (tetrarch) overseeing Galilee (political) who inherited (kinship, wealth) this role from his father King Herod the Great, the Roman appointee as king of the Judeans (Jews) even though he was an Idumean and a lukewarm convert to the Judean religion.

"Jesus was political in a different sense: not as a leader of a movement against Roman rule, but as one who sought a transformation of his own people's socio-political life. If politics is defined as 'what political leaders do,' then it is difficult to see a political thrust to Jesus' message and mission. But if 'politics' is understood as concern for the shape of the city (polis), and by extension as concern for the shape of any historical community, there is considerable evidence of a strong sociopolitical component in Jesus' teaching."

—*MARCUS J. BORG*
"The Teaching of Jesus" in *The Anchor Bible Dictionary* (1992)

On the third level are the Judean leaders (political) who come from the wealthy (civic economics) priestly (civic religious) families (kinship—note how the high-priestly office goes from Annas to his son-in-law Caiaphas, Jn 18:13) and represent the highest ranks of all the realms of Judean society. Their hostility to Jesus is an important clue that his kingdom message and agenda for an alternative organization of society is such a threat to them and their privileges and entitlements from the Temple and from their imperial patronage that they decide that Jesus must be killed using the power of the state to do it for them (Jn 11:50).

3. We Can't Individualize Jesus' Message
Although our culture emphasizes a rather naïve idea of rugged individualism—as if anyone could exist without relationships!—their cultural world emphasized belonging to the group first, and then being an individual. Thus the kingdom message is first meant for a group to embrace and thus become the alternative community that Jesus envisions.

The root of the image Jesus' kingdom community is their experience as Yahweh's covenant people. Recall that the covenants God makes are always with groups—Noah and his family, Abraham and his descendants, Moses and the Hebrew people, Jesus and his disciples—and never just with an individual. Thus a "Jesus and me" understanding of his kingdom message is completely misplaced.

"There can be no Christian life except in community: in families, parishes, communities of consecrated life, base communities, other small communities, and movements. Like the early Christians who met in community, the disciples take part in the life of the Church, and in the encounter with brothers and sisters, living the love of Christ in solidarity, in fraternal life."

—*LATIN AMERICAN BISHOPS (CELAM)*
Fifth General Conference (Aparecida. Brazil, 2007), #278

---

4. We Can't Spiritualize Jesus' Message

Since persons must respond to the kingdom message, that response requires that it be embodied in oneself by assimilating the vision and values of Jesus' message, and then living those values out by using one's personal power to join with others into a community where their combined power is then used to bring about the kind of community that God wants (religion) and incorporates governance (political) under a heavenly patron (kinship) model with Jesus as its broker to ensure survival and well-being (economics) for all.

"The gospel is not just a remedy for domination. It also deals with sickness and death, finitude and faithlessness, tragedy and meaninglessness. But failure to acknowledge the centrality of its emancipatory message has often rendered the gospel politically reactionary and spiritually repressive. Perhaps we can begin to see the gospel for what it has always been: the most powerful antidote for domination the world has ever known."

—*WALTER WINK*
Engaging the Powers: Discernment and Resistance in a World of Domination (1992)

With these caveats in mind, let us now examine more specifically the message that Jesus proclaimed about God's forthcoming kingdom and the alternative community that it would create for those who would respond and embrace it.

CHAPTER TWO

God's New Rule Is Here!
Jesus' Message & Ministry

In the Gospels, Jesus is presented not only as the revealer of God but also as the proclaimer, teacher and builder of God's new kingdom—both the place where God rules and the people over whom God rules. The kingdom is best understood as a new way of community life that is grounded in the kingdom worldview which includes both a vision—an integrated way of seeing the world and of being in it (the kingdom worldview) that is focused on God's presence in our world—and a vocation to work with God to transform the world from a place marred, disordered and dominated by Satan and the powers of evil into a world characterized by God's rule. This requires reordering all distorted relationships, eradicating evil and transforming all creation once again into the obedient service of God.

"God's vision is not a vision of accumulation and monopoly so that those who have the most when they die win. This vision is not about heaven but about God's kingdom coming on earth as it already is in heaven. God's rule where the practices of justice and mercy and kindness and peaceableness are every day the order of the day. It is a vision of the world as a peaceable neighborliness in which no one is under threat, no one is at risk, no one is in danger, because all are safe, all are valued, all are honored, all are cared for. And this community of peaceableness will come only when the vicious cycles of violent accumulation are broken."

—*WALTER BRUEGGEMANN*
Inscribing the Text (2004)

Jesus' goal was to make this kingdom vision become a reality, first in the hearts and minds of his audience, and then in their everyday lives. And after his death, this then became the goal of the kingdom community of his disciples. He envisioned a new way for people to relate to God and to one another. Then he put this vision into practice by starting and building this ideal community with his disciples. This experiment in kingdom living with his followers kept Jesus busy day after day.

But having a **goal** like realizing God's kingdom cannot be accomplished unless one identifies the practical **tasks** that need to be done and the specific **strategies** that must be invented to accomplish these tasks. Jesus demonstrated a keen awareness of these practical tasks needed to bring God's kingdom into being on earth and so he acted in **roles** that would have been familiar to his audience and devised appropriate strategies to accomplish his goal of proclaiming and building God's kingdom.

"Jesus was the most dangerous kind of rebel—a rebel who had seen the Kingdom and knew it was the only reality. He not merely talked about the Kingdom; he lived and manifested its splendor in the beauty of his presence, in the clarity and inner coherence of his teaching, in his fearlessness in the face of opposition."

—*ANDREW HARVEY*
Son of Man: The Mystical Path to Christ (1999)

As a **prophet,** Jesus used parables to teach people how to discover God's presence in their ordinary lives. As a **priest,** Jesus used the common meal to teach people how to celebrate God's presence. As a **king,** Jesus offered his wisdom and deeds of power (miracles) to teach people how to reorder their lives around God's presence. (For a fuller explanation of Jesus' use of these roles and their correlative strategies, see my *Who Do You Say I Am: The Catechist's Guide to Jesus in the Gospels,* chapters 8-13.) These choices, however, led him directly into a conflict with the Judean leaders, who with the help of the Roman provincial governor, had him crucified. Although this ended his earthly life, it did not end his presence with us because God raised him from the dead to a new life with God.

Jesus' New Kingdom Language

Jesus announcement of God's rule reveals a distinctive understanding of who God is and how God is interacting with us. He reaches back into the Yahwist tradition to reemphasize the idea that God is the king who desires to exercise sovereign rule over both the covenant community and the world in order to restore them to their original condition at creation.

Jesus had many alternative ways to describe God that are taken from the four social realms that we described in chapter 1. Kingdom language is taken from the political realm and describes the ruling power for the social organization for the larger community. The ruler is identified as a *king* and *lord* and can also be characterized by the various roles in which the ruling power is exercised—warrior, judge, priest and leader.

"If Jesus had wanted to avoid the political connotations of kingdom language, he could have. He could have spoken of the family of God, or the people of God, or the community of God, or the kinship of God. But he didn't. He used the word 'kingdom': what life would be like on earth if God were king rather than the rulers of this world."

—*MARCUS J. BORG*
Convictions: How I Learned What Matters Most (2014)

Although it is not a precise distinction, it might be helpful to recall that God is often called *creator* and *lord*. *Creator* refers to God's original use of power to establish order in the universe from its original chaos. *Lord* describes the active way that God intervenes in creation to order it and then reorder it after it was corrupted by evil. Thus when speaking of God's rule on earth, it is appropriate to describe this as *lordship* (dominion or power over all of creation) and call God *lord*.

But the other realms also contribute their perspectives. The kinship realm describes the rule of God as a father (patron), mother, master, husband, protector, nourisher. In relation to the economic realm, God is characterized as owner of the whole earth (1 Chr 29:11) and of the promised land (Lv 25:23). God is the master and the people are God's servants or slaves. The religious realm describes God as the holy one, the most high, almighty, everlasting, steadfast (loyal), gracious and merciful to whom we must give worship, praise, thanks and honor. But Jesus takes this traditional emphasis and gives it a new twist, declaring that God was now beginning to rule through him as God's new agent or mediator.

Jesus' New Worldview Builds on the Yahwist Worldview

Our Christian worldview is rooted in and shares much of the Yahwist worldview that was fashioned during the millennium before Christ. It proposed a mental ordering of the world (a way of seeing) and practical cues for deciding on the right values and behaviors (a way of being). We have constructed our Christian worldview by adapting the Yahwist worldview found in the Old Testament. It tells the story of Yahweh's choice of Abraham and his descendants to be God's own people and of their many subsequent endeavors to create and maintain the ideal community desired by God in the land which God gave to them.

The Bible tells this story of the realization of God's dream for establishing this ideal covenant community. By recounting the steps God takes to realize that dream and how the chosen communities have fared in accomplishing this ideal, it provides clues about the deepest meaning of our lives. When this story becomes our own, we discover the "plot" or meaningful coherence of events that forms not just a history but a salvation history of humanity's relationship with God.

"The New Testament writers have simply taken over what was more explicitly expressed in the Old Testament. It is because the New Testament writers simply assumed the faith of their fathers, and could assume that for the most part these assumptions were equally axiomatic for their audiences, that they evidently felt it unnecessary to spell out these beliefs afresh."

—*JAMES D. G. DUNN*
New Testament Theology (2009)

Through this story we also learn about the characters (who God is, who we are and who others are) and the kinds of appropriate actions between the characters, that is, the "roles" that we are called upon to play with the other characters in the unraveling of the plot's narrative sequence. Christians must know this Old Testament story because it is the background for the story of Christ and the Christian community. These Old Testament stories furnish the repository of typical characters and stock images that New Testament authors take advantage of to convey their message. They expected their audiences to be familiar with the basic people, events and themes of the Old Testament and make connections from these to their own lives by the typical associations linking the two.

Jesus' new kingdom worldview suggests that, despite all its efforts to implement God's covenant agenda, Israel had actually failed to fulfill their covenant obligations so a new community needed to be formed. Jesus' kingdom is now going to be the fulfillment of God's search for a community in which lordship would be held by God alone and evil would be overcome because the people would live in right relationships based on justice, held together by love, providing the fullness of life for all.

Our Christian worldview also parts company with the Yahwist one concerning the issue of Jesus as God's promised messiah, God's chosen agent for bringing about salvation. Our Christian beliefs center on Jesus as God's divine son and the promised messiah, who died and rose for our salvation, and who will come again to inaugurate the final age when the covenant people will finally realize God's dream for the ideal human community. This narrative shapes the pattern for our Christian lives.

"The work of the Spirit is the bringing to be of the vision of God—the capacitating of persons to 'see visions' and 'dream dreams'. The birth of the Church is the beginning of the End. The Kingdom of God makes its impact on history in the creation of a visionary community. In this birth of the Church, the risen and ascended Lord takes to himself a Body on earth with eyes opened by the Spirit to see the future."
—*GABRIEL FACKRE*
The Christian Story (1996)

Within a half century after Jesus' death, particularly through the missionary work of Paul which opened the Christian community to the Gentiles, this traditional Yahwist worldview and the emerging Christian worldview became disconnected. The fundamental Christian beliefs about God bringing salvation definitively through Jesus of Nazareth, who was proclaimed as the promised messiah, as risen from the dead, and as both a divine and human person, separated Christians from their Yahwist neighbors. As time passed, Christian communities became even more distanced as distinctively Judahist practices like circumcision, strict *Torah* observance, Temple worship and *kosher* food regulations were abandoned.

Israel's Kingdom Hopes

For centuries the Israelites had been steeped in "kingdom" promises. Throughout the Old Testament there are many indications of this deep-seated idea that God alone was the real ruler of the covenant people, its true "king" and "lord" with dominion over the covenant people, the nations and all creation (e.g., Pss 10:16-18; 22:27-28; 44:4-8; 47:1-9; 74:12-13; 93:1-5; 95:3-7; 96:10-13; 99:1-5; 145:1, 10-13).

Moreover, the most important formative stories shaping their community character—their original relationship with God as a covenant community through Abraham, their liberation from Egyptian slavery

GOD'S NEW RULE IS HERE!

through the exodus, their existence as a tribal confederacy in the newly conquered land, their morphing into a nation under a human monarch, the evolving royal dynasties and the building of their Jerusalem Temple, the exile and loss of dynasty and Temple, the restoration after the exile and rebuilding of the Temple—all gravitated around the experience of God as a loyal and reliable covenant partner, faithfully fulfilling the obligations of providing and protecting that went with being their God.

"Storytellers also helped monarchs solve problems during the course of their reigns. People in modern Western industrial cultures expect future research and future discoveries to solve present problems. People in the world of the Bible looked for solutions to their problems in past experience. Today a crisis sets research in motion. In the world of the Bible, a crisis set storytelling in motion."
—*VICTOR MATTHEWS AND DON BENJAMIN*
The Social World of Ancient Israel (1993)

Each time their oppression became intolerable and a wicked tyrant oppressed them (e.g., Egypt's pharaoh, their own bad kings or the rulers of Assyria and Babylon), God had intervened through various human agents (Moses, various military leaders like Joshua, the tribal Judges and kings—both Israelite like David and foreign like Cyrus of Persia who ended their exile) to right what was wrong, to free the oppressed people, bring them to their land and make them once again secure and prosperous.

Kingdom hopes, then, had always been a constant thread in the life of the covenant people and the primary fuel for their hopes of liberation. Thus whenever the pain of oppression weighed them down, it was natural to yearn for relief through the hope for God's rule or kingdom that would free them from their present oppression. So Jesus proclaims the idea that God the king now desires to exercise sovereign rule over the covenant community and the world in a surprising new way.

Jesus' New Kingdom Message

Jesus proclaimed a simple yet radical message of God's new kingdom, which was his code word for the transformed reality where God rules as the center of meaning and the object of all action. Everything must be reordered with God as the center and the primary concern must be the relationship of covenant friendship. But most importantly, he invited some persons to become his disciples, following him and learning how to realize that dream of a kingdom community by starting to live now in the way that God had wanted everyone to live since the time of creation—in right relationships with God and with one another that were grounded in love, expressed in justice and oriented to the well-being of all.

"We can define God's Kingdom as *the redemptive presence of God*. This redemptive (saving) presence of God can be found in everyday personal experiences. Whenever people love one another, forgive one another, bear one another's burdens, work to build up a just and peaceful community—wherever people are of humble heart, open to their Creator and serving their neighbor—God's redemptive and liberating presence is being manifested. God's Kingdom and loving rule is in operation there."
—*RICHARD P. MCBRIEN*
"What Is the Kingdom of God," *St. Anthony Messenger* (June, 1980)

Jesus' kingdom message, which Mark calls "God's good news," is this: "The time is fulfilled, and the kingdom of God has come near; repent, and believe in the good news" (Mk 1:14-15). This formula not only proclaims that God was once again coming to rule over Israel but also notes the responses that disciples would have to make—first, changing one's whole life (conversion, refocusing one's whole worldview around God's presence in Jesus) because of this message and second being loyal to God the ruler as a member of the new community. God's new rule would be a welcome change considering that Jesus' audience was suffering from the harsh exploitation of the overlapping rule both of the Romans and of the wealthy Judean families who collaborated with Rome.

If we take another look at the five different agendas advocated in Jesus' time for revitalizing first-century Yahwism, we can see that each of them responds to their present experience of painful oppression under Roman rule by linking their hopes for freedom to the traditional kingdom hopes. They have various ideas about how God should rule over the people, what that kingdom would be like and who should be God's chosen agent for its realization.

The Priests and Sadducees, religious conservatives who accepted only the five written books of Moses' *Torah* (instruction or law) as their guide, just wanted to retain the current political relationships with Rome and their own monopoly on Temple worship (in which with Roman authorization they alone acted as God's agent and greatly profited from their exclusive role as God's mediators) and so they were prepared to stop at nothing to keep it going as the source of their wealth and power.

The Pharisees, a more progressive lay group who advocated dedication not only to the books of the written *Torah* but also to the traditions associated with it, wanted a holy kingdom that throughout the land would conform in every detail of daily life to God's guidelines found in the *Torah*. Through their scrupulous interpretation of the *Torah* they would lead the people by example to the kind of covenant life that God desired.

The Essenes, religious purists who fled to the wilderness to live their Yahwism in a purer form, wanted a new and holy kingdom that would be completely purified by creating a new priesthood and a new temple to replace the polluted one in Jerusalem. They also believed that their community and its leader would be the chosen agent through whom God would bring about this wondrous transformation into a new holy people.

The Zealots, a shadowy group often considered terrorists, wanted a political kingdom that through the agency of warrior leaders would be free and independent from the brutal and greedy domination of Rome so that they could once again control their land in their own way.

And into this mix of alternative kingdom hopes, **Jesus** announced a new version of God's rule in which he would be God's chosen agent or messiah. His proposed kingdom was like no other, free from the oppressive domination systems that plagued all the current political, family, religious and economic social institutions people were familiar with.

Jesus' New Kingdom Worldview

Reading the Gospels invites us out of our familiar world into a new and mysterious world of which we are usually only dimly aware. Here the invisible and usually hidden God becomes audible through the words and visible through the actions of Jesus. This new world is different because God is revealed as present and active everywhere. When we realize that this is really how our own world also is, we will never be the same.

Engaging with the Gospels offers a new awareness of the mysterious presence of the hidden God who is luring us into a life-changing relationship. We are transported out of our ordinary worldview and confronted with a new worldview that reveals a new vision of the way reality is, a new set of values to guide our lives, and new behaviors that ought now to characterize our Christian life.

"If Jesus could have told us exactly what the Kingdom was in discursive language, he would have told us. But the proper way of knowing a mystery such as the Kingdom is through metaphor and story. One may try to discover the meaning of the parable, of the metaphor, of the story. But the meaning is no substitute for the parable, or the metaphor, or the story. They must always remain. The true graven image is meaning in place of the story."

—*BERNARD BRANDON SCOTT*
The Word of God in Words: Reading & Preaching the Gospels (1985)

Every culture and every individual has a particular worldview that describes the customary way that those who adopt it see the world, evaluate it and act in it. It provides the coherent and ordered understanding of the way things are and how they work by integrating the complex, interlocking network of ideas, values, symbols, aspirations, attitudes and beliefs of those who share it. It has social, political and religious consequences for every group because it supplies the crucial context which is necessary for determining the meaning, meaningfulness and truth of their existence.

Our worldview provides a whole system of cues to guide our responses and actions: how to perceive objects and situations, how to name them, how to feel in response to them, how to act or perform for praise or blame, what to believe or not believe, what to hold in awe or marvel at, and who to imitate as a hero or model. Because this worldview reveals the organization of reality, it tells us where everything belongs. Its symbolic maps and stories, which we learn simply by being part of a community, provide the overarching context in which everything takes its meaning.

Every Christian also has a distinctively Christian worldview that understands the meaning of reality in relation to Jesus Christ. Since it expresses our unique way of combining the miscellaneous aspects of our experience into a comprehensive understanding of the world, this worldview provides the structures of meaning that make our world intelligible and suggests the best way to live in it. Thus it is crucial to set out the broad outlines of the Christian worldview as proclaimed by Jesus in his kingdom ministry and as embedded in the Good News of the gospel narratives.

The New Christian Worldview

Our Christian worldview is the distinctively Christian understanding of how things are and how they fit together. All Christians share its basic components but, like creating a mosaic from the same colored stones, each individual and group can put the pieces together in different configurations to emphasize one or other aspects. These particular emphases create distinctive communities within the larger Christian worldview.

"Jesus is a vivid challenge to our notion of reality. He proclaims first that there is a dimension of reality beyond the visible world of our ordinary experience, a dimension charged with power, whose ultimate quality is compassion. Second, the fruits of a life lived in accord with the Spirit are to be embodied not only in individuals, but also in the life of the faithful community. What if it is true that the world of our ordinary experience is but one level of reality, and that we are at all times surrounded by other dimensions of reality which we do not commonly experience? What if reality is other than we ever dreamed it could be?"

—*MARCUS J. BORG*
Jesus a New Vision (2009)

Our Christian answers to the basic questions about our worldview are found in our Bible. They provide us with the elements necessary for our Christian identity. Our worldview provides a structure, a story and an understanding of our situation as the context in which the meaning of our lives can emerge. Our Christian way of seeing the world (vision) and of being and acting in it (vocation) gives us a new way of interpreting the meaning of the events happening to us.

In sketching out any religious worldview, there are six basic questions that we must ask. The different answers to these questions distinguish the worldviews of the world's religions from one another. The questions are:

- who is God?
- what is God is doing?
- who are we in relation to God?
- where do we situate ourselves in space and time?
- what is wrong with our situation?
- how can it be remedied?

As we briefly sketch out the generally held Christian answers to these worldview questions, note that the biblical authors do not make abstract statements of their beliefs in this systematic format but incorporate them into images and stories and practical guidelines for behavior in particular situations. Thus our answers must be sifted out from these stories.

1) Who Is God?

Jesus identifies God as the king, the all-powerful yet benevolent ruler of the cosmos and of history. Jesus' theology does not emphasize God's distant, transcendent mystery but rather God's activity in our world in search of a relationship with humanity. God is a mystery transcending our finite powers of understanding and appropriation but at the same time a presence coming from beyond us that is also working in us and in our world.

"The whole New Testament is a record of mystery—the mystery of Jesus. The mystery of the kingdom hidden in parables. The mystery of the Father hidden in Jesus. The mystery of the sending of the Spirit. What a series of mysteries! Christianity is basically mystery. And all is contained in the mystery of Christ."
—WILLIAM JOHNSTON
Christian Mysticism Today (1984)

God is benevolent (heavenly patron/father/savior). God is not hostile but a generous and favorably disposed patron who controls all resources for life. God always does what is best for all creatures by giving everyone what they need and disposing all things for good. God is a bountiful gift-giver, a benefactor who does not hoard resources, wealth or the necessities for living. Instead God is constantly giving gifts and, because of God's covenant obligations, God is concerned with saving us from difficult situations and mending any breakdowns in the relationship.

God's greatest act of salvation occurred through the person and work of Jesus of Nazareth, the chosen messiah or agent of God for salvation. Through his death and resurrection, Jesus reveals that what God had in store for all humanity at the end time has now occurred in the middle of history. The Good News is that like Jesus death is no longer the end of our relationship with God, but the passageway to a new life with God.

God is the ruler (king/lord) over the cosmos and over history. One of the major biblical emphases is that God alone creates and rules over the ordered universe (Gk: *kosmos).* The prerogative of any divinity is power, and for monotheists their God alone is all powerful. As almighty, God is the sole lord and master over both creation and history.

God's wisdom and power establish the order of all reality. Nothing happens without God's knowledge and consent. As creator, God fills the world with good things and makes everything fruitful. As ruler, God orders creation and directs whatever happens among the nations. God the almighty maintains this divine order as judge of creation, designating the appropriate rewards or punishments for disorder.

> "Prophetic proclamation is an effort to imagine the world as though YHWH, the creator of heaven and earth, the deliverer of Israel, the Father of our Lord Jesus Christ whom we Christians name as Father, Son and Spirit, is a real character and the defining agent in the world."
>
> —*WALTER BRUEGGEMANN*
> *The Practice of Prophetic Imagination: Preaching an Emancipating Word* (2012)

The death and resurrection experience of Jesus taught Christians that neither human empires nor the power of death can thwart God's desires for relationship. Death might end a life, but it cannot end a relationship if God wants it to continue. As Paul summarized it, God "gives life to the dead and calls into being what does not exist" (Rom 4:17).

2) What Is God Doing in Relation to Us & Our World?

God's presence and activity are always for the sake of relationships. God's purpose and plan are revealed in the historical drama of **God entering into a covenant with humanity.** Thus human history is, at its core, a salvation history—the story of God in search of a people who will form the kind of community that God envisions and thus re-order the world that is now disfigured by evil. The covenant is God's antidote to sin.

If we take a quick overview of the Bible, we find that God's desire for relationship is the purpose of all God's activity. God's dream for a covenant community is told in the stories of four different communities: the Eden community of Adam and Eve (who represent all humanity) found in Genesis 1–11, the community of Israel told in Genesis 12 to the end of the Old Testament, the kingdom community of Jesus reported in the Gospels, and the discipleship community of Christians recounted in Luke's Acts of the Apostles (which continues to today). Each of these four versions reveals the same general pattern of God's search for a community in which dominion would be held by God, where justice would regulate human relationships based on love, and the blessing of peace—the fullness of life (Heb: *shalom*)—would result for everybody.

"God's plan of revelation is realized by deeds and words having an inner unity: the deeds wrought by God in the history of salvation manifest and confirm the teachings and realities signified by the words, while the words proclaim the deeds and clarify the mystery contained in them. By this revelation, then, the deepest truth about God and the salvation of humanity is made clear to us in Christ, who is the mediator and at the same time the fullness of all revelation."

—*VATICAN COUNCIL II*
Dogmatic Constitution on Divine Revelation (Dei Verbum) (1965), #2

As God engages in the covenant relationship, the familiar salvation story unfolds and reveals God's characteristic roles as life giver (creator), rescuer (savior), covenant maker, lawgiver and judge (lord) in relation to the covenant communities. God's presence to judge and to save transforms not only the covenant communities but also all creation.

3) Who Are We in Relation to God?

Our core identity as Christians is established in relation to God. Since God's power and action are directed toward establishing a relationship with humanity through Jesus, **we are the people who are called to be in relationship with God, the new covenant people, the new Israel.** To symbolize this connection with the twelve tribes that constituted the original Israel, Jesus chose twelve disciples as the foundation of his new kingdom (Mk 3:13-19; Mt 10:1-16; Lk 6:12-16). We are the gathered assembly (Gk: *ekklēsia*, the root of our word *ecclesial*) of God's people chosen to realize God's dream for a community that will live according to Jesus' guidelines. So what distinguishes us is that we are called by Christ to be in relationship with God and with others in the kingdom community. We are hearers of God's word, receivers of God's revelation who respond by giving our commitment to God and to the realization of our relationship.

4) Where Are We in God's Plan?

Identifying our location is an essential factor in our worldview. How we understand the framework of reality, its principles of order and its processes will allow us to situate ourselves in these wider contexts. Just as we can use maps to discover our location and calendars to place ourselves in time, so in a Christian worldview we must answer where we are in relation to God's map of the cosmos and God's timetable for salvation history.

At creation, God's world had been rightly ordered but then was disordered through human sin. This disorder needs to be eliminated and the original right order restored. Genesis chapters 1–11 describe how God began this reordering first after Adam and Eve's sin, then after the flood through a covenant with Noah and his family, then after Babel through a covenant with Abraham and his descendants (Israel), and finally brought it to a final reordering through the covenant with Jesus and the Christian community, and is now working in our world to bring it to completion. Jesus imagines and describes this reordered world as the kingdom of God and invites us to cooperate with God in its realization.

"The mystery of God's wonderful love is that you come with it into the world and it blesses you whether you know it or not. Your life is in God's universal embrace of the whole human family. So if you look with eyes of faith you discover that you are son or daughter, brother or sister, father or mother in the most deeply spiritual way."

—*HENRI J. M. NOUWEN*
Finding My Way Home (2001)

Jesus proclaimed that he and his audience lived **at the moment when the final transformation of all reality according to God's plan was now beginning.** He described this event as a "new age" (Mt 19:28, NABRE, see also 1 Cor 10:11; Heb 9:26) when the right order desired by God would finally be established. The first Christians described this as a new creation (2 Cor 5:17; Gal 6:15). We must remember, however, that creation for them did not stress the production of something from nothing but rather the establishing of right order and relationships.

5) What Is Wrong?

If you ask people what is wrong with our world, you get answers like the economy, or politics, or the breakdown of family values or lax moral standards. **If you asked Jesus, his answer was sin, which can be generically described as whatever breaks down relationships.** Jesus reminded us that our world and our history are dominated by evil powers rather than by God, and hence right relationships are distorted and impaired.

The biblical authors not only detect the toxic presence of sin but also recognize that it is not some accidental factor but an active power that permeates our world and seeks to disorder its divinely established order by setting up an alternative system of disorder in its place. Evil lurks closely beneath the surface of our ordinary reality and remains hidden by disguising itself behind established systems of domination. Unmasking evil and keeping it in check is a constant task. One must be continually vigilant to detect its presence and its practices of disorder and reestablish the right order desired by God from creation.

"What is wrong with the world is most fundamentally that people respond to evil with evil and thereby aggravate the spiral of violence. The key to the good news is that we are freed from prolonging the chain of evil causes engendering evil effects by action and reaction in kind. By refusing to extend the chain of vengeance, we break into the world with good news. This one key opened the door to a restructuring of the entire universe of Christian life and thought."

—*JOHN HOWARD YODER*
The Politics of Jesus (1994)

Since God aims to establish the right kind of relationships between people and God and with one another, sin is whatever breaks down these relationships. The specific types of sins just represent the different ways to weaken and dissolve relationships—rebellion, disobedience, deviation from the way, missing the mark, breaking the law. The disorder created by sin is described as evil, folly, alienation and abomination.

Jesus reminds us that a cosmic struggle is going on in which evil has slowly but surely set up an alternative order to God's original order and rule over the world. Acting through human agents and empires, which personify the disorder and domination of sin, the powers of evil directly contradict God's desire for the right kind of community. The signs of this sinful dominance are evident in the chaos plaguing our cosmos, our history, our nations, our communities and ourselves.

Jesus proposes a worldview that affirms that our real enemies are these evil powers contesting against God for world dominance and demanding our loyalty. Consequently our world is a battleground of good and evil powers locked in a life-and-death struggle for mastery. Because human sinfulness constantly breaks down our relationships with God

GOD'S NEW RULE IS HERE!

and with one another, the history of our world has been the story of the gradual and insidious domination of evil instead of the triumph of the kingdom of God.

"In Jesus' own understanding of the battle he was fighting, Rome was not the real enemy. The real enemy, to be met head-on by the power and love of God, was the anti-creation power, the power of death and destruction, the force of accusation, the Accuser (Satan) who lays a charge against the whole human race and the world itself that all are corrupt and decaying, that all humans have contributed to this by their own idolatry and sin. Jesus has taken the accusations that were outstanding against the world and against the whole human race and has borne them in himself."

—*N. T. WRIGHT*
Simply Good News: Why the Gospel Is News and What Makes It Good (2015)

6) What Is the Solution?

As any doctor knows so well, the remedy for what is wrong must be directly related to the ailment. The remedy is what restores the relationship to health. The metaphor of health is the source of our term for salvation (Lat: *salus,* meaning health). So in a theological worldview the remedy for sin is salvation. Before *salvation* became a technical theological term, it simply meant to rescue someone from a difficult situation. Thus salvation comes when a rescuer (redeemer) or saver (savior) comes to help or rescue those in need.

The biblical notion of salvation centers on God stepping in to remedy the breakdown of the relationship between God and humanity. Humans, who are subject to the seductive powers of evil, introduce disorder into God's creation through their sins which break down relationships. But since God originally initiated and established the relationships, God must act to restore what has been broken down. Salvation history is the story of God's interventions not only to establish relationships but to restore them when they inevitably break down because of human sin.

Jesus proclaimed that he and his message were the necessary remedy for the disordered relationships that have plagued humanity since its beginning. As God's messiah, son and end-times agent, Jesus inaugurates the kingdom of right relationships in which evil and its harmful effects (sickness, disease, suffering and death) will no longer dominate our lives. Because the coming of the kingdom will establish healthy relationships, its arrival can be symbolized by physical healing and the forgiveness of sins, that is, eliminating whatever has broken down the relationship.

"Salvation has long been established as the summary word to refer to the range of human dependency on God. It arises out of a common sense of the fragility of life, constantly threatened by an endless sequence of dangers—illness and disease, bad harvests, famine and flood, hostile armies and banditry, injustice and oppression, human failing, greed and spite, accidents, old age, and on and on. The term *salvation* sums up the help needed, the rescue hoped for, and so, in the end, the condition and situation of one who has survived all such perils and attained to a state beyond such threatening dangers—the state of having been saved."

—*JAMES D. G. DUNN*
New Testament Theology (2009)

Jesus' Achievement

The specifically Christian worldview unveiled by Jesus was new and different from any that had been produced before. It allowed the emerging Christian communities to discover their identity in a culture that was not yet influenced by the Christian vision, values and lifestyle that would eventually permeate Western civilization and finally the whole world.

Jesus' kingdom worldview reveals that through Christ God is now initiating the final transformation of our world into God's reordered world. This new creation will be characterized by justice (God enters to secure right relations), love (we will be bonded to God and others in solidarity and friendship), without evil (God triumphs over evil) and no longer subject to the sting of death. This new world order will bring about peace and harmony both for creation and for all humanity.

As Jesus so clearly demonstrated in his own ministry, to change a person's mind—to offer the person Christ's way of seeing and way of being in the world—is to bring the kingdom. The truly Good News is that in the person and work of Jesus God is reordering the whole universe. Jesus' resurrection is the down-payment on the right ordering of all creation according to God's plan begun after the first sin. No wonder Jesus can tell his audience that "The coming of God's kingdom cannot be observed, and no one will announce, 'Look, here it is,' or, 'There it is.' For behold, the kingdom of God is among you" (Lk. 17:20-21), i.e., in Jesus himself.

GOD'S NEW RULE IS HERE!

A New Kind of King

When reading the Gospels it is always interesting to notice the response of the audience to Jesus' words. So when the people hear Jesus announce the Good News that God's kingdom has now drawn near, they do not seem surprised or even puzzled at all. For them God is and always has been their king so this would hardly pass for "news." The simple announcement that God is king is not the "news." The real "news" is rather what kind of king God will be and how God will rule the community. In fact, it is this characteristic emphasis on God as a new kind of king that will guide Jesus' proposal of a new kind of kingdom community that will be more guided by kinship values than political ones, by mercy not holiness, and by service to others not power over others.

"Jesus' way of teaching through parables was a pastoral act of prophetic imagination in which he invited his community of listeners out beyond the visible realities of Roman law and the ways in which Jewish law had grown restrictive in his time. He tells parables consistent with the rabbinic tradition, but his parables serve to conjure alternative social reality. The stories intend to characterize an alternative society which he calls 'kingdom of God,' but the stories do not offer blueprints, budgets, or programs. They only tease the listeners to begin to turn loose of the givens of the day and to live toward a new social possibility."

—*WALTER BRUEGGEMANN*
Hopeful Imagination: Prophetic Voices in Exile (1986)

Although there are many terms describing and naming God, there is a consistent structural pattern that undergirds them all and cuts across all four social realms. The crucial thing in every realm is its organization of human relationships. Since we usually understand things about God using analogies taken from human experience, we would expect the human experience of establishing and maintaining human relationships also to guide their understanding of the divine-human relationship. But what guidelines did the first-century Mediterranean person have for understanding relationships and how they worked?

Recall from chapter 1 that their culture was characterized by patron/client relationships as the way that relationships between unequals were structured (see p. 27) and through which loyalties were cemented and benefits distributed. To summarize, patron/client relationships are:

- between unequals in power, wealth, status, learning, etc. (in contrast to friendship, which was considered a relationship between equals)
- based on open-ended reciprocity or mutual exchange, in which both the parties give something in order to get something they need or want
- voluntary (not a legal obligation or something "owed" to anyone)
- particular (favoritism is expected and benefits distributed freely)
- binding on both parties (with social rather than legal obligations and clear sanctions if the mutual obligations are not satisfactorily met)

"What kind of a king is Jesus? He does not enter the holy city to receive the honors reserved to earthly kings, to the powerful, to rulers. He enters to be scourged, insulted and abused, to receive a crown of thorns, a staff, a purple robe: his kingship becomes an object of derision. Jesus on the cross feels the whole weight of the evil, and with the force of God's love he conquers it, he defeats it with his resurrection. With his love, God conquered evil."

—*POPE FRANCIS*
Homily (March 24, 2013)

So in their patronage culture people understood their relationship with God (the most powerful patron of all) through what was required of them as subordinated clients in their everyday relationships. Their relationship with God was also illustrated both in their use of patron titles calling God *father, benefactor, savior, lord, master, king*, and in their description of God's benefits as *favors, grace, and mercy (compassion)*.

Thinking in patron-client terms can also help us understand how the dynamics of the covenant relationship gets worked out through history, for example in the crucial exodus experience when the covenant relationship was expressed in a more formal way. The mutual "testing" by God and by the people in the wilderness reveals how each partner is exploring the loyalty and reliability of the other as covenant partner.

From God's side as patron, God's reliability as a faithful covenant partner is proven through the exodus rescue and liberation. God expects exclusive loyalty from the people (who fail by worshiping the golden calf), submission and obedience to God's commands (God's speaks only ten formal commands—the rest are supplied by Moses because the people are afraid to encounter God more directly, Ex 20:1-19).

71

From the people's side as clients, they struggle to give their exclusive loyalty to God and to hear and obey God. But they also expect God the patron to provide for them in the wilderness (thus the accounts of the manna, quail and water) and to protect them from hostile groups who attack them or who must be conquered to possess the promised land.

Jesus' understanding of God as our heavenly patron also influences his idea of God as king. But even though Jesus announces God's kingdom, he does not call or address God as *king,* as is common in many psalms and other Old Testament passages. He prefers to use the kinship language of *father* when talking about God. His vision of God's forthcoming kingdom is one over which God the king rules, but the way God rules is more like the rule of a loving father over a family than a king over a nation. Thus for Jesus the coming restoration of Israel (God's new kingdom) will be governed by a "king" who is a father/patron in heaven, and the consequent reordering of life demands new structures to replace the domination systems and the skewed values and false legitimations that they rest on.

A New Kind of Community

As a Yahwist, Jesus grew up in community of Israel which, for over a millennia, had been trying to realize God's dream of a community that would contrast with every type of human community. As sons and daughters of Abraham, they understood themselves not only as the family of Abraham but also as the family of God.

It is no wonder, then, that Jesus would imagine the ideal community for his disciples as God's family and its members as God's children. Thus in his language Jesus gravitates to the image of God as the heavenly patron, the head of the household, the father or king who protected and provided for everyone in the household. Jesus' image of God's kingdom community was that of a family in which God alone was its head.

Thus all humanity could now be gathered together under God's rule. Thus Jesus recognized something that had often been missed in Judaism, especially in the previous five centuries since the time of the Babylonian exile. In direct contrast to the Judahist idea that their community should be characterized by a separatist and often elitist attitude as God's chosen people, Jesus taught that God's family included all humanity.

In his very first discourse in Matthew's Gospel, known as the Sermon on the Mount (Mt 5–7), Jesus revealed to his disciples his dream for his new community. He identified the benefits bestowed by God as the beatitudes or blessings that those in the community would share (Mt 5:1-12). He dreamed of a kingdom community in which the poor and oppressed would be blessed, those who mourn would be comforted, and the meek would inherit the land. He yearned for a kingdom community in which those who hunger and thirst for justice would be satisfied, where the merciful would be shown mercy, and the clean of heart would see God. In this new kingdom community, peacemakers would be called God's children, and those persecuted for justice' sake and slandered and treated evilly would be rewarded. Anyone who chooses to follow Jesus as a Christian is invited to continue Jesus' work to make this dream of a kingdom community into a reality, to realize it by living the kingdom way now.

"In saying 'Your kingdom come,' we are acknowledging that faith in Jesus is not simply an idea or an emotion. It is a concrete reality of which we are to become part or else be out of step with the way things are now that God has come into the world in Jesus. When the kingdom comes, we are 'to repent' (i.e., change, let go of our citizenship in the old kingdoms) and 'believe the good news' (i.e., join up, become part of the revolution)."

—*WILLIAM WILLIMON & STANLEY HAUERWAS*
Lord, Teach Us: the Lord's Prayer & Christian Life (1996)

The Challenge of Jesus' Kingdom Message

Jesus reveals to us that the kingdom is a mystery, suddenly given and granted, to be lived, and not a thing to possess and control or a place to be. Jesus' kingdom invites us to break through the blinders and boundaries of everyday life to discover something new—a divine mystery that can be encountered but never fully comprehended or expressed in concepts and theories and that requires endless deepening and constant re-interpretation and re-enactment by each individual and succeeding generation.

Since Jesus' kingdom worldview reveals God's transforming presence which normally lies hidden beneath the appearances of our familiar cultural world, it also offers the key to one's transformation into a Christian. To assent to the truth of Jesus' revelation of a God-centered world is the fundamental challenge of Christian conversion.

Hearing and heeding the gospel message will challenge every dimension of our relationship with God and with our fellow believers. It challenges us to hear the words of the biblical message which lays bare the person and work of God in our midst; to make a commitment to the God who is disclosed through it; to adopt this theological worldview and to see and evaluate the world as God does and act in it as God does. It challenges us to link our hope for a new order with the cosmic and historical work of God to realize the divine dream for the right kind of community. Finally, it challenges us to engage in the real power struggle between God and Satan, good and evil, which wreaks so much havoc in our world today.

"Our task as image-bearing, God-loving, Christ-shaped, Spirit-filled Christians, following Christ and shaping our world, is to announce redemption to a world that has discovered its fallenness, to announce healing to a world that has discovered its brokenness, to proclaim love and trust to a world that knows only exploitation, fear and suspicion. I believe if we face the question, 'if not now, then when?' if we are grasped by this vision we may also hear the question, 'if not us, then who?' And if the gospel of Jesus is not the key to this task, then what is?"

—*N. T. WRIGHT*
The Challenge of Jesus: Rediscovering Who Jesus Was and Is (2015)

Jesus not only invites us to follow him but to see the world as he does and so live the way he does. Adopting his new kingdom worldview changes everything for those who accept it. The Good News about God's kingdom begun in Jesus' life, death and resurrection challenges our commonly accepted view of the world. What if things are not as we think they are? What if things could be different? What would our world be like if God really were recognized as its ruler? What then?

CHAPTER THREE

If God Rules, Then What?
Turning the World Upside Down

In the Acts of the Apostles, Paul and Silas his missionary companion entered a synagogue in the Greek city of Thessalonika and argued from scripture that Jesus was God's promised messiah sent to put the world right again. The congregation became so enraged that they formed a mob and complained to the city magistrates that these Christians "who have been turning the world upside down have come here also…acting contrary to emperor's decrees, saying that there is another king named Jesus" (Acts 17:6). Here in a nutshell is what happens when you make Jesus' worldview your own—it will turn your old world upside down.

"Jesus had come to say that God was becoming king, that God was accomplishing the new exodus, that this was the long-awaited good news that would change everything. People were healed—a sign of new creation reaching out to embrace actual human bodies and lives. People found forgiveness, as the power of new creation reached into their moral and spiritual lives with the warm assurance of God's love. People who had seen themselves at the bottom of the pile, economically, socially, morally and physically, suddenly found their lives turned upside down."

—N. T. WRIGHT
Simply Good News: Why the Gospel Is News and What Makes It Good (2015)

Adopting Jesus' Kingdom Worldview
Every worldview entails both **a vision** of a coherent structure of how one sees, understands and organizes reality and **a vocation** or call to realize these meanings in their lives. Thus whoever wants to make Jesus' kingdom vision their own must then use it to make God's rule real and effective in the world. Jesus' kingdom worldview offers a new vision of a God-centered community, a God-ordered universe, a God-dominated salvation history and a God-governed new creation. Because one's worldview influences one's values, which in turn impact behavior, adopting Jesus'

worldview and living it require the change of heart and mind that Jesus demanded (Mk 1:15; Mt 4:17; Lk 5:32) and everything will be changed. And because worldviews tend to be exclusive, adopting Jesus' kingdom worldview demands a rejection of all other worldviews.

"The first impact of conversion is to modify our sense of values: God being at the center of all, everything acquires a new position and a new depth. All that is God's, all that belongs to him, is positive and real. Everything that is outside him has no value or meaning. But it is not a change of mind alone that we can call conversion. We can change our minds and go no farther; what must follow is an act of will and unless our will comes into motion and is redirected Godwards, there is no conversion; at most there is only an incipient, still dormant, and inactive change in us."

—*ANTHONY BLOOM*
Living Prayer (1966)

When the early Christians adopted Jesus' worldview, they had to give up their previously held worldviews, whether Israelite which would not include Christ or Hellenistic which allowed multiple loyalties to many gods. Affirming Christ as the lord and center of our universe brought the early Christians into opposition with all other claims of dominion and sovereign authority and tested their loyalty to God.

A Reordering of Loyalty

Adopting Jesus' worldview meant proclaiming "Jesus is lord" as the first step to salvation (Rom 10:9; 1 Cor 12:3) and demanded complete and exclusive loyalty if one wanted to receive the benefits/gifts (grace) that God our heavenly patron/father distributes. This demand for loyalty is the fundamental question for any Christian—Who is your lord and God (*dominus et deus*) whom you will you serve (Lk 4:8; 1 Thes 1:9)? Is it Caesar or Christ (Jn 19:12)? Is it *Mammon* (wealth) or Christ (Mt 6:24; Lk 6:13)? Is it God or Satan? This was also the basic first commandment issue for all Yahwists (Dt 10:12; Jos 24:15). Would Yahweh alone be their God, or would they put idols or false gods in Yahweh's place?

Thus in relation to God, exclusive loyalty or fidelity was always the most crucial issue, for it identified one's allegiance to the primary power that controlled one's life. Since ancient peoples felt they were at the mercy of many layers of overlapping powers and gods, everyone sought to enter into and to maintain relationships with this hierarchy of divine powers in order to maximize one's chances of survival by trusting that their loyalty would be rewarded. But this required carefully calculating which loyalties would work best in one's relationships.

> "A phrase such as *Kingdom of God* must be understood within, first, the absolute conjunction of religion and politics and, second, the situation of imperial domination and colonial exploitation. The phrase evokes an ideal vision of political and religious power, of how this world here below would be run if God, not Caesar, sat on the imperial throne. As such it always casts a caustically critical shadow on human rule. It includes especially a basic, fundamental, radical, utopian, counter-cultural, or eschatological rejection of the world as it is currently run."
>
> —*JOHN DOMINC CROSSAN*
> *The Essential Jesus* (1994)

A crisis arose when one was forced to choose loyalty between two masters (Mt 6:24; Lk 6:13). The decision to align oneself with one master not another was always a potentially dangerous situation that often led to perilous results. Powerful masters when rejected could turn on a weaker person and ruin them. Moreover, to lose favor with a powerful master often meant being rejected and excluded from the community of his followers who benefited from his protection and his preferential treatment. In a society in which survival depended on belonging to the group, being excluded could often mean death.

A Reordering of Power

Maintaining exclusive loyalty to God as sovereign ruler and Jesus as God's messianic agent demands complete loyalty, and thus no allegiance to other rulers or lords, whether thought of as divine (idols) or experienced as human (emperors, kings, priests, wealthy patrons or males in the household). Thus this reordering of loyalty also demands a reordering of power to serve God's goals for the restoration of creation and the human community to its right order—just relationships held together by love and resulting in well-being for all instead of unjust domination relationships held together by violence and resulting in conflict and exploitation.

In the Bible, God's power is described as God's Holy Spirit. Since breath or spirit is the sign of life and always accompanies power expressed

77

either in words (a spoken word always requires breath to make it happen) or in actions (action requires having life or breath, and the more that power is exerted in our actions, the more we breathe). Thus God's power is revealed when the divine Spirit descends on an agent, as happened at Jesus' baptism, empowering him for his mission of doing God's work.

"Jesus gave his followers a new way to live: a new way to deal with offenders—by forgiving them; a new way to deal with violence—by suffering; a new way to deal with money—by sharing it; a new way to deal with problems of leadership—by drawing upon the gift of every member, even the most humble; a new way to deal with a corrupt society—by building a new order, not smashing the old; a new pattern of relationships between man and woman, parent and child, master and slave, in which was made concrete a radical new vision of what it means to be a human person."

—*JOHN HOWARD YODER*
The Politics of Jesus (1994)

God's kingdom, then, is imagined as a new kind of godly domination whose benefits will establish new relationships that will reverse present unjust dominations and realize the hoped for restoration of Israel, which will be an alternative community, governed by a "king" who is really our father/patron in heaven. Since loyalty must be total and all-consuming, we must use our power to reorder the world as God wants it to be. This reordering will also require a new social organization and institutions that can replace the unjust human domination systems and the values and legitimations they rest on.

Jesus' Alternatives to Unjust Dominations

The consequences of the conflict between the kingdom worldview and the worldview embodied in the four realms of the social world will always turn that old world upside down and challenge the entrenched domination hierarchies that structure it.

Although the issues here are complex and require a much more thorough analysis, we can summarize by recalling that domination systems depend on certain assumptions (e.g., that one group is entitled to rule over others and use its power to generate privileges like honor, wealth and food), which in turn create dualistic value categories that are embodied in hierarchical "ranking" systems (masters/servants, men/women, rulers/

ruled, rich/poor, us/them) that generate consequences when they become the fundamental guidelines for the organizing the structures of a social system (see the chart on pp. 34-35).

If, as Jesus claims, God indeed rules as our lord and a new alternative society is demanded, then each of the four realms will be affected and those now dominating those realms will have to be deposed and their domination systems that control and distribute social power, wealth and privilege (kings to subjects, citizens to foreigners, husbands to wives, adults to children, business patrons to clients, masters to slaves) must be reordered in relation to God's transforming presence now at work.

"Not only did Jesus and his followers repudiate the autocratic values of power and wealth, but the institutions and systems that authorized and supported these values: the family, the Law, the sacrificial system, the Temple, kosher food regulations, the distinction between clean and unclean, patriarchy, role expectations for women and children, the class system, the use of violence, racial and ethnic divisions, the distinction between insider and outsider—indeed, every conceivable prop of domination, division and supremacy. The gospel, is a context-specific remedy for the evils of the Domination System."

—*WALTER WINK*
Engaging the Powers: Discernment and Resistance in a World of Domination (1992)

Jesus recognized not only that individuals were responsible for the evil that wreaked havoc in their lives, but also that the structural domination systems, corrupted by evil powers that remained invisible (Mt 4:8-9; Lk 4:5-8), perpetuated and disseminated evil. If the kingdom were to come, as we pray daily in the prayer to God our patron in heaven that Jesus gave us, (Mt 6:9-13; Lk 11:2-4), then this kingdom will necessarily conflict with all unjust domination systems. In Jesus' prayer, the first set of petitions indicate how we, as God's clients or dependents, must fulfill our part of the patronage relationship by respecting God's holy name (or person) and share God's aim of creating the kingdom community here on earth. The second set of petitions asks God to fulfill the God's patronal obligations by providing food ("our daily bread"), forgiving our offenses (conditioned on our forgiveness of others), and protecting us from evil.

Thus, if God really does rule, then what does that imply for those who thought they were the rulers of this world? Let us briefly examine

IF GOD RULES, THEN WHAT?

each of the four social realms to show how Jesus' teaching and example demands reordering our basic loyalty and how our power must be redirected to build God's kingdom. In this way we will also discover how our institutionalized human domination systems are challenged by Jesus' kingdom vision of God as a beneficent heavenly father or patron and God's community as his followers joined by a bond of loyalty (faith) to God and one another in a covenant community of solidarity and care.

"Our Father in Heaven": The Family Challenge
If God Rules, then the Father Doesn't

We begin with the realm of the family and kinship, which was the most tenacious bond for most ancient people. The family was the necessary context without which life was practically impossible, for it provided the "safety net" which helped people survive and succeed. Because choosing to follow Jesus reorders one's loyalty, it brings "not peace but division" into families (Mt 10:34-7; Lk 12:49-53) in which the father or patron of the household had complete power over all the members and used it to provide for them and protect them from harm.

The Gospels reveal how Jesus challenged many of the traditional norms of family life because of his own loyalty to God his heavenly father. He insisted that loyalty to the kingdom and the demands of discipleship must take precedence over family obligations (Mk 3:31-35; Mt 8:21-22; 12:46-50; Lk 9:57-62), which was also illustrated in his relationship with his own family when at age 12 he visited Jerusalem and stayed behind to question the learned teachers (Lk 2:42-52) in the Temple.

Jesus did not choose any of his brothers to be apostles, though from Paul we know that his brother James (Mk 6:3; Mt 13:55) was an important leader with Peter and John in the Jerusalem Christian community (Gal 1:19, 2:9, 2:12). And when his family—mother, brothers and sisters (Mk 6:3; Mt 13:55)—came to take him back to Nazareth because his healing and exorcisms were dishonoring the family and people were saying "he has gone out of his mind" (Mk 3:21), Jesus' identified his disciples as his real family (Mk 3:31-35; Mt 12:46-50; Lk 8:19-21).

But despite this apparent family tension, Luke portrays Mary in a very favorable light, and, as we will see when studying his Gospel, for him

Mary is the model disciple (see pp. 183-184). John also portrays Mary favorably and frames Jesus' ministry with two events involving her. The wedding at Cana (Jn 2:1-12) launches Jesus into his kingdom ministry and from the cross Jesus seems to reconcile his mother with the disciple whom he loved (19:26-27)—thus preventing any enduring friction between his family and his disciples in the new kingdom community.

Jesus also challenged the inferior family status of women by urging an end to divorce practices which gave women no rights, arguing instead that the Old Testament norm was monogamy, understood as an equal relationship between a man and woman (Mk 10:2-12; Jn 4:7-29; 7:53–8:11). He also included women as his followers (Lk 8:2-3) and suggested that they could be spiritual leaders as well as domestic workers (Lk 10:40-42).

He also challenged the inferior status of children by using them as examples of true discipleship (Mk 9:33-37; 10:13-16). It is clear, though, that his intention was not to abolish the family, but to challenge conventional assumptions about family loyalties (Mk 7:9-13; 10:1-12; Lk 18:18-30; Jn 19:26-27) and encourage human father's to use their power and authority the same way that God does as a father (Mt 7:21; 11:12-13). Human fathers must imitate the characteristics of the "father in heaven" as outlined by Jesus' emphasis on mercy instead of holiness as the key to right relationships: "Be merciful, just as your Father is merciful" (Luke 6:36).

"Jesus' metaphor, kingdom of God, defines the world in which we live. If Christ is King, every thing and everyone has to be re-imagined, re-configured, re-oriented to a way of life that consists in an obedient following of Jesus. This is not easy. A total renovation of our imagination, our way of looking at things—what Jesus commanded in his no-nonsense imperative, 'Repent!'—is required."

—*EUGENE H. PETERSEN*
The Jesus Way (2007)

Jesus reminded his disciples that "you have one father—the one in heaven" (Mt 23:9) and consequently through their relationship to Jesus, who is God's son, now they are also "children of God" (Jn 1:12.). Thus their primary loyalty must be to God their father in heaven. To become a disciple means to reorder one's loyalty away from one's human father and family to one's heavenly father and kingdom family.

IF GOD RULES, THEN WHAT?

"Thy Kingdom Come": The Political Challenge
If God Rules, then Caesar Doesn't

The reordering of loyalty and the use of power required by adopting Jesus' kingdom worldview also challenges one's loyalty to the political rulers and their use of power to create and sustain systems of domination. In a Temple-state like Judea where the religious and political realms were so tightly connected, Rome delegated the responsibility for keeping local populations under control to the religious leaders and elite families who could continue their domination ways as long as they made sure that Rome's revenues flowed in and any disturbances were stopped. Thus Jesus' Good News challenges both the Roman empire (whose interests are administered by the local governor Pontius Pilate) and the Judean religious leaders (who are appointed to administer the Jerusalem Temple and the affairs of Judea), who, if they want to retain their power and privileges, must show their loyalty to the imperial domination system.

"God's kingdom, said Jesus, was coming. When Herod heard, he was angry; he was King of the Jews, and rival claimants tended not to live long. When the Chief Priests heard, they knew that it meant a challenge to their power base, the Temple. If Caesar had heard, he would have reacted similarly. What none of them could figure out, and what even Jesus' closest associates had difficulty understanding, was what kind of a challenge Jesus intended to pose: what sort of a kingdom he was advancing, and what kind of a king he considered himself to be."

—*N. T. WRIGHT*
"God and Caesar: Then and Now," (June 30, 2003)

One way to illustrate Jesus' challenge and their responses might be to examine why Jesus was crucified, which reveals the interconnecting political-religious realms in which the distinction between politics and religion was not sharply drawn and so every public religious claim could also have political ramifications. Although Jesus did not seek political power, as he explains to Pontius Pilate: "My kingdom is not from this world" (Jn 18:36), nevertheless any claim even remotely perceived by the Romans as a threat to their domination was swiftly and ruthlessly dealt with.

In the Gospels, we note that hostility to Jesus and his kingdom message do not just erupt suddenly at the end of his life. Early on in his ministry the Judean authorities begin resisting his kingdom message with various objections that soon turn lethal when the Pharisees "conspired with the Herodians against him, how to destroy him" (Mk 3:6).

John's Gospel also highlights this hostility, but gives the reason why Jesus must die to preserve the domination system of the Judean priests in their collusion with Rome. When the chief priests and the Pharisees are afraid that because of Jesus' signs, "everyone will believe in him, and the Romans will come and destroy both our holy place (the Temple) and our nation," Caiphas the high priest assures them that "it is better for you to have one man die for the people than to have the whole nation destroyed" so "from that day on they planned to put him to death" (Jn 11:41-53).

"Crucifixion was the ruling elites way of dealing with rebellion (along with other means of execution). It was an institution of humiliation, torture and execution designed to deal with the people considered most threatening to the establishment and its interests. It was public, demeaning and painful and designed to strike fear into the hearts of any who would dare pose a threat to the status quo. Normally, the Romans and Judeans reserved crucifixion for the most heinous crimes: rebellion (including social banditry), treason, military desertion and murder."
—*K.C. HANSON & DOUGLAS E. OAKMAN*
Palestine in the Time of Jesus (2008)

When this escalating conflict between Jesus and his opponents over his identity, mission and ministry culminated in his political murder by the Judean and Roman leaders during the Passover in Jerusalem about the year AD 30 (or perhaps 33), the Gospels' accounts of the events highlight how all the participants must make a choice of loyalty to God or to Caesar and the reordering of power to achieve God's desired ends.

Accusations by the Judean Leaders

The interests of the Judean leaders were both religious and political. Their zealous monotheism and refusal to tolerate other gods had more than once brought them into conflict with their Roman overlords. Loyalties to Yahweh and Caesar did not coexist very well because each loyalty was required to be exclusive.

After his arrest, Jesus was taken before the Judean leaders where witnesses accused him of terrorist activity: "We heard him say, 'I will destroy this Temple that is made with hands, and in three days I will build another, not made with hands'" (Mk 14:58; Mt 26:61). For Mark and Matthew this charge is presented as a false accusation because Jesus never says this earlier in their Gospels. But in John's Gospel, after his first public sign at Cana, Jesus goes to Jerusalem and, after driving the merchants and money changers from the Temple precincts, he does say this (Jn 2:19). But then in a kind of editorial aside, John explains that Jesus did not really mean the Temple building but "was speaking of the temple of his body" (Jn 2:21). Still this incident reveals the conflict between Jesus and the Temple and John's continuing concern about where God dwells—in the Temple or in Jesus, God's incarnate son (Jn 1:14) who replaces the Temple as the primary location of God's presence among us.

"For a genuinely Jewish vision of theocracy, you need God in the midst of it. But what the gospels offer us—especially John, but actually all of them—is a God who is in the midst in and as Jesus the Messiah, and a God who is then committed to remaining in the midst, through Jesus, in the person of the Spirit. Jesus himself is the new Temple at the heart of the new creation, against that day when the whole earth shall be filled with the glory of God as the waters cover the sea. And so this Temple, like the wilderness tabernacle, is a temple on the move, as Jesus' people go out, in the energy of the Spirit, to be the dwelling of God in each place, to anticipate that eventual promise by their common and cross-shaped life and work.

—*N. T. WRIGHT*
How God Became King (2012)

When the testimony of the witnesses did not agree, the high priest formulated the charge as a direct question about Jesus' identity as God's chosen messiah (the Christ), the son of God. When Jesus affirmed these two claims, the Judean leaders considered this to be blasphemy (meaning a dishonoring of God by these claims), which was punishable by death. But because they did not have the power to execute Jesus (Jn 18:31), they had to take their case to the Roman governor, Pontius Pilate (Lk 3:1), who was in Jerusalem during the Passover festival as a precaution because when large numbers of Jews congregated for this festival to recall their escape to freedom, their religious zeal could trigger political unrest.

Accusations by the Roman Governor
Recognizing that Pilate would not put Jesus to death for blasphemy, the Judean leaders refocused their accusation in a way that would catch

Pilate's attention. They presented Jesus as a would-be messiah, interpreted in a political way as a king, thus directly challenging the rule of the Roman emperor (Caesar), claiming that Jesus was "perverting our nation, forbidding us to pay taxes to the emperor, and saying that he himself is the messiah, a king" (Lk 23:2) and "stirring up the people by teaching throughout all Judea, from Galilee where he began even to this place" (Lk 23:5).

Jesus would not respond to these slanderous accusations, but did respond truthfully to Pilate's direct question about his identity as the "king of the Judeans" (Mk 15:2-5; Mt 27:11-14; Lk 23:2-5). Pilate found no crime in this and recognized that the accusations of the Judean leaders were motivated by malevolent envy (Gk: *phthonon),* which was a powerful force that always sought to destroy good by producing hatred, malice and the desire to do serious harm. The first-century Jewish author Philo of Alexandria calls it "the most grievous of all evils" *(Special Laws,* III.2).

"We are accustomed to speaking of the death of Jesus as the 'passion' of Jesus, and the stories of his death as the 'passion narratives.' When we do so, we typically think of 'passion' as meaning 'suffering.' And it does mean that. But it has an additional meaning as well. The death of Jesus—his execution—was because of his passion for God and God's justice. And because we see Jesus as the revelation of God, we see in his life and death the passion of God."

—*MARCUS BORG*
The Heart of Christianity (2009)

Jesus' dialogue with Pilate in John's Gospel reveals clearly how everyone had to choose their loyalties. After Jesus assured Pilate that his kingdom was not a worldly one, then the religious establishment's real charge against Jesus surfaced. The Judeans cry out, "We have a law, and according to that law he ought to die, because he made himself the son of God" (Jn 19:7, NABRE). Full of fear at this revelation, Pilate questioned Jesus about his origins but Jesus again remained silent. When Pilate threatened him by claiming power over him, Jesus showed his own loyalty and trust of his heavenly father by reminding Pilate that his power was only from those above him. Pilate then wanted to release Jesus, but Jesus' enemies now played their trump card.

In the Roman social situation, loyalty to one's patron was the highest honor that a client could offer. Clients prided themselves on their special

IF GOD RULES, THEN WHAT?

relationship to powerful patrons and styled themselves "friends" even though there was great inequality in their relationship. But to deny one's loyalty reduced the supposed friend to a conniving traitor. So when the Judean people cried out, "If you release this man, you are no friend of the emperor. Everyone who claims to be a king sets himself against the emperor" (Jn 19:12), Pilate, who owed his governorship to his relationship with his "friend" the emperor, was now forced to reaffirm that loyalty.

But Jewish loyalty was also tested when Pilate asked the Judean mob, "Shall I crucify your king?" The chief priests answered, "We have no king but the emperor" (Jn 19:15). This reply is laced with irony because throughout their history the Israelites had recognized God alone as their king (Pss 47:1-9; 74:12; 145:1; Jer 10:10; Ez 20:33) and endured human kings who constantly infringed on God's kingship (Jgs 8:23; 1 Sm 8:7; 12:12).

"God remains, as he must in this unique theocratic kingdom, the only true king of Israel. Israel will have her human king as well, but he is not to be like the kings of the nations but a representative of God, the true King. He is to be the instrument through which God will work out the ultimate destiny of Israel. He must, therefore, be subject to the Mosaic law and the admonitions and guidance of God's prophets."

—*PETER F. ELLIS, CSSR*
The Men and the Message of the Old Testament (1975)

Now by rejecting Jesus and pledging their loyalty to the Roman emperor, the Judeans at the instigation of their priests were rejecting their covenant loyalty to God as their king and directing their power not for God's goals but for their own selfish desire to retain the power, wealth and privileges enjoyed because of their unjust domination system.

We must note, however, that Jesus' aim was not to replace human political systems, as he explained to Pilate (Jn 18:36). He desired instead to reorder any blind loyalty to rulers who are not loyal to God and do not use their power for the good of the people but rather for the good of those who dominate and use violence to keep the domination system in power. This aim echoes the Old Testament position of Yahweh who allowed the Israelites to have an earthly king, but only on the condition that he acted according to the *Torah* (a recurring prophetic theme). Jesus reminds Pilate that political power and authority are also a gift from God the all powerful heavenly patron: "You would have no power over me unless it had been given you from above" (Jn 19:11). Since power to rule comes from God, it must be used to achieve God's desired ends not human ones.

"Thy Will Be Done": The Religious Challenge
If God Rules, then the Temple Priests Don't

As we noted regarding Jesus' trial, the primary motive of the Judean leaders' hostility was their fear that nation and the Temple might be destroyed by the Romans (which it actually was three decades later). And it is no accident that their concern focused on the Temple. Jesus stressed both in his words and in his deeds that God's powerful presence was not confined to, or even primarily located, in the Temple. Consequently, access to God for worship and sacrifice, for healing, purification and forgiveness was not to be limited to the Temple, its priesthood and its various rituals. But since the Judean priestly families maintained a monopoly on Temple worship through which, with the authorization and support of the Romans, they alone acted as God's agents, they devised many ways to profit from their exclusive role as God's mediators and so were prepared to stop at nothing to keep their control over the Temple as the source for their domination, power and wealth.

The Jerusalem Temple: Where God & the People Meet

To better understand Jesus' conflict with the Temple and the Judean leaders who administered it, we must have a better understanding of what the Temple was and how it functioned in their political-social-economic system. (Note that the usual use of the word *temple* in the Gospels designates not just the sanctuary building that served as God's house, but most often the larger surrounding area encompassing the temple building itself.)

In ancient times, a temple (Lat: a consecrated space) was both where heaven and earth met (thus the Judeans built theirs on Mount Zion, God's holy mountain) and a splendid house where God dwelt as their loyal patron, to protect and provide for them by dispensing divine gifts, thus making the temple sacred because of God's holy presence there.

Holiness described God's unique quality, hence it had no earthly counterpart and characterized God alone. So anything on earth that we might call *holy* (the Temple, the altar, the vessels on the altar, the offering, the priest, the people) can only be made holy through direct contact with God. Because the Judeans believed that their Jerusalem Temple was the only place on earth where God dwelt and should be worshipped (although there were other Yahwist temples in Samaria on Mt. Gerazim, see Jn 4, on Elephantine Island in Upper Egypt, at Leontopolis in Lower Egypt, and possibly at Iraq al-Amir in Transjordan), they measured their holiness by their proximity to the Temple from which God's holiness emanated.

Thus the closer one was to the holy land of Judea, the holy city of Jerusalem, the holy Temple, and in it to the Holy of Holies (i.e., the holiest place of all where God lived), the more intense was the experience of holiness or contact with God. Thus as the worshipper drew closer to God's sanctuary, the Temple area was further divided according to a social hierarchy of graded holiness: non-Israelites (Gentiles), women, Israelites (men), Levites, priests and the high priest who alone could enter the Holy of Holies once a year on the Day of Atonement. Each area was clearly delineated lest its boundaries be crossed and its sacredness defiled.

To have a realistic idea of what their Temple was like, we cannot imagine it as if it were one of our modern day churches, quiet and serene and filled with orderly, reverent worshippers. It was instead more like a large and diversified "government center" with many different bustling departments. To accommodate the large number of participants attending the annual festivals and to comply with the limitations placed by Jewish law on the sanctuary's dimensions, king Herod the Great built a great plaza around it (today's Temple mount with its famous remaining section of the original stone foundation called the Western or Wailing Wall). Near the entrances were ritual baths for purification before entering the Temple precincts.

The actual sanctuary "house" where God dwelt was a shining white marble and gold cubical building with massive bronze entrance doors, "adorned with beautiful stones and gifts dedicated to God" (Lk 21:5). Hidden behind a veil, it was a strictly private area that also contained the ark of the covenant (the box containing the tablets of the covenant law).

The much larger surrounding area was divided into various public areas. One was reserved for worship and sacrifice (Lat: to make holy), which set apart something as a gift for God (thus making it "holy"). A completely burnt offering (Gk: *holocautōma*, a holocaust*)* insured that the giver could not take back the gift. The roasted meat was divided up with portions for God and for the Temple priests and Levites. Every morning and evening there was the sacrifice of a lamb together with an offering of flour mixed with oil, a libation of wine and an incense offering. To provide the animals for sacrifice, there was also a market where persons could purchase "cattle, sheep and doves" (Jn 2:14) and have them slaughtered.

Other areas were designated for law courts and for general gathering and study (where Jesus taught and healed, Mk 12:35; Mt 21:14, 26:55; Lk 2:46; 19:47; 21:37; Jn 7:28; 18:20). There were also thirteen different trumpet-shaped chests into which people put their specific types of contributions, e.g., yearly taxes, tithes and other offerings (recall the widow Jesus sees contributing to the treasury, Mk 12:41-44) which were transferred to storage rooms inaccessible to the public in which were kept not only the things needed for worship but also the money gathered for its upkeep.

Israelites throughout the world were obligated to pay a special tax each year to provide for the maintenance of the Temple. But since foreign coins were usually stamped with images of their gods and emperors (Mt 22:19-21), these coins could not be used for Temple business. Thus money changers congregated in the outer court of the Temple and exchanged these foreign coins for Judean coins for Temple use. Tithes (one tenth, 10%) were also collected as a religious tax that served as a proof of one's piety and religious dedication. They were levied on grain, wine, oil and the firstborn offspring of animals. Some of the tithes supported the Temple personnel and some went to the poor.

Jesus Challenges the Old Ways of Accessing God

Thus the Temple was a large and lucrative operation, whose proceeds in wealth and food (especially meat, grain, wine and oil) supported the priests and Levites who administered the Temple and profited from its various political, religious and economic operations. But upon closer examination, we can see how the Temple and its administration also created and maintained a political-religious-economic domination system whose power derived, like all dominations systems, from controlling important resources for the benefit of those in power. And the primary resource that the Judean priests controlled was access to God and the benefits that God bestowed on those in right relationship with God.

Thus Israelites had to come to the Temple to meet God in worship, to receive God's gifts of healing and forgiveness for whatever sins had broken down their relationship, and to learn what God required of them according to the complex legal regulations (Torah) that ordered their covenant lives. And since it was precisely this controlled access to God through the mediation of the priestly class that Jesus most challenged, no wonder he provoked the greatest hostility from the high priest, the Pharisees and the Judean leaders (Jn 11:47-52), whose power and livelihood depended on retaining control over the Temple and its lucrative business.

In contrast, Jesus' signs revealed that God's power was at work in his healing and exorcisms and so God' gifts of life, a loyal relationship, bodily health and protection from evil spirits—"salvation"—did not depend on mediation through the Temple and its priests. Instead, Jesus himself, because he was God's messiah or agent in whom God dwelt and through whom God's power or Spirit was at work, was the true and effective mediator or broker providing access to God's gifts.

No wonder Jesus' signs provoked an extremely hostile reaction even early in his ministry. Thus when Jesus healed a leper (Mk 1:40), whose healing would normally require the validation by the priests because they decided whether or not a skin eruption was leprous and whether or not a cured leper could be readmitted to the community, Jesus merely sends him on his way, which when his opponents found out about it would be one more reason to "seek to destroy him" (Mk 3:6) for usurping the priestly control over God's gift of healing.

But an even more serious denial of the mediating function of priests and the Temple was Jesus' forgiving sins, which would lead the Judean priests to want to destroy him. When a person's sin was committed against God, the Israelites believed that only God, who had been offended and dishonored by the sinner, could forgive the offense (Mk 2:1-12; Mt 9:2-8; Lk 5:17-26), which meant going to the Temple priests to offer the specific payment to remove the sin/debt/obligation to God in the form of songs, prayers and offering sacrifices. So when Jesus declares that a paralyzed man's sins are forgiven and then demonstrates that this is so because Jesus can just as easily heal him as forgive his sins (because God's power is at work through Jesus in both of these acts), his opponents consider this blasphemy, which is a direct act of disrespect for God by denying God's special power and thinking that one can assume this power for oneself.

"What was it about Jesus' forgiveness of sins that would have caused offense? The answer seems to be that he pronounced the man's sins forgiven *outside the cult and without any reference* (even by implication) *to the cult.* It was not so much that he usurped God's role in announcing sins forgiven but that he usurped the role of God which God had assigned to priest and cult. God could forgive sins no doubt when and as he chose. But man could only promise and pronounce the forgiveness of sins when he operated within the terms and structures provided by God—the Temple, priesthood and sacrifice. In that sense, as usurping a prerogative of God in disregard for the terms laid down by God, what Jesus said and did could be counted a kind of blasphemy."

—*JAMES D. G. DUNN*
The Parting of the Ways (2006)

Another way that Jesus challenged the mediation of the Temple concerned prayer, by which we enter into communion with God. He told people to pray in secret without multiplying words as if trying to attract God's attention or to impress God (Mt 6:5-7) and followed this guideline himself by often praying alone in deserted places and high on mountains (Mk 1:35; 6:36; 14:32-39; Mt 14:23; 26:36; Lk 5:16; 6:12; 9:18; 9:28; 22:41). Although Jesus visited and taught in the Temple, apparently he did not think that Temple worship and rituals were the primary way to encounter God. This was in keeping with his primary emphasis on God's mercy not holiness, which no longer meant for him being separate from everyday life but rather being immersed in everyday life because God was also present there and not just in the Temple through the mediation of the priests.

Jesus' ministry, then, provides several examples demonstrating his revelation of a more direct access to God, who as our heavenly patron or father makes his gifts more directly accessible to us as his children. By challenging the Temple's role in controlling access to God, Jesus diminishes dependence on the Temple, which requires a reordering of the power of the Temple and its exploitative domination patterns and a return to its original function as "a house of prayer" (Mk 11:17; Mt 21:13; Lk 19:46) and not a market or treasury that reinforce the religiously legitimated domination system of the Judean priestly families.

"Forgive Us Our Debts"
The Economic Challenge: If God Rules, then the Rich Don't

Much of Jesus' teaching and many of his parables reveal his concern for the economic realm, in particular its impact on village families who were at that time being subjected to the crushing demands of Roman and Judean taxation and increasing indebtedness to rich landlords. Perhaps one way to explore this is to consider the area of debts. Debts are "what is owed" to someone, hence an obligation that must somehow be "paid."

"The teachings of Jesus have put us on a collision course with the world that needs to divide us into those with the power and those without it. Instead, Jesus preaches a social order in which true charity is possible, a way of relating by which cooperation and community make sense. Jesus offers a world where all share the power of the Spirit 'each according to his or her gift.' And that 'Spirit is given to each person for the sake of the common good' (1 Cor 12:7). And that is the key to Christian community and Christian social justice. It is not a vision of totalitarian equality, nor is it capitalist competition (read: 'domination of the fittest'), but a world in which cooperation, community, compassion, and the charity of Christ are paramount—and to which all other things are subservient."

—*RICHARD ROHR*
Grace in Action (1994)

As we have discovered, in their world the primary pattern of social relationships was "patronage," which was a system of reciprocal gift giving that created "debts of honor" that must be paid in order to maintain the favorable relationship and reward the client's loyalty to the patron. All gifts required something in return. Thus there were "debts" or obligations in each of the four social realms. Political debts or obligations to patrons and to the community at large (tribe, city, nation), kinship debts to members of the household, economic debts to patrons and lenders (money, property, taxes, bills), and religious debts to God (obedience, worship and sacrifice), which, as we noted in the previous section, Jesus forgave without requiring the mediation of the Temple and its priesthood. Thus the experience of indebtedness permeated their social world and when these various debts became oppressive, anyone who could help was indeed considered a "savior" (Mt 11:28).

As with the other social realms, Jesus aim was not to replace the economic realm or eliminate wealth but rather to point out its dangers for the individual and the community (Mk 4:19; 10:23; Lk 16:1-14; 16:19-31; 18:24) and so transform the attitude with which it is acquired and distributed. He favored the traditional Israelite economic practices enshrined in the *Torah* that encouraged the voluntary sharing of wealth because, except for assistance from a person's extended family, charity or almsgiving were the only form of social assistance available to those in need.

While not a landowner himself but an itinerant preacher, Jesus' approach was influenced by the belief that the earth does not belong to the Roman emperor but to the one creator and patron God Yahweh (Ex 9:29; Ps 24:1) who distributes the land as a gift to whomever he wishes. And since it is to this God that exclusive loyalty is required and one cannot serve God and wealth (Mt 6:24), the community must care for or steward the land according to Yahweh's aims for sustenance and nourishment rather than simply for exploitation and profit (Mk 8:37; Lk 12:16-31), for the common good rather than common greed (Lk 12:15).

"In Jesus' manifestations of God's action for the people, and in his offering the kingdom of God to the poor, hungry, and despairing people, Jesus instilled hope in a seemingly hopeless situation. The key to the emergence of a movement from Jesus' mission, however, was his renewal of covenantal community, calling the people to common cooperative action to arrest the disintegration of their communities and to revitalize their cooperation and mutual support."

—*RICHARD A. HORSELY*
Jesus and Empire (2003)

As part of his mercy agenda, Jesus favors something like a return to the Israelite idea of "Jubilee" economics and its "forgiveness of debts" (Mk 11:25; Mt 6:14-15; 18:21-35; Lk 17:3-4). The Jubilee (Heb: *yobel,* meaning horn, which was blown to proclaim the year's beginning) was an ancient Jewish tradition (Lev 25:8-17, 29-31) of pardon and reconciliation celebrated every 50 years (after a "sabbath of sabbaths," 7 times 7 years) when the community imitated God's mercy and forgiveness by forgiving one another's debts and by each family returning to its own allotted land and not cultivating it during the jubilee year.

Moreover, in contrast to the takeover of more and more family land by the wealthiest landowners, Jesus favors traditional village economics characterized by neighborly care (Mt 25:32-46), sharing without demanding repayment (Mk 4:24-25; Mt 5:42, 7:12; Lk 6:30; 11:5-13; 12:33) and non-exploitation as expressed in his demand to "love your neighbor as yourself" (Mk 12:31-33; Mt 22:39; Lk 10:25-37). For him, only a radical trust in God allows one to feel confident enough not to try to secure one's own life through hoarding possessions but to give up one's life in service to the poor and the community (Mk 8:35; Mt 16:25; Lk 9:24).

"Jesus is not against wealth as such and definitely does not center his message directly on a redistribution of worldly goods. The essential thing for his followers is to be with Jesus, to be Christlike. To be like Jesus leads to a new type of life, a life that leads unavoidably to love and care, to justice and peace and to the development of anything that would bring those qualities about. Our wealth, our gifts and our talents should be used to help bring about God's Kingdom."

—*JOSEPH G. DONDERS*
Scripture Reflections Day by Day (1991)

Jesus also encouraged practices of neighborly solidarity: feeding the hungry, clothing the naked, tending the sick and visiting those in prison (Mt 25:31-46). In this way, he upended the usual uncaring and exploitative ways of thinking and acting toward others characteristic of domination systems, urging his followers to open their hearts and minds, to give without expectation of reciprocity (Lk 10:29–37) and to commit themselves to a genuine conversion of life.

"Deliver Us From Evil"
The Cosmic Challenge: If God Rules, then Satan Doesn't

Besides these challenges to the domination systems in the four human realms, there is also an even greater cosmic struggle between God and the powers of evil that dominate our world and lie hidden behind the various human domination systems. This cosmic realm also requires an ultimate reordering of loyalty and the use of power to reorder the whole world.

GOD'S GOOD NEWS

Recall that without much technology, ancient peoples did not really think that they could change their lives in any significant way. They felt always at the mercy of greater powers—family or tribal customs, wealthy landowners, authoritative priests, cruel rulers and mighty emperors, good and evil spirits that roamed the earth, deities residing in the forests, rivers and stars, and finally God almighty in heaven above. Life was a struggle to satisfy the demands of these many diverse and ever more powerful beings who controlled one's fate. This meant making constant trade-offs by choices about whose power could most influence any current situation and thus maximize the benefits and minimize the risks or dangers.

In the ancient world, Sin (often personified) was not an abstraction but an active power that sought to disorder God's rightly-ordered creation and set up an alternative system of disorder in its place. Thus the outward appearances of our world cloak a hidden evil power lurking just beneath the surface of our ordinary realities, disguising itself in order to remain hidden, but always trying to take control and wreak havoc whenever the opportunity arises. Thus keeping evil in check took an immense amount of energy and one had to exert power to re-establish the right order that God desired.

"In the ancient conception, everything earthly has its heavenly counterpart, and everything heavenly has its earthly counterpart. Every event is thus a simultaneity of both dimensions of reality. If war begins on earth, then there must be, at the same time, war in heaven between the angels of the nations involved on earth. Likewise, events initiated in heaven would be mirrored on earth. There is nothing uniquely biblical about this imagery. It was shared not only by the writers of the Bible, but also by Greeks, Romans, Egyptians, Babylonians, Assyrians, Sumerians—indeed, by everyone in the ancient world—and is still held by large numbers of people in Africa, Asia and Latin America."

—*WALTER WINK*
Engaging the Powers: Discernment and Resistance in a World of Domination (1992)

When the ancient Israelites and then Christians surveyed their world, they recognized that for all practical purposes, our world is a battleground of good and evil powers locked in a cosmic struggle for mastery. Since humanity's first sin in Eden, which broke down human relationships with God and with one another, our history has been the conflict between the

If God Rules, Then What?

domination of evil/Satan/the devil instead of the domination of good/ God, and God's constant attempt to overcome evil and return creation to its original "good" condition through specially commissioned human agents—Noah, Abraham, Moses and finally Jesus messiah—and those who join them in their covenant communities.

"As the kernel and center of his Good News, Christ proclaims salvation, this great gift of God which is liberation from everything that oppresses humanity but which is above all liberation from sin and the Evil One."

—*POPE PAUL VI*
To Proclaim the Gospel (Evangelii Nuntiandi) (1975), #9

In place of God's original good order at creation, evil has slowly but surely set up an alternative order whose unjust domination system is personified for the early Christians by the Roman empire. (Nowhere is this more clear than in the New Testament Book of Revelation). Through it, Satan has created a disorder in our world that actively contradicts God's desire for the right kind of community. The signs of this sinful dominion are evident in the disordered cosmos, history, communities and individuals all around us. In fact, the whole of human history is one long story of how Satan influences humans to disorder their relationships with God, with one another, and with creation through their sinful ways. Thus the Christian worldview exposes our most dangerous enemy as the evil powers that oppose God for domination and demand our human loyalty.

Humans, who are subject to the seductive powers of evil, relinquish their loyalty to God and serve Satan, the ruler of our world (Mt 4:8-11; Lk 4:4-8) and use their power to further his aim to destroy God's creation and murder his messiah. By introducing disorder into God's creation, human sins break down relationships. But Christians recognize that there has been an even more powerful force at work for good in this sad history. Since God originally established the right relationships at creation, God acts to restore what has been broken down. Despite the apparent domination of our world by sin, ever since the first sin God has been working within our history to make these disordered relationships right. Salvation history is the story of God's interventions not only to establish right relationships but to restore them when they have been broken down.

This constant struggle that we now experience between the desires and forces of good against those of evil makes our present world a hard place to live in. Though the appearances lead us to believe that the forces of evil are often winning, the truth is that since God is involved in this struggle, the final ending of our history will be God's triumph over the evil powers and a completely new re-ordering of creation, which the first Christians expected was about to happen when the representative of Satanic power embodied in the Roman empire would soon be conquered. God's almighty power and plan for salvation could not be thwarted by Satan's powers, no matter how dominant they might appear to be now.

> "The dark power that stood in the way of this kingdom vision has been defeated, overthrown, rendered null and void. Its legions will still make a lot of noise and cause a lot of grief, but the ultimate victory is now assured. This is the vision the evangelists offer us as they bring together the kingdom and the cross."
>
> —*N. T. WRIGHT*
> *How God Became King* (2012)

Jesus' Good News proclaims God's sovereign rule over all creation and God's plan to inaugurate the final transformation of our evil-dominated world through Christ himself, which will bring about God's ultimate triumph over evil so that God's new and just world order can at last be established on earth as it is in heaven. Thus the key to understanding God's kingdom rule is that Jesus is the presence of the transcendent and immanent God in our history. His kingdom worldview refocuses everything with himself as God's chosen agent, the pivotal figure both in the universe and in salvation history. Christ's enduring presence in the kingdom community, in the cosmos, and in our history inaugurates God's final transforming victory over evil. Jesus, who by his death and resurrection is the final victor over sin and evil and death, also enacts God's final judgment so that the ultimate transformation of our world into a "new creation" can finally be realized.

Realizing God's Dream of a Kingdom Community Today

At our baptism, we were anointed with oil or "Christened." So as Christians we commit ourselves to a life-long conversion through the adoption of Jesus' worldview and to the continuation of his mission to build the kingdom by sharing in his priestly, prophetic and kingly tasks through which we reorder our values and relationships. Christ's kingdom begins in the community of people who adopt the vision of his worldview and live in a new and different way because of God's presence in their lives. As Christians, our vocation is to make God's dream for a kingdom community into a reality—to realize it by living the kingdom way now.

This Christian kingdom community that we are called to create will always be a "contrast" society, free from unjust dominations because it will incorporate God's ideas for a radically different type of social existence that so far we have never achieved. So we must continue use the Gospels' stories, examples, instruction, wisdom and information to realize God's dream of a community of non-domination, nonviolence and peaceful conflict resolution. To live this way will ensure that this goal of building God's kingdom on earth will be realized.

"For the Church it is a question not only of preaching the Gospel in ever wider geographic areas or to ever greater numbers of people, but also of affecting and as it were upsetting, through the power of the Gospel, mankind's criteria of judgment, determining values, points of interest, lines of thought, sources of inspiration and models of life, which are in contrast with God's Word and the plan of salvation."

—POPE PAUL VI
To Proclaim the Gospel (Evangelii Nuntiandi)(1975), #19

But taking God's dream from vision to reality is something that we cannot do alone. It only becomes possible when we cooperate with God. Alone we cannot make God's kingdom come on earth, God must do this. But we can begin now to cooperate and create a community that is modeled on God's dream for a community of right relationships.

Realizing God's dream for a contrast community is not a question of theory but something that begins in our lives right now by starting with little things first. Build a family community, build a parish community, build a neighborhood community, build a church community of disciples dedicated to justice and right relationships, grounded in love and recognition of the essential dignity of each other person, and peace will follow. To live this way ensures that Jesus' goal of transforming our world into God's kingdom will be fulfilled.

GOD'S GOOD NEWS

Just as the magnificent view of our planet from space shows no human boundaries, so God's worldview disregards the human ways we organize our world. Our evaluations of people based on gender, race, religion, citizenship, wealth, status and authority are not necessarily God's. Jesus challenges our human communities to embody this openness and inclusiveness. Like Jesus, we must acquire a view of people that refuses to exclude them or deny them their dignity as God's children and Jesus' brothers and sisters. We must imitate God's impartiality by inviting everyone to belong to Jesus' kingdom community.

"The Church of Christ exists for the sake of the world outside it. Consequently it must be an open society; since it aims at its own extension without limit. It must welcome to its membership anyone who wishes to join it, provided he understands its commitments and accepts its style of life. The attractiveness of the life of the community, their love of one another and trust in one another is a major instrument for the extension of the kingdom and particularly in its contrast with the life styles of the Pharisees or of the peoples of the Roman Empire."

—*JOHN MACMURRAY*
The Philosophy of Jesus (1974)

Hearing and heeding God's Good News will continue to draw our attention to God's powerful reordering of our world and of our everyday lives. It refuses to let us separate God from anywhere, from anyone, from anything that is happening to us. It invites us to wonder, to seek and discover the presence of the God who created us, sustains us, searches us out and finds us to call us into a relationship that will never end.

The Christian worldview provides a new vision that allows us to understand, organize and act in our world in accord with God's transforming presence. Adopting it gives us a new identity as "Christians." So when the early Christian communities were overwhelmed by the power of the Roman empire's worldview, their existence and identity as Christians were in danger. In response, the Gospel authors provided a new framework for their Christian identity and invited them to discover the power for transforming themselves and their whole existence. As Paul noted: "The gospel is the power of God for the salvation of everyone who believes: for Jew first, and then Greek" (Rom 5:18).

As we will discover in the following chapters, the Gospel writers

IF GOD RULES, THEN WHAT?

shaped their texts to encourage their audience (and ourselves) to adopt the vision of the kingdom worldview and the vocation to create the kingdom community. These community catechists knew that if the community members accepted this Christian vision of the world and of history, then they would understand their own Christian identity as followers and disciples of Jesus. If they adopted the vision and values Jesus proclaimed, then they would begin to behave in ways that could transform this vision and these values into reality.

This Christian worldview provided the foundation for their Christian identity. By adopting this Christian worldview as their own, they could understand how God was re-ordering the world in relation to God's presence and plan for salvation. This understanding, in turn, would allow them to situate themselves in this rightly ordered world and to locate themselves in the unfolding story of God's salvation history.

"Christian hope is not about avoiding disaster, but hope for a new creation by God after disaster. What appears to be a catastrophic end is also a new beginning. The future is open-ended. There may be no hope for the particular structure on which the people depend. Like a potter, God is not committed to any particular shape for the clay but is creative and will eventually find another, perhaps better, shape. When everything we value seems to be falling apart, God may be moving us toward a future we cannot imagine."

—*MACRINA SCOTT, OSF*
Bible Stories Revisited (2013)

So likewise, for us today to become Christians by adopting Jesus' worldview and be true to our vocation to continue his mission to build the kingdom of God's rule, we need to explore the Gospels more carefully to learn the details of Jesus' kingdom worldview and discover just how we are to continue his mission and ministry for changing the world.

CHAPTER FOUR

Why the Gospels Were Written
One Message, Four Versions

As catechists we need to understand clearly what a written Gospel is and recognize what the Gospel can do for us and our spirituality. As we noted earlier, the Greek word for gospel *(euangelion)* meant simply a message of "good news," often about a great national victory in war. The Christian Good News was about God's victory through Jesus' life, death and resurrection over the forces of evil, sin and death that were disordering and spoiling our world. This victory made possible for everyone a new relationship with God (salvation) in a new community (God's kingdom).

The written Gospels, narratives of the Good News of our salvation, came into existence around AD 70–100. But before this time, the gospel message had been transmitted in oral and fragmentary written forms for almost forty years, for example in the preaching of Jesus' disciples and in the letters of Paul, who often talks about "the gospel of God" (Rom 1:1-6; 15:16; 1 Thes 2:2, 8-9) and "my gospel" (Rom 2:16; 16:25; 2 Tim 2:8), but who never wrote it down as the story of Jesus' life, death and resurrection.

From Spoken Words to Written Gospels

During the last half of the twentieth century, biblical scholars and historians concluded that in the first century the proclamation of the gospel message developed in three general stages primarily distinguished by their form of expression, not their content. These three general stages of development are concisely summarized in Vatican Council II's *Dogmatic Constitution on Divine Revelation*, #19, which also notes that each stage proclaimed the gospel message in a way appropriate to its audience.

Each proclamation—whether by Jesus, the preaching apostles or the writing evangelists—actively sought to adapt the same gospel message to the needs of the audience. So the Gospels did not just fall ready-made from the heavens or get whispered into the ears of the evangelists.

THE THREE STAGES OF GOSPEL FORMATION

Stage 1: The Lived Gospel

Holy Mother Church has firmly and with absolute constancy held, and continues to hold, that the four Gospels just named, whose historical character the Church unhesitatingly asserts, faithfully hand on what Jesus Christ, while living among us, really did and taught for our eternal salvation until the day he was taken up into heaven (see Acts 1:1-2).

The actual events of Jesus' life :(the facts) he lived, suffered, died and rose from the dead (and their significance) these events are the good news of our salvation.

Stage 2: The Oral Gospel

Indeed, after the ascension of the Lord the apostles handed on to their hearers what he had said and done. This they did with that clearer understanding which they enjoyed after they had been instructed by the events of Christ's risen life and taught by the light of the Spirit of truth.

The oral preaching of the disciples [their proclamation about the events of stage 1].

Stage 3: The Written Gospel

The sacred authors wrote the four Gospels, selecting some things from the many which had been handed on by word of mouth or in writing, reducing some of them to a synthesis, explaining some things in view of the situation of their churches, and preserving the form of proclamation but always in such a fashion that they told us the honest truth about Jesus. For their intention in writing was that either from their own memory and recollections, or from the witness of those who themselves "from the beginning were eyewitnesses and ministers of the word" we might know "the truth" concerning those matters about which we have been instructed (see Lk 1:2-4).

The written narratives of the evangelist's meaning and message of Jesus' life story [proclamations based on the oral testimony in stage 2, which is about the events in stage 1].

[from Vatican Council II's *Dogmatic Constitution on Divine Revelation (Dei Verbum)* (1965), #19]

In summary, the four canonical Gospels are:
(1) The Good News of our salvation first realized in the life and ministry of Jesus,
(2) then proclaimed and taught orally by his followers after his death,
(3) and finally written down in the form of narratives shaped by the story of the life, ministry, death and resurrection of Jesus of Nazareth. Their literary form is narrative, but they are more than biographies because they are proclamations of the gospel truth—the Good News of our salvation.

GOD'S GOOD NEWS

Stage 1: The Living Gospel of Jesus

The first stage of God's Good News is the message of God's kingdom rule proclaimed by Jesus during his life on earth. He announced that, as promised in the Old Testament, God was now powerfully present in Jesus himself and in his words and deeds for the final confrontation with the powers of evil in our world, which would transform the world back to the way God had originally ordered it at the time of creation. In this first stage, the primary gospel was Jesus himself, the living personal gospel.

Stage 2: The Oral Gospel of the Apostles

In the second stage, the disciples, who at Jesus' command began even during his lifetime to proclaim the message they had heard about God's kingdom (Mk 6:6-13, 30-31; Mt 10:7-14; Lk 9:1-10), continued after his death and resurrection to proclaim his message but now in a new and modified form (Acts 2:14-36). Their Good News was no longer just about God's kingdom, but now included that the decisive events that actually inaugurated God's kingdom rule over our world were Jesus' life, death and resurrection. They also now invited others to share his ministry and mission to build the kingdom. This new message was proclaimed both orally and in several letters by Paul and other Christian missionaries.

Stage 3: The Written Gospels of the Evangelists

Finally, in the third stage of development, around AD 70 Mark invented a new written form of the Good News that proclaimed the gospel message by using the story of Jesus' life, death and resurrection. Once he did this, other Christian teachers recognized its essential power and appeal and knew that what Mark had invented could be revised, but not duplicated. So they composed their own versions using his basic narrative structure but adding other things they knew from the oral tradition.

"The relationship of Stage 3 to Stages 1 and 2 is the problem for twentieth-century readers of the gospels, and herein lies the crucial need of the historical-critical method of gospel interpretation. To disregard it and to equate Stage 3 with Stage 1 is the path of Fundamentalism."

—JOSEPH A. FITZMYER, SJ
Scripture, the Soul of Theology (1994)

WHY THE GOSPELS WERE WRITTEN

In summary, then, we can describe the literary form of the four Gospels as **written narratives** (stage 3) **proclaiming** (stage 2) **the good news of our salvation** (stage 1). Or moving forward in the stages: (1) The good news of our salvation is **realized** in the life and ministry of Jesus, (2) **proclaimed and taught orally** by his followers after his death, (3) and finally **written in the form of narratives** of the life, ministry, death and resurrection of Jesus of Nazareth.

God's Good News and its meaning or significance for the Christian community was something the evangelists worked hard to communicate. Just as Jesus presented his message in ways that people could understand, so likewise the evangelists tailored their message for the needs of their readers. The Gospels were successful because they responded to the deeply felt needs of the early Christian communities and satisfied their demand for an appropriate communication of the gospel message by answering the questions that the communities needed to have answered.

The four evangelists as authors were actively and personally involved in the shaping or formulation of what they communicated (*On Divine Revelation*, #19). They composed their narratives according to how our human minds operate. We must also note that authors in the ancient world did not stress creative novelty (as we do today), but "invention"— in the ancient rhetorical sense of artfully putting the text together out of pre-existing materials. We use the term *invention* similarly when we distinguish between *discovery* as the process of finding what was already there but not perceived (e.g., electricity) and *invention* as the process of using what already exists to make something new (e.g., the light bulb). So Mark did not *discover* the gospel but *invented* a new way to communicate it.

Mark wove together (the Latin root of our word *text* means to weave) the relevant Christian oral teaching traditions about Jesus' words and deeds—healings and exorcisms, wonders and signs, shameful death and surprising resurrection—to present the Good News of our salvation in his account of the "beginning of the good news of Jesus the Christ, the son of God" (1:1). He shaped Christ's life story so that it could become the pattern for our *Christ-ian* life story—the story of our individual and communal life in the right relationship with God which is our salvation.

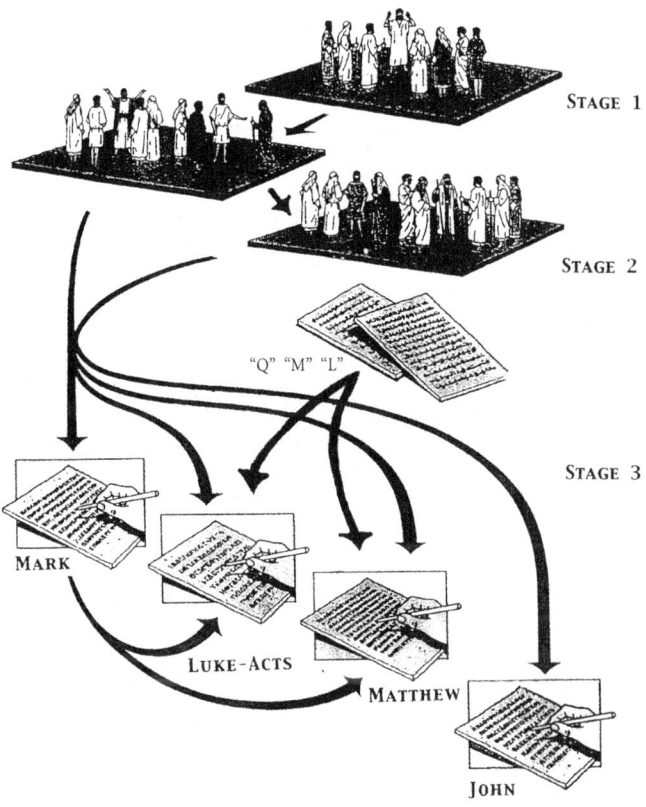

THE THREE STAGES OF GOSPEL FORMATION

STAGE 1

STAGE 2

"Q" "M" "L"

STAGE 3

MARK

LUKE-ACTS

MATTHEW

JOHN

Why Did Mark's Community Need a Gospel?

What prompted Mark around AD 70 to proclaim the gospel message using a written narrative story about Jesus? What you would do if someone asked you to summarize the basic Christian message for them? Would you give them a list of the most important doctrinal formulas? or a copy of the Creed? or maybe a catechism? or perhaps a theological essay explaining Christian beliefs and worship practices?

I imagine that someone in the decade of the sixties of the first century asked the catechist Mark to do just this for his community, and he decided that the gospel story of Jesus was the best catechetical tool to instruct Christians—especially new converts to the Christian way—in the fundamentals of what they needed to know to be followers of Jesus.

Why did communities need something like our written Gospels in order to help them with their Christian existence? The times themselves can perhaps give us some clues. After all, the ancient Christian writers did not just sit down one day and decide to write a new book for the Bible. Indeed, like all writing, we must first look to the historical situation that compelled the writers to write what they did because their readers needed their message. And this will give us clues about why the authors might have decided to write their texts in the particular ways that they did.

Between AD 65–70 the Christian community faced a new and unprecedented crisis that no one anticipated. In July AD 64, a devastating fire burned down a large area of Rome. As the Roman historian Tacitus reported, looking for a convenient scapegoat to blame, the emperor Nero singled out the small and rather insignificant group called *Christians* and arrested and killed many of them in gruesome spectacles. (But note that Tacitus indicates that *Christian* was already a label with very bad connotations among the Roman populace even before the fire because of their "disgraceful acts" and "hatred against mankind"). The important point to note is that Christians were not arrested and killed so much for causing the fire or other crimes but just simply for being Christians. So when Christians were first singled out in Rome for official government persecution for being Christians, it was no doubt very traumatic.

"Therefore, to stop the rumor [that he had set Rome on fire], Nero falsely charged with guilt and punished with the most fearful tortures, the persons commonly called Christians, who were hated for their disgraceful acts. Accordingly, an arrest was first made of all who pleaded guilty; then, upon their information, an immense multitude was convicted, not so much of the crime of firing the city, as of hatred against mankind. Mockery of every sort was added to their deaths. Covered with the skins of beasts, they were torn by dogs and perished, or nailed to crosses, or doomed to the flames and burnt, to serve as a nightly illumination, when daylight had expired."

—*TACITUS*
Annals, 15.44

As Mark's Gospel seems to hint, many Christians might have thought (and even hoped!) that this was the end time when God would come to save them from their suffering. But Mark reminded them that just as Jesus suffered, died and rose to new life with God—so if they remained faithful to Jesus, they too would suffer, die and rise. His Gospel warns them not

GOD'S GOOD NEWS

to expect God' miraculous appearance to save them from their suffering. God did not do it for Jesus and will not do it for them either.

So when Christians began to be singled out for persecution, in order to know who to arrest, the Roman persecutors had to ask: What exactly makes someone a Christian? How can we tell a Christian from a Jew or from members of other religious groups? And not only the Romans but also Christians had to answer this question about their identity because now their lives depended on it.

"Many in the Church thought they were seeing the end. Mark responded with the story of another time when people thought it was the end of the gospel, the time when Jesus was put to death and buried, when everyone abandoned him. The disciples thought it was the end, but it turned out to be the beginning. In effect, Mark was telling his readers, 'Now *you* think it is the end!' To understand the continuation of the gospel in the Church they had to understand the beginning of the gospel. As a preacher and teacher, Mark fulfilled his mission by proclaiming 'the beginning of the gospel.' At a time when nearly everyone felt it was the end, Mark boldly told the story of the beginning. When so many were overwhelmed by what seemed to be bad news, he proclaimed the story of the beginning of the good news."

—*EUGENE LAVERDIERE, SSS*
The Beginning of the Gospel: Introducing the Gospel of Mark, Vol. 1 (1999)

Who are we as Christians? Are we Christians to continue to be a certain kind of Judahist or is there something distinctive that sets us apart as Christians from both Judahists and Gentiles? And just what exactly is this distinctive element? What is really at stake here is the nature of Christian identity, which, until this crisis, Christians had not been forced to answer in such a direct and explicit way. The first written narrative Gospel of Mark came into existence at this particular time to help Christians in their persecuted communities to understand their Christian identity by answering this basic question.

Mark's Narrative Gospel & Christian Identity

For a community struggling with their Christian identity, Mark offers the help they need to know who they are and how they ought to respond to God's presence in our world. He reveals the coherent structure of the Christian worldview that provides them the necessary context in which they can discover their specific Christian identity.

THE EMERGENCE OF CHRISTIANITY INTO

Birth of Jesus c. 4 BC	Death of Jesus AD 30	Start of Christian Mission 35	Paul's Missions & Letters 50	Nero Burns Rome 64

2nd Temple Judahism ——————————————————————

     Mostly Judahist Christianity ——————————————

        Growing Gentile Christianity ——————————

             Romans say:

             "Christians are not Jews"

             Christians ask:

             "Who are we?"

             [MARK]

By the year 100 or so, Christians had emerged in the eyes of both Rome and the Jews as a distinct religious group. They were identified as a public community that had its own distinctive beliefs about God and Christ, its own rituals for worship, its own social organization for the community and its own moral style for living a Christian life. All these aspects joined together to provide a coherent response to the reality of God experienced by the community of believers in Christ through God's Holy Spirit. In this short span of less than a century, Christianity went from a band of a few of Jesus' disciples in Roman Palestine to a network of communities spread throughout the whole Mediterranean world.

THE FIRST-CENTURY HELLENISTIC WORLD

Peter & Paul Martyred	Jerusalem Temple Destroyed	Christians ejected by Jews	Hellenistic Roman Church	
67	**70**	**c. 85**	**90**	**100**

———————————————— Rabbinic Judaism

Hellenistic Christianity

Jews say:
"Christians are not Jews nor
welcome in our synagogues."
Christians ask:
"Who are we?"
[MATTHEW, LUKE, JOHN]

This emergence of Christianity is reflected in the collection of writings called the New Testament that show Christians struggling to find their place in the larger Hellenistic world. The four **Gospels and Acts** serve as foundation documents for their communities and as tools for conversion that explain the meaning of the unique Christian identity for newly-converted Jews and Gentiles. The various **letters** address the needs of the communities for sound teaching and clear guidelines for Christian living. The **Book of Revelation** is an imaginative vision of how God's presence in our world will finally triumph over evil and transform our world into the ordered world that God had envisioned from its creation.

For a community that felt powerless in opposition to the awesome power embodied in the Roman empire and its divinity-desiring emperors, Mark proclaims a vision of the world from God's perspective. Instead of just submitting to the power of the empire, his Good News reveals that God alone is the true ruler of all creation, whose presence in our world and in its history is now transforming everything.

For a community that felt hopeless because on their own they could do little about the overwhelming sin and oppressive evil dominating their world, Mark proclaims that through Jesus God has now begun the final conquest of evil in our world. The community's mission is to participate with God's Holy Spirit in this process of transforming our world into God's "new creation," the kingdom of justice, love and peace.

"Our best text reading does not deny that these narratives might reference actual events, but merely recognizes that this dimension is ancillary to the most important truth they have to tell—the truth contained in the narrative's rhetorical power to create and define a community's identity. To put it somewhat differently, the objective of the narrative is not primarily an accurate reporting of events, but rather the sort of narrative shaping of those events which will lead the audience to believe it is their story, and so constitute their community based on it."

—*DALE PATRICK & ALLEN SCULT*
Rhetoric and Biblical Interpretation (1990)

What is distinctive about the four Gospels is not just their content or message, but also their particular literary form. They were written not as abstract theological treatises or letters or poems or creeds but as narratives. A narrative, or perhaps we might use our more familiar term *story*, indicates a continuous and ordered presentation which has a beginning, a middle and an end. The term *story* here is synonymous with narrative and describes only the literary form of the presentation and does not say anything about whether a narrative is factual or fictional.

We use *story* this way when we are asked about "the story of our life" or are invited "to tell our story." In either case, people don't want us to make up some fictional account but to order and shape the many things that have happened to us into a unified account that is ordered by chronology or maybe by another significant idea (e.g., overcoming obstacles, achieving success, etc.). This is exactly what the evangelists did with Jesus'

GOD'S GOOD NEWS

story by shaping it into a unified narrative with a beginning, a middle and an end. Luke claims at the start of his Gospel that he has written an "orderly account" to help Theophilus "know the truth concerning the things about which you have been instructed" (Luke 1:1-3). Clearly Luke understands his Gospel as a catechetical resource to enhance the basic instruction that the convert Theophilus has already received.

Mark: Why Write a Narrative Gospel?

But why would Mark shape a Gospel in the form of a life of Jesus? Our first response might be that this would preserve the memory of Jesus. While there is certainly some truth to this, preserving memories can be done in many other ways. One could collect and arrange various remembered sayings of Jesus, as both the "Q" source (a scholarly abbreviation of the German *Quelle,* meaning *source)* and the apocryphal (i.e., not recognized in the official list or canon of biblical books) Gospel of Thomas do, or one could present a theological summary of the gospel and its meaning, as Paul tends to do in his letters.

"Mark's gospel presents the Pauline Christ-event (also called a 'gospel') in a narrative form, which weaves together diverse traditions (including the Old Testament) to create a unified story of the saving significance of the public life, death and raising up of Jesus of Nazareth."

—*JOHN R. DONAHUE, SJ, & DANIEL J. HARRINGTON, SJ*
The Gospel of Mark (2002)

In contrast, Mark's great invention was to take Jesus himself and the events of his life story and shape them into something more than a biography. He uses Jesus' story as a dramatic proclamation of the Christian message. Thus Mark's narrative Gospel of Jesus in action not only fixed the general pattern (both temporal and geographical) of Jesus' life—his baptism, ministry in Galilee, journey to Jerusalem to suffer, die and rise to new life—but it also connected the community's numerous memories of Jesus' words and deeds to specific situations in his life. And most importantly, it allowed readers to encounter the personality of the remembered Jesus through his words and deeds and then connect that knowledge with their personal experience of the risen Christ (the foundation of every Christian's faith). Thus believers can recognize the continuity between the remembered Jesus they know from the Gospel and the risen Christ they know from their own faith experience.

"In Mark, the wealth of traditional stories and sayings about Jesus came together in a new kind of literary work. It was not history, biography or travelogue, yet it included elements of these. Nor was it drama or fiction, though there were characteristics of these as well. Mark wrote about the good news, and all he presented was but the beginning of that good news."

—*EUGENE LAVERDIERE, SSS*
"A Guide for Listening to the Sunday Gospel," *Praying*, No. 5 (1985)

Scholars now conclude that soon after its invention, Mark's written Gospel became known to other Christian communities for whom it became the new norm. Then other catechists—Matthew, Luke and John—followed his lead by adapting his Gospel for the situations and needs of their respective communities. Although they had Mark's Gospel, they did not think it was necessary to keep reading it as the only expression of what it meant to be a Christian follower of Jesus. In fact, once their versions existed, they probably did not read or rely very much on Mark anymore.

Matthew and Luke—Why Revise a Gospel?

Once Mark's Gospel was written and other Christian communities became aware of it, community leaders and catechists recognized its essential appeal and its power to bring about and deepen Christian conversion. They could make copies of Mark and use it for their teaching and worship. But what if Mark's Gospel no longer seemed to address the needs of communities as their situations and challenges changed? Once Mark had invented the written Gospel, the basic gospel story could not be reinvented, but its riches could be adapted and emphasized in new ways. Like a tool that could be adapted to new tasks, Mark's Gospel was used by other Gospel writers for their own purposes.

The need to revise Mark's Gospel occurred for the same reasons most books are revised. Revisions (the word means "to see anew") most often occur when the original book is read in a new situation that demands fresh solutions to new problems and hence a new perspective, or when a later author has new material that needs to be added to what the first text said. Both Matthew and Luke are guided by these fundamental motives as they edit Mark's Gospel to respond to problems facing their communities.

Recall that Mark's Gospel was written for a mixed community of Jewish and Gentile Christians in a time of trial, when following Jesus' way meant taking up one's cross and maybe even dying just for being a Christian. He clarified the meaning of Jesus' identity so Christians could use it to discover their identity. Over and over his readers are forced to readjust their comfortable (and in his view misplaced) expectations in the light of the surprising and challenging information about who Jesus really was and what Jesus said God was doing and wanted to do in our world.

Neither Matthew's nor Luke's communities faced such drastic challenges. Matthew's main problem was not persecution but how to encourage his mostly Jewish converts to embrace both their Israelite tradition and their role in the expanding mission to the Gentiles that was transforming Christianity into a new kind of community. To do this, he portrayed Jesus as an authoritative teacher who built upon Moses' law but transformed it into the foundation for the new Christian covenant community that would live according to right relationships (righteousness).

Luke's primary problem was to show how the new Christian community of his mostly Gentile converts was rooted in the unfamiliar Israelite traditions and to direct their energy into the worldwide mission following the example of Jesus and his disciples. To do this, he portrayed Jesus as a compassionate prophet whose witness both in word and in suffering gathered everyone, especially the poor and those on the margins, into a new community of universal table fellowship, bold witness and loving service.

When Matthew and Luke use Mark's Gospel as a source for their own, they both retain Mark's general narrative framework of Jesus' baptism, ministry in Galilee, journey to Jerusalem and final days in Jerusalem as the schematic pattern for their own narratives. This similarity is what leads us to identify these three Gospels as *synoptic,* that is, *seen from the same perspective,* because they narrate the events using the same general framework although many of the details are changed.

But in their careful reading and adaptation of Mark for their own versions of the Good News, Matthew and Luke did not simply add their communities' traditions to Mark's. Rather they felt free to change Mark's text where it did not make sense, re-orient Mark's text to accommodate the needs of their respective communities, eliminate what was no longer necessary or applicable, and add what might be more meaningful and relevant from their community's many remembered traditions.

Both Matthew and Luke add new material about Jesus' words and deeds to Mark's overall structure. Their first source was a shared collection of Jesus' sayings (the "Q" source) with which they supplemented Mark in different ways. Matthew uses most of these sayings to create five extended discourses of Jesus' teaching (chapters, 5–7, 10, 13, 18 and 24–25). Luke lumps most of this material into a great insertion (chapters 9–19) in which Jesus the teaching prophet sets his face toward Jerusalem and on the way reveals the meaning of God's dream for a community of persons who are related as God wants them to be.

Shared Verses in the Synoptic Gospels

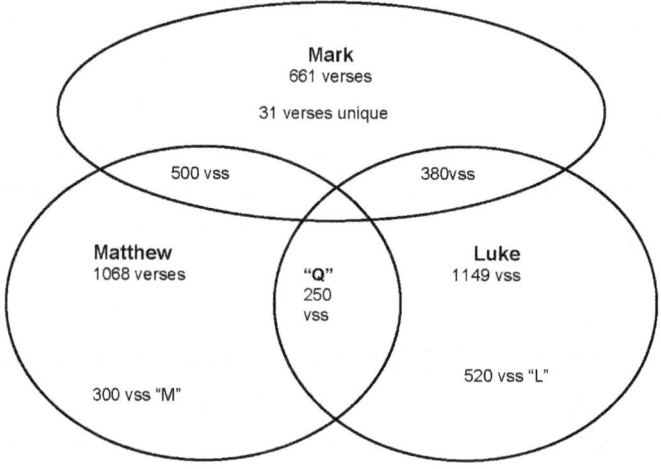

But besides these added sayings of Jesus, Matthew and Luke also had other sources that were unique to their respective communities (scholars call these "M" and "L"). Much of this unique material occurs in their infancy narratives (chapters 1–2 in each Gospel), in which each author in his own way expressed the meaning of Jesus as God's son, and in their accounts of Jesus after his resurrection (Mt 28; Lk 24). Thus both Luke and Matthew not only expanded Mark's Gospel with new material, but also reshaped the perspective and emphasis of Mark's Gospel to meet the new needs and different problems of their communities.

John—Why Write a Different Gospel?

Although not directly based on the other three Gospels, John's version of the Good News depends on similar Christian traditions. Living near the end of the first century in a situation of increasing conflict with the Jews about the divine status of Jesus, John's community needed a Gospel that stressed Jesus' divinity as God's Son and the community's equality as Jesus' friends. Thus John shifts his emphasis to the divinity of Jesus—God's son sent from the father for our salvation.

Although John also adopts Mark's basic structure, he radically changes many of the details to focus not on the coming of God's kingdom, but rather on the coming of Jesus the Christ as divine being from heaven—God's Word made flesh—who reveals how through faith in him believers can attain eternal life because of God's victory over evil and the beginning of the new creation. Instead of short sayings and parables, Jesus teaches in long speeches, in particular to his disciples at the last supper (chapters 14–17). Instead of miracles and exorcisms revealing the powerful presence of God's kingdom, Jesus does "signs" to show how believers come to believe in him and begin now to share eternal life. John also reconfigures his passion narrative to emphasize Jesus' death and resurrection as the final victory over sin and death. Finally, before Jesus returns to his heavenly father who sent him as emissary, he bestows the Holy Spirit on the disciples to empower them to carry on his work once he is gone.

The Narrative Gospel Presents the Christian Worldview

The gospel story, like every narrative, creates a unique world and invites the reader to use his or her imagination to enter into that world and understand the worldview of this particular author. The way we envision the world will influence our values, which in turn will impact our behavior. What we see influences what we want and how we act to get it.

In chapter 2 we explored the basics of the Christian worldview. Recall that the gospel worldview claims that God's holiness and power are now unleashed and on the loose in our world. God's kingdom rule is here!

Whenever we read the term *kingdom* we should substitute the words *powerful presence,* which better expresses what the kingdom is all about. God's kingdom is not just a spatial territory but it identifies the realm in and over which God's powerful presence rules. When Jesus preaches about the kingdom he is trying to open our eyes to a world where God actively rules and where God is treated like God ought to be treated.

> "The purpose of a narrative is to give meaning to the world, not to describe it scientifically. The measure of a narrative's truth is in its consequences. Does it provide a sense of hope, ideals, personal identity, a basis for moral conduct, explanations of that which cannot be known?"
>
> *—NEIL POSTMAN*
> *Building a Bridge to the 18th Century (1999)*

The second feature of this gospel worldview is that each neighbor becomes extremely significant and important because of our common relationship to God, whom Jesus reveals as "our father." In other words, we learn who we are and who others are in relation to God and how we ought to live together in a covenant community. This is the basis for Jesus' challenge to love God and our neighbor.

In chapter 3 we considered how worldviews have consequences and why adopting the Christian gospel worldview demands a rejection of all other worldviews. The Christian worldview affirms that through Christ God is now initiating the final transformation of our world into God's reordered world. This "new creation" will be characterized by justice, held together by love and will bring about peace for all creation.

Since this Christian worldview understands the meaning of reality in relation to Jesus Christ, it provides us with the necessary elements for our Christian identity. It provides a structure, a story and an understanding of our situation as the essential context in which the truest and deepest meaning of our lives can now be discovered. Our Christian way of seeing the world and of being and acting in it gives us a new way of interpreting the meaning of the events that are happening to us.

Through their narrative proclamations, the evangelists provide us with an intellectual component that identifies what we believe (doctrines), a moral component that outlines the proper values, attitudes, and choices that should guide our actions (ethics), a ritual component that identifies the specific consecrated actions (rituals for worship) through which we come into effective contact with God, and a social component that describes the proper ways or structures for organizing our life together in community (institutions for justice not domination).

Adopting this new worldview and living according to it is another way of describing the basic experience of conversion. Hearing and heeding the biblical message will challenge us to recognize God's presence and activity in Jesus of Nazareth and to make a commitment to this God. It challenges us to see the world as Jesus does, evaluate it as he does, and act in it as he does. It challenges us to link our hope for a new order with work realizing God's dream for the right kind of community. Finally, it challenges us to engage in the real power struggle between God and Satan, good and evil, which wreaks havoc in our world today.

"There is a divine dream which the prophets and rabbis have cherished and which fills our prayers, and permeates the acts of true piety. It is the dream of a world, rid of evil by the grace of God as well as by our efforts of establishing the kingship of God in the world. God is waiting for us to redeem the world."

—*ABRAHAM J. HESCHEL*
Between God and Man (1981)

Each Gospel writer provides a whole system of cues to guide our responses to these challenges and tells us where everything belongs and so provides the overarching context in which everything takes its meaning. And although all Christians share the same Christian worldview, each Gospel writer can put the basic pieces together in different configurations to emphasize one or other aspects that are most important for his community. These particular emphases help create several distinctive communities that share the general Christian worldview.

How the Gospel Narratives Work on Us as Readers

Everything in Mark's Gospel story has been chosen to have an effect on his readers. His choice of a narrative form subtly works its persuasive force on us first through its structure and then through its characters, especially the portraits of Jesus and the disciples. Thus the first masterstroke of Mark's Gospel is its structure. His narrative reveals what he thinks is most significant in Jesus' life and should therefore be most meaningful to us his readers. His written narrative not only fixed the general pattern of Christ's life—baptism, ministry in Galilee, journey to Jerusalem to suffer, die and rise to new life—but also encourages us to use this same pattern as the model for our *Christ-ian* lives.

"The gospels were written by different men of different abilities and outlooks, whose lives had been transformed by the impact of Jesus upon them, in all cases probably an indirect impact through the witness of others who had known him directly. It would be unthinkable that these men who were responsible for the tradition had not been anxiously concerned to get it right and to keep it right."

—JOHN MACMURRAY
The Philosophy of Jesus (1974)

Engaging with the Gospels narratives has several implications for us as readers. The first thing a narrative does is to create a bond of community between the author and the reader. Every communication, whether spoken or written, creates a community of speaker/author, listener/reader and the word/text that is shared between them. The audience is invited into the world of the text in which through their hearing or reading they are shaped by the text and better able to understand who they are and how to relate with others. The story becomes their own through their participation in it. So the community for whom the Gospel is written is also bonded by their encounter with the gospel story. The Gospel writers choose the narrative form because their communities are faced with the threat of fragmentation. Their Gospels help them create and rebind their Christian communities using the example of Jesus and his gospel message.

Reading the Gospels shapes us as readers first by shaping our ideas. The Gospel writer "invents" (in the sense of putting it all together in a unified, coherent and believable way, whether he was historically part of that world or not) the world of Jesus and the disciples, the scribes and Pharisees, the parables and miracles, Jesus' death and resurrection. The author then invites us through our reading and imaginative participation to enter into this new and strange world to encounter and be with Jesus. But the Gospel authors not only present us with this world but try to persuade us that this new world they are describing is so important that if we

GOD'S GOOD NEWS

adopt it, it will change how we see and act in our world now. Thus we are invited to make the reality of this gospel story world our own.

But the most important thing about the narrative form is that you don't have to be a theologian or even highly intelligent for it to work. Stories work differently from abstract logical arguments. For theologians in universities, logic might be persuasive, but it has never been so to most Christians. But a narrative works on us because it invites us into the story to get involved. We are expected to use our imagination to see what Jesus is doing, to hear his words and to let this have some impact on us.

"As a narrative rather than an epistle, homily, or some other form of writing, Mark has a narrator who tells the story to an implied reader, a cast of characters who interact with one another, and events or scenes that cover a span of time and form a more or less coherent plot. Mark is also based on the history of Jesus' life and set in a particular historical context."

—*R. ALAN CULPEPPER*
Mark (2007)

Another important way that the narrative works is through the example of the people in the story. These characters and their interactions evoke in us the desire to imitate them. The attractiveness of their personalities, the wisdom and beauty of their words, the grandeur of their deeds and struggles invite us to be and do likewise. The invitation to act like them is a persuasive invitation. To each of the disciples, Jesus offered the inviting command and commanding invitation to "Follow me," to be as he is and do as he does. The Gospels now make the same invitation to us when we read them. "Follow my story," they plead. If you do you will enter into a world where God is present and ruling, where each neighbor has his or her unique personality respected and cherished. This world is like ours in many respects, and yet it is very unlike ours. This unlikeness challenges us most as we are transported into the world of the Gospels.

Each evangelist has shaped Jesus' life into a story. But his story is meaningful because it is contextualized by the Old Testament story of God's creation of the world and the nurturing of the covenant people of Israel who are to express in their lives the right relationship to God and others. Through the Gospels, the Israelites' story of faithful covenant living becomes Jesus' story, and in turn his story becomes the story of every Christian. His story is our story. This is how the Gospel works on us— story shaping story as it ties together the great stories of God's presence and activity in our world to transform it and us into a "new creation."

So if we are looking for the pattern of our life—the context in which to discover what our life is all about—then we should turn to the Gospels because they give us the context in which we can understand the real meaning of our life. Jesus' story is shaped by the same pattern that was acted out by the Israelites and is now being acted out by ourselves. Reading the Gospels helps us learn what the true story of our life is, and thus recognize the wrong stories that we might now be using that keep us from achieving a right relationship with God and others.

Thus we can now clearly recognize that the Gospels were invented to help Christians find and shape their own identity and thus to know what it means to be a Christian in a world that was not particularly Christian. As documents for forming Christian identity, the Gospels provide the guidelines for the Christian way of following Jesus and the blueprints for building Jesus' kingdom community here on earth. The gospel life of Jesus reveals the gospel life that every Christian is called upon to live. So if we read and study the Gospels and let their power work on us, we will be invited to change and be transformed. The Gospels help us to recognize God's powerful life-changing presence in our world and encourage us to commit ourselves to sharing in making God's kingdom come.

How the Narrative Gospels Shape Us as Christians

It is clear that the Gospel writers shaped their Gospels not only to work on us as readers but also to shape us as Christians. By fixing the structure of Jesus' story as God's model disciple, they also fixed the structure of our story as Jesus' disciples. His relationship to God holds the key for understanding our relationship to God through Jesus in the Holy Spirit.

Since the narrative form of the Gospel holds together the times of Jesus' life story, it will also hold together our life story. Thus the ending of the Gospel is very important for we learn that although death ends our earthly life, it does not end our relationship with God. Just as Jesus rose to new life through God's power, so will we. And since one person has

The Gospels as Tools of Conversion: His Story Is Our Story

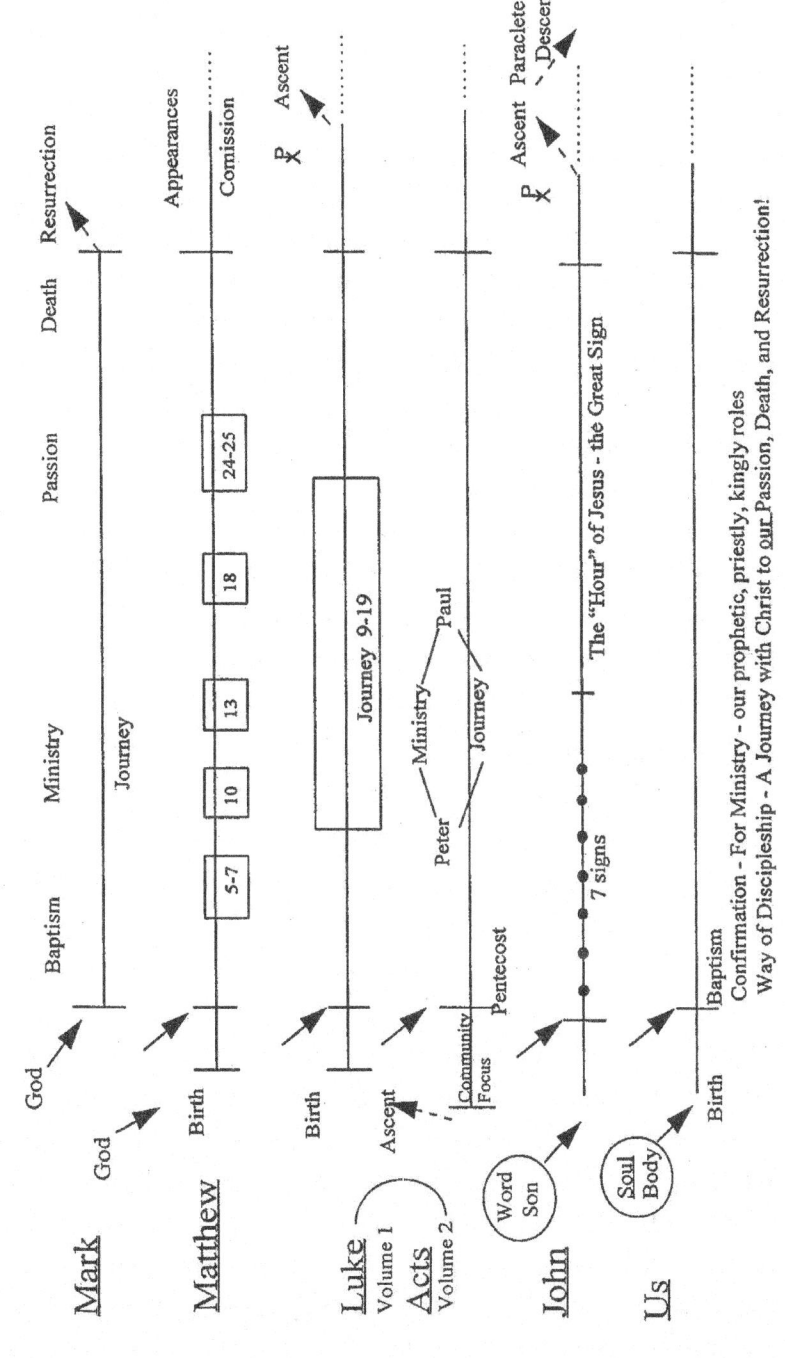

Mark
God
God
Baptism
Ministry — Journey
Death
Resurrection

Matthew
Birth
Baptism
5-7   10   13   18   24-25
Passion
Death
Appearances
Comission

Luke   Volume 1
Acts   Volume 2
Birth
Ascent
Community Focus   Pentecost
Journey 9-19
Peter — Ministry
Paul — Journey
P ☧ Ascent

John
Word / Son
Baptism
7 signs
The "Hour" of Jesus - the Great Sign
P ☧ Ascent   Paraclete   Descent

Us
Soul / Body
Birth
Confirmation - For Ministry - our prophetic, priestly, kingly roles
Way of Discipleship - A Journey with Christ to our Passion, Death, and Resurrection!

already risen, the new order that God promised from of old—the way
of God's salvation—has indeed already begun with Jesus' life, death and
resurrection. The new age is here, the kingdom of God has begun!

Like Jesus' parables, the gospel story proclaims God's Good News
and so provokes a crisis in the hearer/reader, which will in turn bring
about a new way of relating to God and to others as Jesus' disciples. Thus
the Gospels will challenge us as disciples to a relationship that entails:

- a vivid experience of our **call** to follow Jesus on the way of discipleship
- a renewed **commitment** to the relationship with God through Jesus in
  the power of the Holy Spirit (what we need is faith not fear!)
- a **conversion,** by which we dare to face all the changes in ourselves and
  our lives that we must make to live out the implications of our discipleship commitment. This demands following the way of Jesus through
  suffering service to death and through death to new life with God
- a **co-mission** to continue the work of suffering service begun with
  Jesus in our own time as we carry on the challenge of building the
  kingdom community and overcoming evil in our world
- a greater willingness to pay the **cost** of following Jesus on the way to
  God—even to the point of death if necessary.

Responding to God's Good News

We really only learn what the Gospels mean when we relate them to our
lives. As with reading any book, the Gospel's story, characters and themes
take on increased significance only when we decide that they mean more
than what we first find in the book. When we connect what we read with
something in our life, then we will remember what we read and let it
shape us. For this reason, engaging with the Gospels does not just inform
but transforms us as we move beyond simply amassing scraps of information to being shaped by the meanings we discover.

As we examine the Gospels, then, we will be shaping our own gospel
spirituality (for more on this, see chapter 9). These four gospel patterns
for genuine Christian existence are ways for us to shape our lives. So if we
want the Gospels to help us with our Christian identity, what we first have
to experience is the story itself. As we read each Gospel, we must consider
how each evangelist portrays Jesus, who is the primary example of what a

Christ-like life will be. He is the model for our lives as his followers. When we find out who Jesus is we can then discover who we are.

As we will discover in the following chapters on each Gospel, each evangelist shapes a portrait of Jesus that is unique and distinctive. Like individuals who are making mosaics, the evangelists share many common elements but the mosaic that each produces is distinct because of the way that each has shaped the tiles, integrated their color, size and shape to produce a distinctive picture of Jesus that they think will be most helpful to their community and its needs.

As Christian readers, meeting Jesus in the Gospels can be a life-changing experience. No matter how much you think you already know about the God of the Bible or about Jesus, you will constantly be surprised when you begin to meet them anew in the Gospel story. Whatever you might know about Jesus comes alive as you hear his words and consider his actions and discover his agenda for right relationships with God and one another. No one can encounter Jesus through the Gospels and remain untouched by this experience.

"The kingdom comes into being after a deep shift in vision, understanding and values. Anyone can choose the new imagination of what it means to be a human. In making that choice, you exit the dead-end values of the age and enter the Gospel kingdom. If you follow Jesus' example and listen for your destiny and fate, you will have to go your own way, adapting the simple, radical, teachings to your own calling and circumstances. You will evoke the kingdom in your own style, making your own life a tiny mustard seed, cultivating the seeds of your thoughts, making yourself the embodiment of the moral beauty and spiritual intelligence found in the Gospels."

—THOMAS MOORE
Writing in the Sand: Jesus & the Soul of the Gospels (2010)

In the Gospels, besides the example of Jesus, there are good and bad examples of discipleship. It is up to you to detect which is which and which is most relevant for your life today. All of the characters in the story exemplify some dimension of ourselves in relation to Jesus. As you read the Gospels, you are invited to discover that part of yourself that is like Peter, or James, or John, or the Pharisees or the woman at the well or the good thief. The spectrum of characters reflects the spectrum of possible responses to Jesus and his Good News message.

Each of the evangelists has a shared sense of what being a Christian is about and a distinctive sense of what is most important. Engaging with the Gospels will be full of surprises, a mixture of anticipation and anxiety, fun and fear. The unknown stirs up anxieties because we never know what we will face and whether or not we will be able to handle what does come. This Gospel encounter is a chance to think about your own spirituality by seeing it against the spiritualities offered by the evangelists to be challenged by the Gospels so that you can grow and not allow your Christian life to be stunted by old habits, old ways of seeing and old ways of being.

"Today too, Jesus lives and walks along the paths of ordinary life in order to draw near to everyone, beginning with the least, and to heal us of our infirmities and illnesses. To you who are well disposed to listen to the voice of Christ that rings out in the Church and to understand what your own vocation is. I invite you to listen to and follow Jesus, and to allow yourselves to be transformed interiorly by his words, which 'are spirit and life' (Jn 6:62)."

—*POPE FRANCIS*
Message for World Vocation Day (May 11, 2014)

The aim is that you will become, as Paul says, "transformed by the renewal of your mind, so that you can find out what is good" (Rom 12:2). You are invited to use your imagination to enter into Jesus' story and to make his story your own. To enter into a world that is different from your own and to ask: What if that vision of the world that is portrayed in Jesus' story is true? What if that script for Jesus' story becomes the script for my story? What if, as Jesus says in Mark's Gospel, "The kingdom [presence] of God is here" (1:15)? What happens when you discover God's awesome, mysterious, powerful transforming presence in your self and in your life? If you do, then you know that the time of decision is at hand. To shape and reshape your self and your life will be your way of responding to God's Good News.

Part 2
The Good News
in Four Versions

"We make a mistake to think of the four Gospels
as all of a type, and even to think of the Synoptic
Gospels as similar. They differ as much from each
other as the Fourth Gospel differs from any or all of
them. Different conditions in the different churches
from which they variously come underlie the differences in form."

—AMOS N. WILDER
Ancient Christian Rhetoric:
The Language of the Gospel (2014)

THE GOSPEL ACCORDING TO MARK

THE PROLOGUE: PREPARING THE WAY OF/TO THE KINGDOM
1: 2-13 John the Baptizer, Jesus' Baptism & His Testing by Satan as God's Son

PART 1. THE WAY THROUGH GALILEE:
JESUS' MINISTRY INAUGURATES GOD'S NEW WAY
1:14–3:12 The Kingdom Community Begins in Galilee

1:14-15	summary: Jesus proclaims "the good news of God"
1:16-20	call of first disciples, initial positive response
1:21-45	a day in Jesus' ministry (teaching/healing/exorcizing)
2:1–3:6	5 conflict stories: Jesus' honor and power challenged, negative response
3:7-12	summary: people come to Jesus

3:13–6:6a Building the Kingdom Community: God's New Family

3:13-19	choice of the twelve as apostles
3:20-35	Jesus' true family
4:1-34	guiding the new family by teaching in parables
4:35-41	Jesus' wondrous actions as leader of the new family

5:1–8:26 Opening the New Way: One Family for Jews & Gentiles

5:1-43	cures for Gentiles and Jews
6:1-6a	rejection at Nazareth
6:6b	summary: Jesus teaches in the villages
6:7-13	the twelve are sent to share in Jesus' mission
6:14-29	the identity and fate of John the Baptist
6:30-34	the twelve return, a time for withdrawal and rest
6:35–8:26	wondrous events and controversy while building the community

PART 2. ON THE WAY TO JERUSALEM:
FOLLOWING THE WAY OF THE SUFFERING SERVANT
8:22–10:52 Jesus Teaches about Himself & Discipleship "on the Way"

8:22-26	healing a blind man in two stages
8:27-30	Peter's confession: Jesus, God's son, is the messiah/Christ who "must" suffer
8:31–9:1	1st passion prediction & discipleship as a way of suffering
9:2-29	Jesus' transfiguration: God confirms Jesus' messianic identity; teaching
9:30-50	2nd passion prediction & discipleship as a way of service
10:1-31	Jesus teaches in Judea and beyond the Jordan
10:33-45	3rd passion prediction, discipleship as a way of redemptive service for many
10:46-52	healing of another blind man who follows Jesus "on the way"

PART 3. THE WAY OF TRIUMPH & TRAGEDY:
THE FINAL WEEK IN JERUSALEM
11:1–13:37 Preliminaries to the Passion (Sunday to Thursday)

11:1-11	the 1st day: the triumphant entrance of the messiah
11:12-19	the 2nd day: teachings, cursing barren fig, disrupting the Temple business
11:20–12:44	the 3rd day: more teachings and final controversies with opponents
13:1-37	Jesus final teaching: a vision (apocalyptic) of God's final work in our world

14:1–15:39 The Way of the Cross & the Death of "the King of the Judeans"

14:1-17	plotting, anointing, betrayal
14:17-31	the last supper, prediction of Judas's betrayal & Peter's denial
14:32-52	Jesus' prayer and arrest in Gethsemane
14:53–15:15	Jesus' trial by Judean leaders, Peter's denial, trial by Roman governor Pilate
15:16-39	Jesus' crucifixion and death

THE EPILOGUE: THE WAY TO THE FUTURE
15:40–16:1-8 Jesus' Burial, the Empty Tomb & Easter Message to the Disciples

[16:9-19	other resurrection materials added later to Mark's original ending]

126

CHAPTER FIVE

Mark's Gospel
The Beginning of the Good News
& the New Way of Salvation

Mark's Gospel pulls together many strands about who Jesus is and who we are if we wish to be his disciples. But since the text is shaped to communicate a message to his readers, we must first ask historical questions about the author, the audience and their situation, and then literary questions about the form (structure), content and function of the text.

Thus we will discover Mark's special emphasis about Jesus as the promised messianic prophet, teacher and kingdom-community builder who "must" suffer, and ourselves as his all-to-human disciples who model our lives on his. Mark's Gospel is a way of remembering Jesus to re-member the community which is threatened with identity problems, challenged by failures of faith and leadership, and distanced from the time and person of Jesus who is no longer physically present with them.

"It is challenging to read Mark as the first gospel—as if the other gospels didn't exist and this is our first encounter with the story of Jesus. It requires imagining that we haven't already heard about Jesus from the other gospels, from Christian preaching and teaching, and from what is taken for granted about Jesus in Christian and popular culture."

—MARCUS J. BORG
Evolution of the Word: The New Testament in the Order the Books Were Written (2012)

Since we do not have the time or space to deal with all the scholarly differences of opinion regarding Mark and his Gospel, we will rely on the consensus of scholarship. More complete answers to all of these basic questions can be found in greater detail in scholarly commentaries.

Mark & His Community

First of all, we must note that the identity of all the Gospel authors is a problem that is resolved only by historical study and not by faith. Most scholars recommend caution in accepting the traditional identifications of the Gospel authors. Moreover the author's identity has little to do with our belief that the Gospels, like all Scripture, are revealed, inspired, without error regarding revealed truth, canonical and helpful for our salvation.

Who Was Mark?

Since nothing in the Gospel itself identifies the author by name, and the description "according to Mark" was added later, we can probably never know who he was personally because he reveals no information about himself or his life or his motives for writing. Moreover, he never claims to be an eyewitness of the events he reports. Most importantly, since Mark was not trying to become a famous author but rather to do something important for his community, he would not want his audience (then or now!) to focus unnecessary attention on him but rather to concentrate on his Gospel and on Jesus whose message and mission it proclaims.

"Mark was essentially a pastor addressing a beleaguered and persecuted community and offering them moral guidance and spiritual consolation. The story of Jesus' miracles, death and resurrection spoke of a power which could overcome all obstacles and sustain the community through the fires of persecution. The story of the disciples' faltering progress in understanding Jesus' message and moral instruction would provide comfort to those who themselves were in danger of breaking under the pressures to betray one another and their faith."

—*JOHN K. RICHES*
Conflicting Mythologies: Identity Formation in the Gospels of Mark and Matthew (2000)

According to the constant tradition of the early Church, the author was one Mark, the "interpreter of Peter." Many think he was the John Mark in Acts 12:12, to whose house Peter goes after escaping from prison, who then accompanied Paul and Silas on their early Christian missionary journeys (Acts 12:25; 13:5-13; 15:37-39; see also Col 4:10; Phlm 24; 2 Tim 4:11) and is associated with the missionary work of Peter since he is also referred to metaphorically as "my son Mark" (1 Pet 5:13). The earliest testimony describing Mark as author of the Gospel is given by Papias (c. AD 120–140), the bishop of Hieropolis in Turkey, as reported by the Church historian Eusebius (c. 325).

Most scholars now recommend caution in taking Papias's claims at face value and many are slower to give it immediate consent. Whoever wrote the Gospel drew on early tradition of Jesus' miracles, teachings and passion, and thus interpretation must begin with the Gospel itself rather than tradition about its authorship. The Gospel reveals much more about the evangelist and his setting than does the tradition of Papias.

Mark's Community

Who needs the good news as Mark announces it? What was the situation of his community that demanded the communication of the Good News of their salvation in the narrative shape or form that Mark chose?

Mark wrote about the year 65–70, probably in Rome (although some scholars argue for a location closer to Palestine), to a community that was a mixture of both former Jews and Gentiles. This was a dangerous time for Christians both in Palestine and in Rome. In Palestine, the Jewish rebellion during the years 66–74 shattered the peace of the eastern Roman empire. Both the Jews and their Christian neighbors were treated with equal harshness by the Roman occupational force. In the year 70, the Romans destroyed the Temple in Jerusalem, which was the only place on earth where the Judahists believed God dwelt.

And in Rome, for the first time in their history, Christians were singled out for persecution by the emperor Nero who blamed them for the burning of Rome in the summer of 64. Until this time, the Romans had always thought of Christians as just a fringe Jewish group. But now Christians could no longer hide their identity. How would Mark's community respond when their faithful following was threatened by persecution and martyrdom? Did these persecutions mean that God had now abandoned Mark's Christian community?

Why Did They Need a Gospel Like This?

Like every text, the Gospels were written to meet the needs of the audiences who found them important for their lives. Mark's Gospel responded to the challenges posed by the first Christian persecution, when following Jesus' way to God really meant taking up the cross to follow him.

Mark's community was suffering for their faith and scrambling to discover their true identity as faithful followers of Jesus. Their persecution created a time of decision when the community had to discover God's kingdom or presence anew. They had to make choices about following Jesus' way or failing to be with him for the whole journey. Could they choose to suffer the way Jesus suffered or would they choose to abandon their faithful following of his way because it was getting too difficult?

Using Jesus as his model, Mark gives his community new answers to the urgent questions of who they are and what they must do to follow Jesus in the chaotic experience of war, persecution and apparent abandonment. The stakes are high because in the face of persecution it is tempting to deny one's Christian identity rather than to suffer. In this time of heightened anxiety, when old ways are ending and new directions are not yet clear, Mark shapes his Gospel as the haunting story of the messiah who suffers so others can live, whose death and apparent abandonment culminate in new life with God.

Mark emphasizes the reality of suffering and the inevitability of the cross, which for him is the only way to new life. He encourages his community to recognize that Jesus as the suffering messiah is the key to their relationship to God. Anyone who thinks there is another way, or that there is another gospel which does not demand your whole loyalty and your whole life, then that is not the Good News of Jesus.

A New Community of both Jews & Gentiles

Not only is Mark's community suffering but it is also deeply divided about the status of Jews and Gentiles gathered into one group. As the Gentiles came flocking into the communities because of the missionary work of people like Paul, they created the demand to rethink the community's relationship to the Jewish practices and views that had been so natural for the earliest disciples. Since the original core of disciples were all former Jews, they thought of the Jewish way of life as the right way to please God. But as the number of Gentile converts increased, the communities had to accommodate themselves to a more Gentile-oriented way of life. In twenty years (AD 40–60), the whole makeup of the community had shifted so dramatically that the split between Christians and Jews was inevitable.

By the end of the century, the vast majority of Christians throughout the world would no longer be former Jews and so would not be familiar

THE GOOD NEWS IN FOUR VERSIONS

with Jewish traditions from a first hand experience. Mark's community is already caught in this tension. Mark's stress on Jesus' struggle to build one community out of Jews and Gentiles by doing the same things for each group is an indication of how deep this rift was within Mark's community. Jesus gathers together the divided community into one eucharistic community who shares the "one loaf" (8:14) which can feed them all.

Mark's Gospel: Structure & Style

As we noted in chapter 4, Mark invented the written Gospel, that is, a consecutive narrative account or story of Jesus' life, ministry, death and resurrection that models for us who we are as Christians and what we ought to do to follow Jesus. His narrative also gave new meaning to the many isolated events and sayings that the Christian community remembered about Jesus by locating them in specific times and situations in his life story.

"In content, Mark's Gospel was a story of the gospel of Jesus and his disciples. In form, Mark's Gospel was an act of proclamation. It made Jesus, the one who was crucified but had been raised from the dead, present to Mark's readers and listeners. Through the Gospel, the gospel proclaimed by Jesus and the Church became the gospel that was Jesus."

—EUGENE LAVERDIERE, SSS
The Beginning of the Gospel: Introducing the Gospel of Mark, Vol. 1 (1999)

As with any narrative, Mark has a basic temporal structure related to Jesus' life that can also be loosely organized geographically—baptism in the Jordan River by John the Baptist, a ministry of teaching and healing and establishing God's kingdom community in Galilee and other northern regions, and then a final journey to Jerusalem where he openly confronts those who want to kill him, is betrayed, suffers, dies and rises to new life with God. Mark's Gospel thus has a general threefold schema after the prologue (1:1-13): the first unit is Jesus ministry in Galilee and regions nearby (1:14–8:21); the second is Jesus roundabout journey to Jerusalem (8:22–10:52); and the third is Jesus' final days in Jerusalem (11:1–16:8).

Like any good narrative, Mark's plot is constructed through the revelation of many conflicts. Jesus first appears as a popular teacher, prophet and wonder worker who like Moses and Elijah preaches God's message, performs many miracles and exorcisms, and gives guidelines or laws for living out the right kind of relationship with God. But Jesus and his proclamation of a new way to live the Yahwist faith seems always in conflict with those advocating alternative agendas. Mark's narrative charts how Jesus and his message are constantly misunderstood and rejected, resulting in the transformation of his followers and the hardening of the hearts of his opponents. These conflicts also embroil Jesus in the cosmic conflict of God and Satan, good and evil, for ultimate control of our world.

Despite all conflict and opposition Jesus resolutely follows the way to Jerusalem and then the way of the cross. The mystery of Jesus is finally revealed in his death and resurrection. The cross casts its shadow all through Mark's Gospel. It is the key to understanding what Mark writes and what he is trying to proclaim to us who now read and respond to his Gospel.

Mark's Portrait of Jesus

Mark's invention of this new Gospel form was immediately recognized as exactly what the Christian community needed. He gave Christians a new identity by showing both who Jesus was—the Christ who had to suffer—and who they were as his disciples—people who were called to take up their own cross and follow Jesus.

"The theme of the cross can be compared to a magnet that attracts the other motifs that appear throughout the gospel. The shadow of the cross, opposition from powerful leaders, divisions among Jesus' followers, persecutions, and betrayals—all these themes in Mark's Gospel would have been especially meaningful to an early Christian community that had suffered for the name of Jesus and was expecting even more suffering."

—*JOHN R. DONAHUE, SJ, & DANIEL J. HARRINGTON, SJ*
The Gospel of Mark (2002)

Jesus: the Messiah Who Suffers

Mark's Gospel is constantly concerned with the mystery of Jesus' identity. His main effort is to show that "the Christ, the son of God" (1:1) is God's chosen servant who does God's work by suffering, as described by the prophet Isaiah in four poems or "servant songs" (Is 42:1-4; 49:1-6; 50:4-9; 52:13–53:12). In their original Old Testament context, these poems helped the Israelite exiles make sense of their suffering. But for Mark this servant who is innocent and just, chosen and empowered by God, yet who then is killed, is the way to comprehend the meaning of Jesus' death as the fulfillment of God's plan for salvation. Mark reminds his audience that the messiah *must* suffer to enter into his glory, which is also the essential way of discipleship that eventually all Christians must follow.

Throughout the first half of the Gospel, Mark emphasizes that Jesus is really human like us. He has emotions, gets tired and is subject to the plots of his enemies. Under stress he can almost despair. He is not the grand and glorious messiah whom many people waited for. He is not a flashy wonder-worker who demanded fame or money for his miracles. Instead Jesus was a messiah who is willing to give his life for others.

Mark first confirms some of the conventional Jewish expectations about the messiah. Jesus is a prophetic teacher and lawgiver like Moses, a miracle worker like Elijah and a kingdom builder like David. Mark then negates all of these common expectations. Jesus is indeed the messiah, but he "must suffer greatly, be rejected, and be killed, and rise after three days" (8:31). The rest of the Gospel shows how the suffering messiah fulfills God's plan for salvation and builds the kingdom community.

Jesus: the King Who Is Crucified

Mark presents Jesus' suffering as the great reversal of the common expectation that the messiah would be a glorious king like David who would free the Israelite people from their oppressive Roman overlords. Unlike Matthew or Luke who provide clues about Jesus' royal identity in their infancy narratives, Mark gives no hints about Jesus' royal character until the passion. Then surprisingly enough, these royal associations appear with tremendous irony. That is, when the characters in the story mock Jesus as a king, they think it is not true. But we readers know that he is indeed a king, despite being crowned with thorns, mocked, scourged, spit upon, clad in royal colors, given an impotent scepter and finally enthroned on a cross with a sign mocking him as "the king of the Judeans."

What kind of a king is this? This is hardly the way a real king would be treated unless he had been defeated. Is Jesus passion a defeat? Is he a victim? If his crucifixion is his coronation, then this is a very strange way to be declared a king! This is important if we are going to understand how Mark is working on us as readers. Our expectations of a prophetic messiah and of a conquering royal messiah are not the way God has chosen for the plan of salvation to be realized. God's way is to save us through Jesus' suffering. Mark's final picture of an abandoned Jesus dying alone outside the holy city challenges all the usual expectations about Jesus as a glorious and triumphant messiah, and reveals how God's suffering servant through his death opens a new way to life with God.

Mark's Portrait of Discipleship

Mark's portrait of Jesus as God's suffering servant who gives his life for all is also the clue to his portrait of genuine discipleship. What happened to Jesus will happen to us. Following Jesus means not expecting that God will save us *from* our suffering, but that God will save us *through* our suffering. The cross is the only way to the crown of new life. But Mark stresses that Jesus' way of the cross is not a dead end. Paradoxically, Jesus' way of dying is the only way to find new life in God!

Jesus: Mark's Model Disciple

In Mark, only Jesus is really a positive model for being a Christian. He reveals how to be God's disciple by fulfilling in his own life all the characteristics of a genuine disciple: "to be with him, and to be sent out to proclaim the message, and to have authority to cast out demons" (Mk 3:12-14). For Mark Jesus is the only disciple worth imitating, which can be somewhat shocking because we are so used to imitating the example of the disciples

But this expectation of the disciples as our role models is just one more instance of Mark's general pattern of reversing our cherished expectations. Not only do we have to reverse our ideas about who Jesus is, but we have to change our ideas about what it means to be his disciple. Mark would admonish us not to be like they are. Whatever they are doing, be prepared to do the opposite! Rather, be like Jesus and do like Jesus does.

Although Mark offers Jesus as the model for Christians who are suffering and feel themselves abandoned by God, Mark offers no easy comfort. Jesus will not return miraculously to save us from our suffering. The only solution is to take up one's cross as Jesus did. For only by living through the suffering and death does resurrection follow. Suffering is not the end but the door to a new existence with God, who never abandons us.

THE GOOD NEWS IN FOUR VERSIONS

Mark's Negative Portrait of the Disciples

Since Mark wants to show that Jesus is the only true disciple of God, he presents a consistently negative portrait of the disciples who always fail in their attempts to follow Jesus. They are very human, never really understand who Jesus is, and serve as negative examples for us to learn from for shaping our own discipleship.

When Jesus chooses the apostles he goes up on the mountain and chooses the twelve to "be with him" (3:14). As we move through Mark's Gospel, it becomes clearer and clearer that the disciples are not "with" Jesus mentally since they never seem to be able to get their minds aligned with his vision and values. After their first generous response to Jesus' call, the rest of their experience with Jesus becomes more and more a tissue of misunderstanding of just about everything that Jesus tries to tell them. They always have other ideas about who Jesus is, what Jesus should be doing and how he should be doing it.

Nor are they physically "with" him when the chips are finally down in the passion, for when the guards come to arrest Jesus in Gethsemane they all abandon him and flee. Peter does return to follow along "at a distance" (14:54) but then when confronted by a serving maid he three times denies that he even knows Jesus and goes off to weep. In the end, there is no indication that any of the apostles are near the scene of the crucifixion. In Mark's Gospel, Jesus dies alone and completely abandoned both by his chosen followers and even apparently by God.

No Privileged Discipleship—Carry Your Own Cross

Mark also emphasizes that a Christian disciple is one who must take up his or her cross and follow Jesus on this way of suffering. His negative portrait of the disciples allows him to show that there is no privileged discipleship. By systematically undermining all the popular claims of privileged discipleship—e.g., by having family connections, being one of the twelve apostles, having a personal knowledge of Jesus or being a member of the Christian community—Mark shows that these discipleship claims are not enough and will always end in failure. Only those who faithfully follow by taking up their cross can be genuine disciples.

A Brief Reading Guide to Mark's Story of Jesus

In the chapters on each Gospel, I will provide a brief Reading Guide to encourage you to encounter the four Gospels themselves and explore their versions of Jesus' Good News that the forthcoming kingdom of God is here. Reading the Gospels and engaging with them directly is the only sure way to begin to understand both their life-changing message and how that message can change your life too.

The Title (1:1)

Mark's first line seems like a title and perhaps was written on a small tag of parchment to identify the contents of the rolled-up scroll. This title, "The beginning of the good news of Jesus the Christ, the son of God" (1:1), summarizes the central concerns of his Gospel narrative. He wants to help us to understand Jesus as both God's chosen one or messiah (Gk: *christos*) who will fulfill the promises to the Israelite people and who is at the same time the son of God.

Mark's first emphasis helps his audience grasp through his narrative that Jesus is the promised messiah/Christ. But he also wants to indicate the kind of messiah Jesus is. The title takes away any mystery for the readers that Jesus is the messiah, but only by progressing through the Gospel do we discover exactly what kind of messiah he is and how he will act.

Mark's second emphasis helps his audience understand what it means for Jesus to be the "son of God." He does this by taking people back to the events of Jesus' life and ministry. But he is always shaping those events so that his readers don't just read about them but experience them through their participation in his narrative and so can grasp what it means to be a disciple and faithfully follow Jesus in their own lives.

Since in Greek, the "good news *of* Jesus" can mean either *from* Jesus or *about* Jesus, Mark's Good News includes both the message from Jesus' to us about a new kind of kingdom community that he was building to include everyone—both Jew and Gentile—and the message about Jesus as God's messianic agent for the forthcoming victory over the forces of evil, sin and death by his life, death and resurrection.

The Prologue:
Preparing the Way of/to the Kingdom (1:2-13)

The way a story begins is important. Mark's prologue situates Jesus story within the prophetic matrix of the Old Testament. The "beginning of the good news" (1:1) is the realization of what was promised long ago in the prophets about the messiah/Christ whom God would send to show the way for people to rebuild their relationships with God. In a combination of prophetic quotes which Mark attributes collectively to Isaiah as the great prophetic spokesperson of the coming messianic age, he indicates that the one who is coming is the one the whole Old Testament points to.

Note that in Mark's Gospel there are no familiar infancy stories—Jesus is already an adult when his story begins with a baptism. For us as readers, this suggests that for Mark our real life—our significant life with God—begins with our baptism and not just with our birth.

Jesus' Baptism in the Jordan for His New Ministry

Mark describes the preaching of John the Baptist that sets the stage for Jesus entry into the story. The adult Jesus leaves his family to begin his public ministry of announcing and building God's new kingdom community. He journeys from Nazareth to the Jordan River to reaffirm his commitment to God's rule by being baptized by John the Baptist.

"In Mark God has ripped the heavens irrevocably apart at Jesus' baptism, never to shut them again. Through this gracious gash in the universe, God has poured forth his Spirit into the earthly realm."

—*JOEL MARCUS*
Mark 1–8 (2000)

Mark uses Jesus' baptism and God's voice from heaven to affirm Jesus' identity as God's chosen son (1:1). God's approval is also accompanied by the descent of God's Holy Spirit to empower Jesus for his coming kingdom work. Like the dove that signaled to Noah and the people in the ark that God's new creation was waiting for them, this dove signals that Jesus will now begin renewing creation according to God's ways.

Confronting Satan in the Wilderness

After the heavenly confirmation of Jesus' identity as God's son with a mission, he journeys into the wilderness for 40 days to consider what kind of son he is going to be. Being the right kind of son will mean that he must dedicate himself with complete loyalty to God and use his power for building God's kingdom community. His loyalty is tested in confrontation with the powers of evil, which now rule our world.

Part 1. The Way Through Galilee: Jesus' Ministry Inaugurates God's New Way (1:14–8:26)

The Kingdom Community Begins in Galilee (1:14–3:12)

Jesus' first words are significant for they summarize his whole message and ministry. After his baptismal calling or vocation, he journeys from the wilderness back to Galilee to begin his Spirit-empowered ministry by announcing that God's promised kingdom rule is here and if people want to belong to this community and follow this new way, then they must change their lives and believe in this Good News (1:14-15).

Jesus begins to alert people to God's presence in their lives and their need to begin to live differently. Through his preaching in parables and through his deeds of power (we usually call them miracles, which in Mark are also "teachings," 1:27), Jesus reveals that God's powerful presence has now broken anew into our world to begin the final transformation of all relationships through the process by which we are converted, re-formed and transformed.

He called this new way of relating to God and others *the kingdom of God,* and he invited followers to change their lives and become part of the kingdom community. From his base in the village of Capernaum by the Sea of Galilee, he announces that God's salvation breaks across all our humanly created boundaries. Like a magnet, Jesus draws the poor, the outcasts, the sick, women, and foreigners to himself for healing. But his words and actions threaten the Judean leaders, who even at this early stage know that they must find a way to eliminate Jesus (3:6).

Building the Kingdom Community: God's New Family (3:13–6:6a)

Jesus calls followers to share his way of seeing the world and to live as God intends. His first followers are Galilean fishermen who are invited to put their fishing skills to work catching people for the kingdom. Then from among the disciples he calls twelve "apostles" to "be with him" and share his mission and ministry as they learn what it means for God's presence to break into our world through the person and work of Jesus.

Jesus spends his days traversing the Galilean region teaching about God's kingdom, demonstrating its reality through his healing, and celebrating it through shared meals. He offers his wisdom and deeds of power to teach people how to reorder their lives around God's presence.

By following Jesus, his disciples (and us) begin the necessary process of conversion. He proclaims his vision of reality and his values. His authoritative teaching challenges us to accept a new motivation for doing God's will and a complete loyalty and dedication to him. He invites us to change and to become his followers.

All the while Jesus is also building a new kingdom community or family for which he acts as the lord or head—but not the father or patron, who is God. Thus Mark portrays him in chapters 1–8 fulfilling many of the various roles of the head of a family: teacher, lawgiver, judge, provider and protector of the members of the community/family

Teaching in Parables (4:1-34)

In chapter 4, Mark gathers together most of Jesus' parables into the most extended teaching that Jesus gives in this Gospel. Jesus first teaches publicly to the crowds about the kingdom, then privately he explains his mysterious teaching to the disciples. Through the puzzling images in the parables (which conceal his meaning from outsiders—"them"—but reveal it to insiders—the disciples—and us!), Jesus reveals how God's powerful saving presence (the kingdom of God) comes to each of us as a gift, requires our response, changes us when we do respond, and empowers us for new action on behalf of this kingdom. The parables also provide examples of the proper responses to God's presence in our lives.

Opening the New Way: One Family for Jews & Gentiles (5:1–8:26)

In chapters 1–4, Jesus is primarily the proclaimer of the kingdom who announces God's transforming presence in our world for salvation. In chapters 5–7, the emphasis shifts to Jesus' work of building the kingdom of God. Mark structures these chapters around the basic theme that what

Jesus does for the Jews, he also does for the Gentiles.

The Sea of Galilee's chaotic waters served as a boundary that divided Jews from Gentiles. By moving back and forth across the Sea, Jesus breaks down the boundary and draws both Jew and Gentile into the right relationship with God and with each other. Through six different boat trips back and forth across the lake, Mark shows Jesus healing the true kingdom community by including both Jews on the West side and the Gentiles on the East. Jesus ministry of unification here serves as an outward sign of what Mark is trying to accomplish in his community through his Gospel.

"Galilee and Jerusalem are not simply the two locales of Jesus' ministry but also have theological import. Galilee is the place of the initial proclamation of the kingdom and of the manifestation of Jesus as a figure of power. Jerusalem functions as a place of opposition where Jesus predicts the destruction of the Temple and where he himself becomes progressively more powerless."

—*JOHN R. DONAHUE, SJ, & DANIEL J. HARRINGTON, SJ*
The Gospel of Mark (2002)

Part 2. On the Way to Jerusalem:
Following the Way of the Suffering Servant (8:22–10:52)

Jesus Teaches about Himself & Discipleship "on the Way"

As opposition to his teaching grows, Jesus makes the curious decision to go to Jerusalem, which is the seat of opposition and the stronghold of his most outspoken opponents. So he sets out on a somewhat roundabout journey to Jerusalem that will take up chapters 8–11. On the way he continues to instruct his followers about what belonging to the kingdom community demands of them.

Mark structures the journey in a series of three affirmations of Jesus' identity (8:31–9:1; 9:30-50; 10:33-45) as God's suffering messiah and a transfiguration experience in which the voice from heaven again affirms Jesus as God's son (9:2-13). This confirms that Jesus' messianic identity can only be rightly understood when connected to the reality that as messiah he must suffer, die, and rise to follow God's way of salvation. The misunderstanding of the disciples invites Jesus' further teaching about what it means to follow Jesus' way, in particular with its new characteristics of suffering and service.

Part 3. The Way of Triumph & Tragedy:
The Final Week In Jerusalem (11:1–15:39)

The increasing conflict between Jesus and his Judean opponents over his identity, mission and ministry climaxed in the turbulent events during the Passover in Jerusalem about the year AD 30 (or perhaps 33) which provide the framework for the story of Jesus' passion and death in the Gospels.

Preliminaries to the Passion (Sunday to Thursday) (11:1–13:37)

Jesus' final week began with a great public demonstration of acclaim (11:1-11). In a prophetic sign mocking the triumphant victory procession of a military messiah on horseback, Jesus rode into Jerusalem on a donkey while people strewed palm fronds on his path.

Once in Jerusalem, Jesus' attention focuses on the Temple, which as we noted was not merely a place of worship but also a market where sacrificial animals were sold and a bank where the state treasury was kept (note the widow' gift in 12:41-44). Jesus performs another prophetic sign by overturning the money changers' tables and disrupting the business going on in the Temple (11:15-17). His action was not really a cleansing of the Temple but rather a forewarning of God's judgment upon it and its consequent destruction when the end times came. He continued to teach in the Temple, reaching out one final time to his opponents who are actively searching for a way to kill him (11:18).

Jesus' Last Teaching: God's Final Triumph (13:1-37)

Although triggered by the disciples' questions about the end of the Temple and the future end of the world as we know it, Chapter 13 provides the disciples with guidelines for how they are to live when he will be hidden from them but never absent. His message centers on God's final judgment and the expectation of the coming of the "son of man," a title describing Jesus as the divinely chosen human agent who ushers in the end times (13:26) when God's kingdom will become the reality for our world.

In Semitic languages, when connected to a collective noun, "son of" designates the individual member of a group. Thus *a son of man* means a human person, especially in contrast to God, and so can mean "someone," "anyone" or even an indirect reference to "I myself" or "me."

But this title also takes on a particularly important meaning for Christians because the prophet Daniel describes God's final agent, to whom all power is given to accomplish God's rule in the world, as a "son of man" (Dan 7:13). Mark also adds further meanings by connecting this son of man with the suffering that the messiah must undergo (8:31; 9:12; 9:31; 10:33) and with the forgiveness of sins (2:10), which only God could do. Thus the title could point to Jesus as just another human person, or as the suffering, sin-forgiving savior or, finally, as God's final triumphant figure brandishing the power of God for the kingdom.

The Way of the Cross & Death of "the King of the Judeans" (14:1–15:39)

Each Gospel presents a distinctive picture of the suffering Jesus. Mark was the first evangelist to gather the disparate oral elements of the passion tradition and shape them into a coherent written narrative. The last two chapters of Mark's Gospel are his account of Jesus' arrest, trial, death and resurrection—his way of the cross. [For a more detailed examination of the passion narratives, see my *Who Do You Say that I Am? The Catechist's Guide to Jesus in the Gospels* (Faith Alive Books, 2015), chapter 12].

Mark shapes the traditional material to reinforce the major themes of his Gospel. So once again Mark reverses the most common expectations about the messiah. One expectation was that the messiah would be a great prophet and teacher like Moses. The other expectation was that he was going to be a king and warrior like David who would restore the freedom of Israel by going to war against its enemies, which were exemplified by the Roman overlords who dominated the Jews. The Judean leaders charged Jesus before the Roman governor Pontius Pilate with being "the king of the Jews" (15:2) so the Romans would be quick to respond to this challenge to their authority with the swift and cruel punishment reserved for these kinds of rebels—crucifixion.

Those who were crucified were made examples so that all could see and fear the power of the Romans. Note that none of the evangelists has much to say about the gruesome details of the crucifixion. They were all too aware, as were their audiences, of the agony which this death brought. They only had to mention that Jesus was crucified and that, apparently, was enough to clue the readers about how much Jesus suffered. We are,

THE GOOD NEWS IN FOUR VERSIONS

of course, more removed from the terrors of crucifixion but the horrible practice of the Nazi death camp doctors who crucified Jews in order to gather "scientific" data about crucifixion is well-known.

Jesus Death on the Cross

As is clear from Mark's Gospel, Jesus never sought death but accepted his death when it came. The conspiracy of the Jewish leaders, the treachery of Judas the betrayer, the complicity of Pontius Pilate and the collusion of the Jewish crowds all contributed to Jesus' crucifixion. But seen from a faith perspective, the meaning of his death emerged only in relation to the larger context of God's plan for the forgiveness of sins and the restoration of right relationships between God and humanity.

THE MESSAGE OF MARK'S PASSION NARRATIVE

1. The death of Jesus is the climax of a life for others.
2. In his passage from death to life, Jesus is proclaimed as the suffering yet triumphant son of man.
3. Jesus' death is a "theophany," revealing God's power at work in weakness.
4. The way of the disciple must be the way of the cross.
5. The church is, through the experience of the cross, to be a non-triumphant, reconciled church.
6. The crisis of the passion reminds the church that it must be open to outsiders.
7. The church is called to be a living "temple," open to all people and suffused with the spirit of the crucified Christ.
8. The passion reveals that the redemptive mission of the church is world-wide and costly.

—*DONALD SENIOR, CP*
The Passion of Jesus in the Gospel of Mark (1991)

Since Mark's passion account is shaped for his community who are being persecuted for their faith, he stresses Jesus' abandonment perhaps because his community felt like it had been abandoned by its leaders—and perhaps even by God (15:34). Jesus is deserted by his disciples (14:27, 50), betrayed by Judas (14:10-11, 20-21, 42-45) and denied by Peter (14:30-31, 66-72). When confronted by the Jewish high priest at his hearing, Jesus openly proclaims his status and destiny (14:60-62). Acclaimed as "son of God" only by the voice at his baptism (1:11), at his transfiguration (9:7) and by the demons during his ministry (3:11), Mark insists that we can recognize Jesus' true identity only by gazing on the crucified Christ and affirming with the Roman centurion that "truly this man was the son of God" (15:39). The torn Temple curtain (15:38) reveals that God is now not to be found not in the Temple but in those who, like Jesus, are suffering. The dark path of the passion is the way to God.

"Mark's theological achievement was that he integrated the traditions of the life and ministry of Jesus with the proclamation of the gospel of the cross. In Mark, therefore, the reader finds that no one confesses that Jesus is the Son of God as a result of hearing his parables or witnessing his mighty works. It is only in the context of his death that his identity can be understood (14:62), so it is only when he is hanging dead on the cross that the Roman centurion can confess his true identity."

—*R. ALAN CULPEPPER*
Mark (2007)

The Epilogue:
The Way to the Future (15:40–16:8)

Jesus died. Nobody—friend or foe—disputed or doubted that fact. He was hastily buried and his disciples then had to wait through the long Sabbath until Sunday morning to prepare his body properly according to the usual burial customs. When Mary Magdalene and other women disciples came to the tomb bringing spices to anoint his body, they discovered that the tomb was empty and his body gone, which stunned and perplexed them. These facts cried out for meaning. Was the body stolen? Who had taken him away? For what purpose? What did all this mean?

What happened next was a complete surprise. Jesus, whom they had known and who had been crucified, died and was buried, was suddenly somehow alive again. Their conclusion was that Jesus' resurrection to new life was God's action, motivated by love, because God did not want the relationship built up over the course of a life to end in death. Rather, through God's animating and vivifying power, Jesus was gifted with new life (a "new creation") beyond the power of death. This new life and the relationship with God it stems from, are therefore deathless or eternal.

The most eventful moment in Mark's Gospel is the ending because everything in the story builds toward it. It ends not with Jesus' death but with his resurrection. Had his Gospel ended with Jesus' death, there would have been no "Good News" for anyone to report and proclaim but only a rehash of the old familiar news that everybody dies, even messiahs.

But the resurrection proclaims that although death ends Jesus' earthly life, his relationship with God continues because God's power to give life triumphs over evil's power to kill. The Good News for us is that what happens to Jesus after his death will also happen to his followers (including us!) who faithfully follow to our death his way of relating to God.

Mark's Puzzling Ending: the Disciples' Fearful Failure

But the way Mark actually ends his Gospel (16:8) is somewhat puzzling, which no doubt encouraged later editors to add other material to make it more satisfying and bring it into conformity with the other later Gospels (16:9-19). In Mark, the chosen apostles are not part of the resurrection narrative nor does Jesus appear to anyone. The only followers are the women who watched the crucifixion from afar (15:40-41, 47) and who come on Easter morning to anoint the body. But they only find a mysterious angel-like figure in the empty tomb who announces the Good News that Jesus is risen and tells them to go and tell the other disciples that Jesus will meet them in Galilee. But strangely enough, rather than doing what the messenger told them to do, the women "went out and fled from the tomb, for terror and amazement had seized them; and they said nothing to anyone, for they were afraid" (16:8).

"The unresolved ending of Mk 16:8 functioned as a summons to the audience to follow Jesus in the way of discipleship, enjoying healings and risking persecution, failing and succeeding 'on the way.' The ending would call the audience to continue the story, expecting both successes and failures. The lack of closure helps to involve the hearer in the continuation of the story."

—*JOANNA DEWEY*
"The Gospel of Mark as an Oral-Aural Event: Implications for Interpretation,"
in *The New Literary Criticism and the New Testament* (1994)

This strange ending of Mark's original Gospel challenges the readers who have accompanied Mark throughout his presentation of the Gospel. Like the women, the community must decide either to be paralyzed by fear and say nothing or to overcome their fear with faith (see Mark 6:36 for Jesus' directives connecting these two attitudes) and go forth to deliver the message that they now have been given.

Mark's Gospel & Us

As modern readers of Mark's Gospel, we are also challenged in exactly the same way. As disciples who believe in the resurrection, we too have been given the task of spreading the gospel message. But how often are we tempted not to speak out or act according to our Christian values in a society which is often hostile to these values? How often do we just want to give reverence to the dead Jesus instead of courageously trying to meet up with the risen Lord in the "Galilee" of our lives?

Galilee was where the disciples first experienced God's saving power through Jesus' teaching and miracles and where God's kingdom first began to be realized. Our world still is searching for Jesus but we find it hard to get back to Galilee. This journey to meet the risen lord is not a geographical trip to the hills of Galilee but rather a spiritual trip to the place where we can begin to live our lives by recognizing that God indeed is the king or ruler of our lives. Living out the kingdom promise means that we will begin to be involved in the transformation of our world.

"Mark's Gospel condemns the self-oriented, fear-filled quest for security, status, and power as contrary to what God wants people to be. People who embrace these standards are destructive of others and ultimately of themselves. The result is a society of conflict and oppression."

—*DAVID RHOADS*
Reading Mark: Engaging the Gospel (2004)

Mark's Gospel was written for Christians who were suffering and persecuted. They looked around at their world and thought it was the end. So he calls it "The beginning of the good news of Jesus the Christ, the son of God" (1:1). Reading his Gospel today is still challenging but it can help us to confront and deal with the reality of suffering in our lives and in our world. The most important thing about suffering is how we understand its meaning. How do we approach our own suffering to discover its meaning and value? Is it something we simply put up with? complain about? sulk about? despair over? get angry at God or the people for? Mark invites us to understand our suffering in relation to Jesus' suffering. The core challenge of our Christian lives is to die with Christ, to die everyday, and not just at our final moment, because we are willing to conform ourselves in faithful following to Jesus' example. Do we have the courage to take up our cross and follow Jesus through our death to new life?

As with Mark's Jesus, our real life begins with our baptism when we are empowered by God's Holy Spirit. This empowerment is renewed by us at the time of our confirmation when our personal gifts of the Holy Spirit for service to the community are received, recognized, embraced as our own, and then used for the building up of the whole Christian community. Our empowerment, like that of Jesus, is an empowerment for ministry, which means acting on the threefold pattern that Jesus instituted for his disciples: "to be with him, and to be sent out to proclaim the message, and to have authority to cast out demons" (Mk 3:14-15). Mark also reminds us that fidelity to this way of ministry leads inexorably to opposition and the way of the cross. Only through death can we arrive at the promised new life with God, whose mysterious hidden presence even now fills our lives and surrounds us.

Mark reveals that what happened to Jesus is also happening to us. But it will only happen if we are willing to be faithful followers and allow the pattern of Jesus life to become the pattern for our own life. As we follow Jesus on the way to God, all we can be really sure of is that to be like Jesus we frame our lives according to his example of empowerment, ministry, suffering, death and new life. All we can predict with certainty is that as we follow our own way to the cross, the Holy Spirit ceaselessly surprises us and reverses all our cherished expectations.

Our challenge today is to use Mark's Gospel, as he did for his community, to discover the power of the Good News of Jesus to change our suffering and alienation, despair and betrayal into a new experience of community life. But the main thing we can predict and depend on is that, however unexpected the events are on our way of faithful following—the apparent tragedy of our life, our suffering, our defeat or abandonment, and the mystery of our eventual death—we know that God is present with us in all these circumstances. Mark invites us into a world where our main question ought to be "what if"? What if, as Jesus says, the Good News is that "The time is fulfilled, and the kingdom of God has come near"?

THE GOSPEL ACCORDING TO MATTHEW

PART 1: THE PERSON OF JESUS MESSIAH

Prelude: The Identity of the Master: Son of David, Son of God (1:1–2:23)
1:1–2:23   *Narrative: Jesus' Origins & Birth*

PART 2. THE MINISTRY OF JESUS MESSIAH

Invitation to God's New Kingdom & Call of His Disciples (3:1–7:27)
3:1–4:25   *Narrative: The Beginnings of the Galilean Ministry*
5:1–7:27   *Discourse: The Challenge of Christian Conversion*
            (The Sermon on the Mount)

Controversy & the New Kingdom (8:1–10:42)
8:1–9:37   *Narrative: Jesus Manifests God's Saving Presence in His Ministry*
10:1-42   *Discourse: Initiation into the Mystery of Missionary Discipleship*

The Mystery of God's Kingdom in Parables (11:1–13:52)
11:1–12:50 *Narrative: Jesus' Ministry Evokes Israel's Negative Response*
13:1-52   *Discourse: Jesus Teaches in Parables to Explain the Kingdom*

Confronting the Opposition (13:54–18:35)
13:54–17:27 *Narrative: The Kingdom Grows Despite Opposition*
18:1-35   *Discourse: Life in the Community of Disciples*

The Journey to Jerusalem to Confront His Opponents (19:1–25:46)
19:1–23:39 *Narrative: Confronting Opposition in Jerusalem*
24:1–25:46 *Discourse: Discipleship in the Master's Absence*

PART 3. THE DEATH & RESURRECTION OF JESUS MESSIAH

Tragedy & Triumph in Jerusalem (26:1–28:15)
26:1–28:15 *Narrative: The Death & Resurrection of Jesus, God's Obedient Son*

Epilogue: The Risen Christ Sends Us to Carry on His Mission (28:16-20)
28:16-20   *The Great Commission of Christ to the Disciples*

THE GOOD NEWS IN FOUR VERSIONS

CHAPTER SIX

Matthew's Gospel
A Handbook for Disciplizing All Nations

Throughout the centuries, the Gospel according to Matthew has played a central part in the life and worship of the Church. Each of the Gospels proclaims that the Good News of our salvation (that is, our right relationship with God) is best understood by attending closely to the life of Jesus of Nazareth. Their strategy was to invite readers to identify first with Jesus and then with the disciples in the story, and follow Jesus as they did.

Matthew & His Community
In the mid-eighties of the first century, Matthew adapted Mark's Gospel to the needs of his primarily Jewish community that was probably located in Antioch, the center of the Christian missionary effort to include the Gentiles. His Gospel is more Jewish than the others and is also the most concerned to work out the relationship of Jesus to Israel's hopes.

"The gospel of Matthew tells the story of Jesus the Son of God. The most important basic theological decision of Matthew was to take the Gospel of Mark as the basis from which alone Jesus' proclamation can be correctly illuminated. This means theologically: He has tied the ethical proclamation of Jesus concerning the kingdom of God to the history of God's actions with Jesus. In this way, it becomes the proclamation of grace."

—*ULRICH LUZ*
Matthew 1-7, A Commentary (1989)

Who Was Matthew?
Although nothing in the Gospel names the author, authorship is ascribed to Matthew, traditionally identified as the tax collector (9:9) who becomes an apostle (10:3). The Church historian Eusebius quotes an early second century Bishop named Papias who claimed that "Matthew compiled the sayings (Gk: *logia*) in the Hebrew language, and everyone translated them as best they could" *(History of the Church, 3.39.16).*

Although many scholars thought this meant that the Gospel was originally composed in Hebrew or Aramaic, the Gospel we have is not such a translation but is written in good non-Semitic Greek. Its Old Testament quotations come from the Greek translation called the *Septuagint* (meaning 70, after the legendary 72 Jewish elders who were said to have translated the Old Testament from Hebrew into Greek in the second century before Christ). One solution might be that Matthew had some kind of compilation of Aramaic or Hebrew scripture quotes or sayings of Jesus for his use, but these were translated into Greek for incorporation into his Gospel.

The author is well-versed not only in the Old Testament but also in other Jewish writings and traditions. Many scholars today think he was a converted scribe, although other scholars think he might have been a learned Gentile. In either case, Matthew 13:52 has often been taken as a self-description of the author and his purpose: "a scribe...trained for the kingdom...who brings out of his treasure what is new and what is old."

Who Was Matthew's Audience?

The Gospel, written most likely during AD 80–90, indicates that the community for whom Matthew wrote was predominantly Jewish in background, but becoming more and more Gentile in membership. A Greek-speaking congregation, it was probably located in a city like Antioch in Syria, since the earliest definite references to the book are by Ignatius of Antioch, about AD 110. Matthew expects his reader to be familiar with the Old Testament, to which he often refers in order to illustrate its fulfillment in the person, ministry and passion of Jesus. He also expects a certain familiarity with Jewish law and ritual practices.

As more and more Gentiles streamed into the Christian communities, Christians faced a decision about their relationship to Judaism. The fall of Jerusalem and the destruction of its Temple in AD 70 forced the decision. Without a Temple, the diverse groups within Judaism struggled to decide how they were going to continue to be Jewish without a temple.

The Pharisees, whose practice of Jewish life focused on the laity and the synagogue rather than on priests and the Temple, became the new leaders within Judaism. They questioned and finally rejected the way of practicing Judaism that Jesus had taught. It may have been to meet this crisis in the community that Matthew's Gospel suggests that the Christian community, not Pharisaic Judaism, was the true embodiment of the covenant community of Israel. He provides his community with a sense of who they are both as heirs of the Jewish tradition and as followers of the new "kingdom way" of relating to God that Jesus taught.

Judaism and Christianity as alternative ways of holiness began to diverge drastically after the destruction of the Jerusalem Temple. By the mid-eighties the Pharisees created a new form of Judaism which no longer had a Temple to worship in and now recognized clearly that many Christian beliefs—especially in the divinity of Jesus—were so different from Judaism's beliefs that Christians were no longer welcome in the synagogues.

Matthew stresses to his community that they, not Pharisaic Judaism, are the true and genuine Israel. So when Matthew's community was expelled from their synagogues, they, like Paul some forty years before, decided to take the gospel to the Gentiles. But this decision apparently created controversy within the community who were caught between loyalty to their Jewish heritage and their new mission to confront the Gentile world.

"Matthew's anti-Jewish polemic should be seen as part of the self-definition of the Christian minority which is acutely aware of the rejection and hostility of its 'mother' Judaism. For a minority struggling to gain its voice and firm up its boundaries, it is as important to indicate what movement it is not a part of in early Judaism as well as what movement it is a part of. The Jesus movement therefore is set over against at least some of the Pharisaic movement here."

—*GRAHAM N. STANTON*
A Gospel for a New People: Studies in Matthew (1992)

Matthew wants his readers to be proud of their Jewish heritage while at the same time embracing their task of realizing God's plan for a new community that is open to all nations and so can come about only if they participate in the Church's worldwide mission. Thus he defends this direction by rooting it in Jesus' ministry. His Gospel assures the community that their Christian identity and the direction that Matthew wants them to follow are the right ones. Remaining true both to their Jewish tradition and to Jesus' example, the community will be prepared to continue Jesus' mission and follow his directive to "make disciples (the Greek is more accurately a verb that we do not have in English, "disciplize") of all nations" (Mt 28:19).

Matthew's Gospel: Structure & Style

Matthew adopts Mark's Gospel for the general framework for his Gospel—arranging the events of Jesus' life and ministry from his baptism to Galilean ministry, then the journey to Jerusalem where he teaches, is arrested, tried, crucified, and is raised to new life. But Matthew also included new material from his community's sources. He uses a collection of Jesus' sayings (the "Q" source) that he shared with other communities like Luke's, which he gathers into five major discourses of Jesus the authoritative teacher (chapters 5–7, 10, 13, 18, 24–25). Between the discourses, Jesus is shown in action doing the things he has taught. Matthew also adds unique material from his community's own traditions which reflect their distinctive theology and christology (the "M" source). He uses this material for his infancy narrative focusing on Joseph, for supplementing Jesus teaching and for the appearances of the risen lord to the disciples after his resurrection.

"While this Gospel is written within shouting distance of Pharisaic Judaism, the community of the evangelist is no longer part of that particular stream of early Judaism; rather it is part of the messianic movement of Jesus. The Evangelist seeks to redefine the course or direction of Israel's history as pointing toward Jesus and needing to be redefined in light of the Christ event."

—*BEN WITHERINGTON III*
Matthew (2006)

Matthew's Literary Style

Matthew writes in a good but rather undistinguished Greek, more polished than that of Mark or "Q" but not as elegant as Luke's. His style is didactic and generally styled for teaching. He normally tightens Mark's narratives to highlight the essential points which he wishes to teach. He is repetitive (a major feature of oral teaching) and relies on many formulas and Old Testament citations, leading words, and inclusions. He is strongly influenced by the style of the Septuagint translation of the Old Testament and rabbinic Judaism. He has a habit of putting things in doublets or triads.

Matthew & the Other Gospels

Matthew's Gospel provides his community with a sense of who they are both as heirs of the Jewish tradition and as followers of Jesus' new way of

Christian righteousness (rightly relating to God). The destruction of the Jerusalem Temple was interpreted by his community as God's judgment on the Jews, just as Jesus had foretold, along with the obligation of the community now to become the new true and genuine Israel.

"What is new in comparison with Mark is the accenting of the 'gospel of Jesus Christ' (Mk 1:1) as a 'gospel of the kingdom,' i.e., as ethical proclamation of Jesus. The community which is confronted by the demand of Jesus knows itself directed first of all to the story of Jesus in which it experience the 'with us'—Emmanuel—of God. New furthermore is the programmatic turning to the Bible of Israel which is claimed for the history and proclamation of Jesus in and equal manner."

—ULRICH LUZ
Matthew 1-7, A Commentary (1989)

Matthew Revises Mark for a New Community Situation

Since Mark's Gospel was written in a time of trial and persecution, following Jesus' way to God meant taking up the cross. Matthew's community did not confront such trials. Matthew's main concern was that his mostly Jewish community was facing marginalization in a Church that was fast becoming almost exclusively Gentile. He realized that his community would not be able to continue unless they could find a place in the increasingly Gentile-Christian community. Matthew needed to encourage his community to embrace their Jewish tradition because it was the foundation for their Christian way of life. But he also needed to stress that their future task was participation in the Church's evangelizing mission to the Gentiles. How could he affirm their Jewish tradition and yet urge them to participate in the growing worldwide mission? His answer is his Gospel.

Matthew Revised Mark to Include New Materials

Matthew also revised Mark because he had new material from his own community traditions that Mark did not have. One source is a collection of many sayings of Jesus which scholars call the "Q" source (from the German word for source, *Quelle*, but we can remember it by thinking of "Quotes"). These materials include mostly "Quotes" from Jesus not found in Mark. Luke also knows and uses of these quotes, but he arranges them differently in his Gospel. Matthew groups these quotes into the five major talks or discourses that Jesus the teacher gives to the disciples.

MATTHEW'S GOSPEL

Matthew also adds some unique community traditions that are not found in the other Gospels (the "M" source). Some of these special passages include his use of Old Testament scriptural citations to show the fulfillment of God's promises and introduce several familiar elements of the story of Jesus' birth: the focus on Joseph, Herod and the Magi or wise men, the slaughter of the innocent children and the flight into Egypt.

"Behind the Gospel of Matthew, Jewish-Christian, partly scribal circles become evident, circles which are interested in Q, the Gospel of Mark, other Jesus traditions, and the Bible. Matthew is influenced in his language and his theology by the community; he does not write in a vacuum."

—*ULRICH LUZ*
Matthew 1-7, A Commentary (1989)

Matthew also includes several parables not found in the other Gospels and reports unique events in his passion narrative such as the dream of Pilate's wife about Jesus' innocence, Pilate washing his hands, the Jewish leaders accepting the responsibility for Jesus' death and the posting of the guard at the tomb. He also provides accounts of the resurrected Jesus appearing to the disciples that were absent from Mark's Gospel.

Matthew's Major Additions to Mark

So when we compare Matthew's Gospel with Mark's, we can see that Matthew adopts Mark's basic structure. Then from his own community sources, at the beginning, Matthew adds the genealogy of Jesus family origins and the birth narratives focused on Joseph to show that Jesus' divine sonship begins from birth, long before his baptism as in Mark.

In the main section of the Gospel, Matthew adds five long collections of Jesus' teaching (mostly from the "Q" source) that include the famous "Sermon on the Mount," Jesus' teaching in parables and other instructions to his disciples on their journey to Jerusalem. Matthew surrounds these five discourses with narratives that show Jesus teaching in action. At the end of the Gospel, he adds stories of the resurrection appearances that emphasizes how the risen Christ continues to be with us.

Old Testament Echoes

An important emphasis in Matthew is how he illuminates the deeper meaning of many events in Jesus' life by connecting them with specific Old Testament prophecies. The formula, "this was to fulfill…" (1:22; 2:15, 17, 23; 8:17; 12:17; 13:35; 21:4) demonstrates this literary characteristic. For example, 2:15 quotes from Hosea 11:1; 2:17-18 quote from Jeremiah 31:15; the reference in 2:23 about Jesus as a "Nazorean" is uncertain.

By connecting these events in Jesus' life to the Old Testament, Matthew reveals that Jesus' life was not an isolated phenomenon, but the completion of a story that was begun long ago. This same theme is also highlighted through the royal genealogy that begins the Gospel by showing Jesus as a highly honored successor to the Judean kings and by characterizing his entry into our world as the end point and fulfillment of the long history of Israel in relation to God as described in the Old Testament.

"In the infancy narrative and the events leading up to the public ministry of Jesus, Matthew introduces the reader to his understanding of Jesus. He connects Jesus to the history of Israel, affirms that the child's conception is an act of God, announces his salvific mission, demonstrates his fidelity and commitment to God's plan, and brings him into the arena of his public ministry. Through the addition of the fulfillment quotations, this majestic overture to the gospel story is welded to the promise of the Scriptures."

—*DONALD SENIOR*
The Gospel of Matthew (1997)

Matthew also relies on several Old Testament passages for the imagery in his magi story. The star and scepter that would "rise out of Israel" (Num 24:17) were identified with the messiah in Jewish thought. Herod's desire to control the magi echoes that of Balak, who tried to control Balaam's blessing (Num 22–24). Matthew adapts Micah 5:2 and 2 Samuel 5:2 to identify the child as the long-awaited shepherd of Israel (Mt 2:6).

Matthew Revised Mark to Include a New Perspective

In contrast to Mark, Matthew refocused both the portrait of Jesus and that of the disciples. Instead of Mark's misunderstood and suffering messiah, Jesus is the master, a teacher and compassionate healer who guides his disciples (and us!) step by step through a process of Christian discipleship. He also has a different approach to the disciples. Instead of Mark's disciples who constantly misunderstand and fail, Matthew presents them in a much more positive way. They are learners, which is the primary meaning of the Greek word for *disciple.*

Matthew's Portrait of Jesus

Matthew portrays Jesus as the royal lord and teacher of the new Israel. Jesus is the authoritative teacher, a compassionate master who proclaims, teaches, and heals as a sign of God's powerful presence in our world for salvation. Some important titles for Jesus are: messiah, son of God, son of David, Emmanuel [God with us], king, lord, and son of man.

He adds to Mark's Gospel an infancy narrative that focuses on Joseph to reveal Jesus as the son of David and establishes that Jesus was God's son from the time of his birth. (For a more detailed explanation of how the Gospel writers each used the titles son of David, son of man and son of God to reveal Jesus' unique identity, see my book *Who Do You Say that I Am?: The Catechist's Guide to Jesus in the Gospels,* pp. 67-94). Jesus' genealogy establishes his royal lineage and Matthew often likens Jesus to the great founding father of the old covenant, Moses. Jesus, however, transcends Moses and is the authoritative lawgiver for the new covenant.

"In Matthew's Gospel, while the disciples repeatedly address Jesus as 'Lord' (see e.g., 8:21, 25; 14:28; 16:22), when a stranger or a Jewish leader addresses Jesus it is as 'rabbi' or 'teacher' (8:19; 12:38; 19:16; 22:16, 24, 36). Notice that only the betrayer Judas among the disciples calls Jesus 'rabbi' (26:25, 49)."

—*BEN WITHERINGTON III*
Matthew (2006)

Woven throughout the Gospel is a carefully developed exposition of Jesus' identity. He is God's messiah, whose coming and destiny fulfill what had been spoken by the prophets. He is God's son, uniquely sent by the Father and completely obedient. He is the authoritative teacher who is like Moses but surpasses him. He is the son of man, who serves and suffers here on earth, but who will return as judge and king. People often call Jesus "lord" and recognize the tremendous authority with which Jesus applied God's word to our daily lives. He is the true teacher, what many Jews were hoping for in the promised messiah.

By portraying Jesus both as the fulfillment of the hopes of Judaism and as the inaugurator of the new Christian way of relating to God, Matthew's

Gospel serves as a powerful tool for conversion and an invitation for his community to be the new people of God with a mission.

Matthew's Portrait of Discipleship

Matthew stresses that Jesus ushers in God's powerful rule over our world. Jesus confronts us with a choice. We must decide to follow him or to reject him. Thus each person who responds to Jesus reflects these positive and negative possibilities of salvation. So instead of Mark's disciples who constantly misunderstand and fail, Matthew presents them in a much more positive way. The disciples respond to the call of Jesus and then tag along with him—listening to his words and observing his actions.

Matthew's Jesus often characterizes the disciples as having "little faith" (6:30; 8:26; 14:31; 16:8; 17:20). Like us, they grow in faith as they learn about Jesus and his challenging demands for discipleship. Becoming a disciple means not just knowing about what Jesus said and did, but putting his demands into action (5:19; 7:21, 26; 10:38; 12:50).

"For Matthew a relationship with God involves gift and demand. God's merciful initiative and gift to human beings is the possibility of a new existence which trusts and enjoys God's mercy and love. But such a life brings with it the difficult demand to do and live God's will. The interweaving of these themes through the actions and teachings of Jesus means that Matthew's God is neither an eternal Santa Claus handing out 'goodies' nor a fierce, punishing judge. Our reading of Matthew's gospel requires us to reflect on life in relation to the God who defies either category, and about how and what sort of God we might experience."

—WARREN CARTER
Matthew: Storyteller, Interpreter, Evangelist (1996)

Answering Jesus' invitation, disciples commit themselves in loyalty to a group characterized by being with Jesus to share his ministry and his suffering. The community of disciples (Gk: *ekklēsia*, an assembly, which Matthew twice uses for the Christian community or church) shares a spiritual bond with Jesus which is deeper than that of family. They are characterized by their "little faith" which must grow through the process of conversion.

Peter: The Model Disciple

One way to see Matthew's idea of discipleship is to concentrate on his depiction of Peter who serves a model for us of both the positive and the negative possibilities of discipleship. Positively, he is the first called (4:18-22), eagerly responds and becomes the leader of the disciples (10:2; 15:15; 17:1-8, 24-27). He represents their faith when he correctly affirms that Jesus is indeed the promised messiah on which a church can be built (16:13-20).

But despite this great privilege, Peter is still a person of "little faith" who needs to grow. He can be the founding rock or a stumbling block. He is challenged to have greater faith (enough to follow Jesus across water, 14:20-33), to avoid being an obstacle to Jesus' suffering (16:21-23), and to be a leader whose forgiveness is unlimited (18:21-35). Even Peter's denial of Jesus and failure to follow during the passion does not keep him from being a leader. It is another way through which he grows. Peter shows the ups and downs of the discipleship challenge. Always a learner, he can be a model for us who know that we are far from perfect in our following of Jesus.

A Brief Reading Guide to Matthew's Story of Jesus

Matthew follows Mark's familiar framework for Jesus' life—baptism in the Jordan by John the Baptist, Galilean ministry of teaching, healing and establishing God's kingdom community, then a final journey to Jerusalem where he openly confronts those who want to kill him, is betrayed, suffers, dies and rises to new life with God.

But Matthew restructures much of this material by inserting his new material into Jesus' five long speeches or teaching discourses to the disciples (chapters 5–7, 10, 13, 18, 24–25). These extended speeches proclaim Jesus' kingdom message. Then alternating between the discourses, Jesus is shown in action doing the things that he has talked about. These narrative sections also reveal how Jesus' message is accepted or rejected, either transforming his followers or hardening the hearts of his opponents.

As we read his Gospel, Matthew invites each of us to follow or imitate this journey with Jesus. Jesus' journey from birth through baptism to ministry and through suffering and death to new life is also the pattern that each of us as Christians must follow. His journey is our journey too.

PART 1: THE PERSON OF JESUS MESSIAH
Prelude: The Identity of the Master: Son of David, Son of God

Jesus' Origins & Birth (chapters 1–2)

Although Matthew adopted Mark's basic structure, one of the unique ways that he changed Mark was to add the events surrounding Jesus' birth. By telling right at the start everything a curious first century reader would want to know about Jesus, Matthew eliminates the Markan emphasis on the gradual unfolding of Jesus' secret identity. Through the genealogy or family tree and the birth events, Matthew reveals Jesus as the royal messianic son of David and the son of God, "Emmanuel...God with us" (1:23). The only mystery is what kind of response he will get when people discover this.

Jesus' Family Origins (Chapter 1)

The opening genealogy situates Jesus' life against the backdrop of the whole Old Testament. Matthew gives Jesus' life its meaning by putting it into relationship with other lives, with other covenant communities and with the events of salvation history. Matthew's message is that if you want to know what Jesus' life and death and resurrection are all about, then you have to see them as the fulfillment of the whole Old Testament story of God creating a covenant people. This old Testament story for Matthew shapes both the story of Jesus and also the story of the community of Christian disciples.

"Worrying about historicity and sources of information distracts from the inspired meaning of the biblical text, which is centered on what the evangelist was trying to teach us, namely, the religious message. We can explore that message under two major points: the first focuses on the identity of Jesus, the second on how Jesus, in his early life, sums up the history of Israel."

—*RAYMOND E. BROWN, SS*
"Why the Infancy Narratives Were Written," *Catholic Update* (Nov 1986)

Jesus is the fulfillment of this salvation story because he is the inheritor of Abraham's promises and David's royal mission. Jesus is an Israelite, a son of Abraham and so the one from whom the new covenant people will now trace their ancestry. He is also a royal messianic figure, a son of David, who will rule the people in God's place in the way that God wishes. He is an ideal figure who fulfills in himself all that Judaism waited and longed for.

Matthew recognizes in the genealogy that God is the driving force behind the story of salvation. The ones chosen to have significant parts in this story are often surprising choices. Matthew indicates some of this surprise by including the names of four women through whom the salvation story was changed significantly. Their presence indicates that when Mary is mentioned this will also be a significant change that signals a new direction in the continuing story of salvation as it will be enacted through Jesus.

Joseph's Dilemma

Matthew describes neither the event of Jesus' conception nor of his birth, but rather the reactions and responses of others to these happenings. He emphasizes first Jesus' surprising origin and second Joseph's actions. Matthew stresses that Jesus' birth is not just an ordinary one. The circumstances of Jesus' birth reveal that he is not merely a human person. God's power to give life was not working in the usual way that it did when human parents conceive a child, but in a very extraordinary and special way to produce Jesus through a human mother but without a human father.

Joseph is a "just man" who epitomizes the goal of Jewish life. He listens to God's revelation, obeys God's *Torah* but tempers it with mercy, and even though he does not completely comprehend what is occurring, he trusts God's signs and diligently fulfills the whole law. By law, Joseph could have chosen to quietly break his betrothal to Mary by sending her back to her family and reject her child that he knows is not his. But he was obedient to God's command and took the crucial step of accepting her child as his own, thus making Jesus his own legal son in the eyes of the community.

Responding to the Messiah: Acceptance or Rejection (Chapter 2)

Matthew's concern is not only to reveal the mystery of who Jesus is, but also to display the possibilities for response when he comes into our lives. These contrasts are illustrated in the persons of the Judean king Herod, the Jerusalem religious leaders and the Gentile magi or wise men who search for the new king to honor him.

For Matthew, there are always two possible responses and thus two types of persons. Some accept Jesus and his message and follow him, while others reject him even to the point of crucifying him. The tension of

Matthew's Gospel revolves around the question of who will follow Jesus and who will reject him. These two possibilities of response also reflect the situation of the early Christian community. While the Jews rejected Jesus even though the Jewish scriptures attested to his identity as their long-awaited messiah, the Gentiles however showed great interest, discovered Jesus as their lord and converted to such an extent that the community was now dominated by their presence and attitudes.

Thus Matthew's Christmas story (Chapters 1–2) reads like the Gospel in miniature. Its themes echo the rest of the Gospel: Jesus comes into the world—and into each person's life—calling and thus demanding a decision about how to respond. Some people accept and follow him (like Joseph, Mary and the magi), while others reject and persecute him (like Herod and the Judean leaders) to the point that he becomes a target for murder and must flee from Bethlehem into hiding in Egypt in order to survive until the family can return after Herod's death and resettle in Nazareth.

PART 2. THE MINISTRY OF JESUS MESSIAH
Invitation to God's New Kingdom & the Call of the Disciples

The Beginnings of the Galilean Ministry (chapters 3–4)
Matthew then skips ahead several years to the time when Jesus, now an adult, leaves his family in Nazareth to begin his public ministry of announcing and building God's new kingdom community.

Baptized in the Jordan for His New Ministry
Jesus journeys from Nazareth to the Jordan River area to reaffirm his commitment to God's rule by being baptized by John the Baptist. This baptism is a central event in Matthew's revelation of God in and through the incarnate son Jesus. Though sinless, he identifies himself with sinful humanity and also shows his obedience to and fulfillment of Old Testament expectations. God's voice from heaven publicly affirms Jesus' identity as God's chosen son, which we readers already know from the account of his birth.

Confronting Satan in the Wilderness
After the heavenly confirmation of Jesus' identity and mission at his baptism, he journeys into the wilderness for 40 days to consider what kind of

son he is going to be. Being the right kind of son will mean that he must dedicate himself with complete loyalty to announcing God's coming rule over us and our world, which will provoke a confrontation with the powers of evil, which now rule our world.

Jesus' confrontation with evil is depicted in his three temptations about how he, as God's son, will use the powers God has given him. Will he satisfy his own hungers, seek his own glory, expect special treatment from God? Or will he be a son who spends his life doing what his father wants?

Jesus then begins to announce that God's promised kingdom rule is here and journeys from the wilderness back to the Galilean hills where he starts to alert people to God's presence in their lives and their need to begin to live differently. Jesus then calls his first followers to share his way of seeing the world and to live together as God intends.

His first followers are Galilean fishermen, the brothers Simon (Peter) and Andrew, and the brothers James and John, who are invited to put their fishing skills to work catching people for the new way of relating to God and to others, which Jesus calls the kingdom of God, or as Matthew often refers to it, the kingdom of heaven. Jesus' ministry includes "teaching in their synagogues and proclaiming the good news of the kingdom and curing every disease and every sickness among the people" (4:23).

1st Discourse: The Challenge of Christian Conversion (Chapters 5–7)
The Sermon on the Mount

In this, the first major discourse of five which form the backbone for the structure of Matthew's Gospel, Jesus is presented as the authoritative teacher of the new *Torah*. The narratives of chapters 1–4 have portrayed Jesus as a "new Moses" and now Jesus the teacher presents the basic principles for life as Jesus' disciples in God's new kingdom. It is not likely that this discourse was actually delivered by Jesus in this form, but is rather a construction by Matthew from his collection of the sayings of Jesus that summarize the heart of his invitation to his followers.

The sermon is not meant to be a complete code of Christian ethics. The Christian moral revolution consisted primarily in "conversion" (Gk: *metanoia*), which was a change of mind and heart that meant the re-valuation of all our commonly accepted values. Jesus offers here the principles

Jesus' Sermon on the Mount

Some scholars think that this discourse is structured according to Jewish rabbinic methods of teaching. One rabbi, Simon the Just, taught that "By three things is the world sustained: by the law, by the Temple service or worship, and by deeds of loving-kindness." The first part of the main body of the sermon deals with the law (5:17-48), the second with true worship: almsgiving, prayer, fasting (6:1-18), and the third with deeds of loving-kindness (6:19–7:12).

I. Opening

1.) 5:2-10   Jesus' beatitudes express the essential spiritual characteristics of a true disciple, who must have the poor person's complete trust in and dependence upon God alone.

2.) 5:11-16   The special character of the disciples is to be salt and light for the world.

II. Main Body of the Sermon

1.) 5:17-19   A declaration concerning the perfection of Jesus messianic *Torah* in relation to the *Torah* of Moses. The perfection and the "more" of Jesus' *Torah* is explained in 5:21-48.

2.) 5:20   A declaration concerning the greater response expected from Christians in contrast with the response advocated by the Pharisees. The greater response is then elaborated in 6:1–7:12.

3.) 5:21-48   Antitheses that establish Jesus' authority as greater than Moses' authority; Jesus' *Torah* is the completion and perfection of Moses' *Torah*.

4.) 6:1–7:12   The contrast between the way of true (Christian) discipleship and the way of false (Pharisaic) discipleship with regard to (1) almsgiving (2) praying (3) fasting (4) material things (5) neighbors.

III. Conclusion

1.) 7:13-23   Three warnings that contrast the two ways of discipleship and indicate the seriousness of the demand of 5:20.

2.) 7:24-27   Matthew's final saying, which serves as a summary of his meaning, likens the doer to one who builds on rock and the non-doer to one who builds on sand. The meaning is clear that discipleship demands doing, not just talking.

In this discourse, then, Matthew summarizes the fundamentals of his understanding of Christian discipleship and then constantly illustrates them throughout the rest of the Gospel. The true disciple, unlike the Pharisees, not only "teaches" the law but "does" the law. He not only "does" the law, but he does "all" the law and governs his life by the radical, "kingdom" will of God. The true disciple recognizes that the law of love is the principle of interpretation and discernment for all laws. Finally, the true disciple is one who lives through faith, i.e., a complete and whole-hearted trust in God. By following Jesus more intimately, the disciple grows from "little faith" (6:30, 8:26, 14:31, 16:8, 17:20) to a greater and more faithful following of Jesus.

for this transvaluation of values and reorienting of our love in a summary way that is intended as a guideline for an ongoing Christian conversion.

Jesus invites his disciples (and us) to begin the process of conversion. He informs us about his vision of reality and about his values. His authoritative teaching now challenges our own attitudes with his beatitudes, our behavior with new motivation for doing God's will, and our commitments with a complete dedication to him. Jesus invites us to change and to do "more" as his followers.

Jesus Manifests God's Saving Presence in His Ministry (Chapters 8–9)

From his base in the village of Capernaum by the Sea of Galilee, Jesus announces God's salvation that cuts across all our humanly created boundaries. Jesus draws to himself the poor, the outcasts, the sick, demoniacs, women and foreigners for healing.

"Jesus now encounters individual Jews and gentiles, rulers and pariahs, men and women, all with distinct needs and distinct responses to his message. By focusing particularly on the interaction between Jesus and those who are outcasts of or marginal participants in the Jewish cultic establishment—lepers (8:1-4), women (8:14-15), demoniacs (8:16, 28-34; 9:32), tax collectors (9:9-13), sinners (9:11-13), the cultically impure (9:20-22) and the very marginal and impure, the dead (9:23-26)—the section exposes an interest in the social rather than the ethnic divisions."

—*AMY-JILL LEVINE*
The Social and Ethnic Dimensions in Matthean Salvation History (1988)

Jesus spends his days traversing the Galilean region teaching about God's kingdom, demonstrating its reality through his healing, and celebrating it through shared meals. Jesus' always focused on the revelation of God's presence with us and how we ought to respond. He taught people how to find God's presence in their ordinary lives, how to celebrate God's presence at their meals and how to reorder their lives around God's presence. During this time, his proclamation of God's kingdom and his healings provoke very little opposition.

2nd Discourse: Initiation into the Mystery of Missionary Discipleship (Chapter 10)

The disciples have observed Jesus in action proclaiming, teaching and healing. Now Jesus invites them one step further into the process of becoming disciples by actually imitating him. They are sent out to proclaim and heal as he has done (but Matthew carefully does not indicate that they can teach—this is left to the end of his Gospel when they will understand the message of the resurrection). Jesus warns them about the hardships of following him, which anticipates his suffering and death, but he also gives them the encouragement they need to carry on his work. In his teaching, Jesus reveals that he will be with them in their mission. Thus as they identify with him in their mission and ministry, he identifies with them to the point that rejecting them is rejecting him.

Jesus Ministry Evokes Israel's Negative Response (Chapters 11–12)

When Jesus' announces God's kingdom rule, everyone must respond. Some will accept and follow, others will resist and reject. In these chapters, Matthew offers several contrasting examples of responses to Jesus and reveals many signs of increasing opposition. The Pharisees and the Jewish leaders constantly argue with Jesus about the meaning of Jesus' teaching and his actions and Jesus is rejected in his hometown of Nazareth. He warns the disciples that this hostility will eventually culminate in his death.

3rd Discourse: Jesus Teaches in Parables to Explain the Kingdom (Chapter 13)

Matthew gathers many parables together in this chapter as Jesus teaches publicly to the crowds about the kingdom. Then privately he explains his mysterious meaning to the disciples.

"Jesus, the parable of God, reminds us that no matter what we think God is, no matter how sure we are of God, be careful. Maybe we don't know God at all. Maybe there is much more, but we can only learn it by staking our life on this story and throwing in our lot with those who become the story and enchant all the others with its power and grace. Jesus tells us that this story, the story of God, comes true when we do too."

—*MEGAN MCKENNA*
Parables: The Arrows of God (1994)

Through his perplexing images of the parables (which conceal his meaning from outsiders but reveal it to insiders whom he helps understand), Jesus reveals how God's kingdom comes to each of us as a gift and demands our response. The parables also provide various examples of the proper response to God's presence in our lives.

The Kingdom Grows Despite Opposition (Chapters 14–17)

As Jesus continues to travel the Galilean countryside, teaching despite the danger from the growing opposition that rejects him and his teaching, Matthew stresses that many are also responding positively to Jesus' presence and teaching. In particular, the disciples, as exemplified in the person of Peter, are growing from their "little faith" to a greater faith. As opposition builds among Israelites, Jesus reaches out to offer the kingdom and its healing power to Gentiles like the Canaanite woman, whose faith Jesus declares is stronger than that of many Israelites.

4th Discourse: Life in the Community of Disciples (Chapter 18)

Life in the community of disciples must be guided by Jesus' teaching about the kingdom of heaven and not simply by human management techniques. In this discourse, Jesus offers guidelines for the community of disciples regarding some essential issues for any community: status (prestige), authority (power) and deviance (non-compliance). Jesus explains that those who serve and care for the least members of the community are the greatest in the kingdom. He also outlines a process for the community to use in dealing with those who sin and deviate from the community's teachings. Finally, Peter learns that forgiveness must be without limits.

Journey to Jerusalem to Confront His Opponents (Chapters 19–20)

As opposition to his teaching continues to grow, Jesus makes a fateful decision to go to Jerusalem, which is the stronghold of his opponents who have been growing stronger and stronger in their negative response to his kingdom teaching and ministry. He seems to understand that his ministry cannot be complete until he confronts the Judean leaders in Jerusalem with the message of God's kingdom and invites their response.

So he sets out on the journey to Jerusalem and on the way continues to instruct his followers about some important challenges for those who want to belong to the kingdom community: fidelity in marital relationships, inclusiveness for the vulnerable, detachment from riches to open oneself for God's unsuspected and undeserved gifts (grace) and suffering service instead of dominance, honor and privilege. Only by giving up oneself and acting for others can the ideal of Christian love become a reality.

THE GOOD NEWS IN FOUR VERSIONS

Confronting Opposition in Jerusalem (Chapters 21–23)

As in the other Gospels, the intensifying conflict between Jesus and his opponents culminates in Jesus' passion and death at the Passover in Jerusalem. Jesus' final week begins with a great public demonstration of acclaim. In a prophetic sign of parody about the triumphant character of the messiah, Jesus rides into Jerusalem on a donkey while the bystanders celebrate his "triumph" and strew palm fronds on his path.

"Conflict is the stuff of Matthew's gospel. From start to finish, the whole gospel is one extended account of Jesus' conflicts, from the genealogy in chapter 1 that legitimates Jesus' familial standing as one of honor, to Herod's quest for the life of the child in chapter 2, to the battle between Jesus and Satan in chapter 4, to Jesus' fight with the Pharisees in chapter 12, eventually to his confrontation with the chief priests in chapter 21–27."

—BRUCE J. MALINA & JEROME H. NEYREY
Calling Jesus Names: The Social Value of Labels in Matthew (1988)

He then proceeds to the Temple to teach and reach out one final time to his opponents by extending an invitation to conversion. He then disrupts the business going on in the Temple as another prophetic sign forewarning the onlookers of God's judgment upon it and its consequent destruction when the end times begin.

5th Discourse: Discipleship in the Master's Absence (Chapters 24–25)

Chapters 24–25 are the last of the five major speeches that Jesus gives. They center upon the last days and the expectation of the coming of the son of man, which for Matthew, is a title that identifies Jesus as God' chosen human agent who ushers in the final time when God's kingdom will become the reality for our world. Although triggered by the disciples' questions about the end of the Temple and the future end of the world as we know it, Jesus instead offers guidelines about how they must conduct themselves as they await his final coming in judgement.

Matthew introduces three parables by which Jesus teaches the disciples that as they await his final coming they (and us) must be prepared at all times, use their talents wisely to build the kingdom, and know that their actions toward others, in whom Jesus hides himself, will be the criteria on which they will ultimately be judged.

The warnings against lack of awareness balance those earlier that stress caution against overzealous or premature expectations of Jesus' final coming, which will indeed bring judgment, not only upon sin, but upon one's state of readiness. The division made by God between the ready and the unready cuts across all human categories. The eternal choice may occur at any moment, therefore constant watchfulness is needed.

PART 3. THE DEATH & RESURRECTION OF JESUS MESSIAH
Tragedy & Triumph in Jerusalem

The Death & Resurrection of Jesus, God's Obedient Son (Chapters 26–28)
Each Gospel presents a distinctive picture of Jesus' death and resurrection. Although heavily dependent on Mark's passion narrative, Matthew revises it in light of his distinctive portrait of Jesus as God's obedient son and of his desire to encourage his community to participate in the continuation of Jesus' mission that now included outreach to the Gentiles.

Matthew's Passion Narrative
In his Gospel, Matthew portrays Jesus as the royal messiah who is completely willing to suffer in order to inaugurate God's plan for a new world. He emphasized that Jesus was God's faithful and obedient son because his community (c. AD 85) needed to persevere in their fidelity to their Yahwist heritage when they were rejected by their former Judahist colleagues.

"Matthew's passion narrative contains all the major prominence titles of Jesus in the gospel and dwells on them more intently than the rest of the narrative: Christ (26:63; 27:17, 22); Son of God (26:63; 27:40, 43, 54): King of the Jews (27:11, 29, 37, 42); Prophet (26:67-68); Son of Man (26:64)."

—*BRUCE J. MALINA & JEROME H. NEYREY*
Calling Jesus Names: The Social Value of Labels in Matthew (1988)

Although Matthew based his passion account closely on that of Mark, he regularly tightened up the narrative and introduced new material not found in Mark's account concerning the betrayal and suicide of the apostle Judas, the warning dream of Pilate's wife, Pilate's washing his hands, the Judean crowd's assumption of responsibility for Jesus' death, the cosmic events occurring when Jesus dies and the deployment of guards at the tomb.

1. Jesus is the obedient Son of God who fulfills the Scriptures and is faithful to God's will unto death.
2. Jesus is the Christ and Servant of God whose redemptive mission comes to its final expression in the cross, which frees God's people from sin and death.
3. Jesus is the Son of man who goes the way of humiliation and death but will come in triumph at the end of time.
4. In the crisis of suffering and death, Jesus is the exemplar of authentic faith/Christian existence.
5. The crisis of the passion reveals disciples of "little faith" and "unexpected disciples" who respond with generosity and courage.

—*DONALD SENIOR, CP*
The Passion of Jesus in the Gospel of Matthew (1990)

God Raises Jesus to New Life to Be with Us Always

Jesus' death was never in dispute. As the Sabbath approached, he was hastily buried and his disciples then had to wait until Sunday morning to prepare his body properly according to the prescribed burial customs. When Mary Magdalene and other women disciples came to the tomb bringing spices to anoint his body, they discovered that the tomb was empty and his body gone. The empty tomb and the absent body stunned and perplexed them. They had no idea what had happened or why. Was the body stolen? By whom? For what purpose? What did all this mean?

"Faith seeks the earthly Jesus not as a dead teacher, but as the living Lord, whose word and work were not merely accomplished once upon a time, but are now made ever present in the community."

—*REGINALD H. FULLER*
The Formation of the Resurrection Narratives (1980)

What happened next was a complete surprise to the women. The Jesus that they had known and who had been crucified was now suddenly alive again and appeared to them as they ran from the tomb to tell the disciples. Jesus tells the women to tell the disciples to meet him in Galilee where, indeed, the risen Jesus also appears to the disciples. Though, as always, two responses are described (some worship, some doubt), the Gospel ends with the risen Jesus sending his disciples out to take the Good News to all nations and use it to disciplize others.

Matthew's Gospel & Us

So we see that Matthew shaped his Gospel to help us understand who Jesus is and how we can follow him. As we listen and read his Gospel, we can connect Jesus' story to our story by focusing on the core pattern: revelation, recognition, response. God's presence is **revealed** in Jesus and his words and actions. People **recognize** that it is God in and through Jesus who is at work for salvation. Then they must decide how they will **respond**. Some accept Jesus and his message and become his followers, while others reject him and his message and become his hostile opponents.

The five major discourses and the passion narrative that structure the whole Gospel can also be viewed as an invitation to a conversion process:

- beginning a conversion of heart (ch 5–7)
- sharing in Jesus' mission (ch 10)
- deepening insight through parables (ch 13)
- directives for life as a community of disciples (ch 18)
- directives for life without the earthly Jesus (ch 24–25)
- the passion as an example of following Jesus (ch 26–28)

So when we encounter Matthew's Gospel, we are also invited to move through this conversion process and deepen our relationship with Jesus and with the kingdom community of other disciples. In this way, Matthew's Gospel becomes our basic teaching tool for accomplishing Jesus' final command to "*disciplize* all nations" (28:19) by teaching those who would be Christians the Gospel's way of discipleship just as Jesus had taught it to his first disciples and Matthew had taught it to his community.

"When the apostles went to preach the Good News and to baptize as the Lord instructed them, they didn't have any catechetical manuals. They had the gospel. They had the Holy Spirit. Why can't we modern Christians adopt the 'techniques' of the apostles and the early Christians? The gospel would be preached to the poor and the kingdom of God would begin at least to have a toehold in our modern world."

—*CATHERINE DE HUECK DOHERTY*
The Gospel without Compromise (1989)

Thus the final section, often called "the great commission" (28:16-20), summarizes Matthew's whole Gospel. Many of the themes which he stressed

THE GOOD NEWS IN FOUR VERSIONS

are echoed here: the authority of Jesus, the process of becoming disciples, the empowerment of the disciples, the mission of the disciples [now including teaching!], doing what Jesus taught, and the continuing presence of Jesus [Emmanuel] with the community of disciples for all time. Matthew unifies all of salvation history by recalling past events, hearing Jesus present command and being consoled by his promise of future presence with them.

"In virtue of their baptism, all the members of the People of God have become missionary disciples. Anyone who has truly experienced God's saving love does not need much time or lengthy training to go out and proclaim that love. Every Christian is a missionary to the extent that he or she has encountered the love of God in Christ Jesus: we no longer say that we are disciples and missionaries, but rather that we are always missionary disciples."

—*POPE FRANCIS*
The Joy of the Gospel (2013), #120

Through his Gospel, then, Matthew challenges us to a way of compassionate disciplizing or evangelization that encourages us to discover the risen Jesus as our mysterious companion—"when did we see you hungry, thirsty, a stranger, naked or in prison?" (25:37-40). Becoming a disciple means carrying on Jesus' mission to respond to God's presence with us and build a community of disciples, overcoming our fear and "little faith" to become teachers of the Christian Way and then sharing it so that others can also become Jesus' followers. Taking up this challenge is the daily work that we are called to do today as Jesus' missionary disciples.

MATTHEW'S GOSPEL

THE GOSPEL ACCORDING TO LUKE

1:1-4 THE PREFACE: AN ORDERLY ACCOUNT FOR YOU

1:5–2:52 THE PROLOGUE: JESUS IN HIS ORIGINS & IN HIS DESTINY
1:5-56 Annunciation, the conceptions of Jesus & John the Baptist
1:57–2:40 Manifestation, the Births of Jesus & John the Baptist
2:41-52 Jesus at 12, foreshadowing Jesus' adult ministry

3:1–4:13 BACKGROUND & PREPARATION: JESUS IN HISTORY
3:1-22 Jesus & John the Baptist's ministry; God's son confirmed
3:23-38 Jesus' genealogy: his place in the history of Israel & of humanity
4:1-13 Jesus & the struggle of humanity: temptations to sonship

4:14–9:50 THE MINISTRY & MESSAGE OF THE SON OF GOD
4:14-44 Introduction: Jesus, his mission & his journey
5:1–9:50 The mission: Jesus & the origins of the Christian community
 5:1–6:11 Jesus & his first disciples
 6:12–7:50 Jesus & the new Israel
 8:1-56 Jesus & the formation of the new Israel
 9:1-50 Jesus & the mission of the new Israel

9:51–24:53 THE JOURNEY: JESUS & THE DESTINY OF THE CHURCH

9:51–13:21 Ministry in Galilee: Orientation for the Christian Journey
9:51–10:24 Introduction: the missionary journey
10:25–11:54 Basic dispositions for disciples
12:1–13:21 Toward the final crisis: persecutions & discipleship

13:22–19:27 From Galilee to Jerusalem: Advice for the Christian Journey
13:22-35 Introduction: the journey of salvation
14:1–16:31 Discipleship, wealth & reconciliation in God's kingdom
17:1–19:27 More teaching & the arrival at Jerusalem

19:28–21:38 In Jerusalem: Rejection & Victory on the Christian Journey
19:28-48 Entry into Jerusalem
20:1–21:4 Jesus in dialogue with the leaders of Israel
21:5-38 Vision of the destruction of the Jerusalem Temple & the end time

22:1–24:53 From Jerusalem to God: Jesus' Passion, Resurrection & Ascension
22:1-13 Introduction: conspiracy, betrayal & preparation
22:14-53 Passover supper, prayer & arrest
22:54–23:25 Peter's denial, Jewish trial, Roman trial before Pilate
23:26–23:56 Jesus' crucifixion, death & burial
24:1-53 Visits to the empty tomb, recognition & the disciples' mission

THE GOOD NEWS IN FOUR VERSIONS

CHAPTER SEVEN

Luke's Gospel & Acts of the Apostles
The Journey of Christ & of Christians

Sometime around AD 75-90, Luke adapted Mark's Gospel for his primarily Gentile community which was probably located in Syrian Antioch, the center of the Christian missionary effort to include the Gentiles. Unlike the other Gospel writers, Luke tells the story of our salvation in two volumes, his Gospel and the Acts of the Apostles, which account for about one fourth of the New Testament. He wanted to show that what happened to Jesus was foreshadowed in the Old Testament and continued after Jesus' death in the lives of his disciples. His "orderly account" (1:1) of God's salvation history for Jews and Gentiles alike is revealed in Jesus' life, death, resurrection, ascension and expected return, which is at once the fulfillment of the Old Testament preparation and the foundation and pattern for its continuation in the ministry and mission of Jesus' followers.

"Luke's gospel is a literary and pastoral interpretation of the story of Jesus, the Son of Adam, the Son of God (3:38). Its purpose is to show how God fulfilled the promise of biblical history, first through the Word and Spirit which thoroughly permeated the person, life and mission of Jesus, and second through the Church which accepted to live like Jesus and to extend his mission to the ends of the earth. Quickened by the Spirit and heir to the Word, the Church would also fulfill the promise of what God had accomplished in Jesus, the Christ, the risen and ascended Lord."

—*GENE LAVERDIERE, SSS*
Luke (1980)

More than any other Gospel writer, Luke structures his gospel life of Jesus according to the familiar pattern of a journey. We often use this journey pattern to chart our experience of changes both in space—going from a starting point through a transition to a new place—and in time—from the past through the present and to the future. This familiar "from-through-to" pattern of a journey shapes Jesus' gospel life. He comes *from* God to become human in Mary's womb. He moves back toward God *through* a life of service dedicated to establishing God's kingdom community in Galilee. He confronts opposition and is killed in Jerusalem. He is rewarded by God with new life and finally returns *to* God to continue his life with God in heaven. After Jesus ascends to the Father, the Holy Spirit comes into the Christian community to empower and direct the community of disciples to give world-wide witness to the Christian message. Through his Gospel, Luke invites each of us to follow Jesus on this journey to God.

Luke & His Community

Who Was Luke?

Linguistic, stylistic and theological considerations all lead to the widely accepted conclusion that both Luke's Gospel and Acts were written by the same author. The early Church's constant tradition identifies this author as a certain Luke, described as a physician and companion of Paul (Col 4:14; Phil 24; 2 Tim 4:11). While many continue to maintain this tradition, other modern scholars think that the evangelist's identity is simply not known. From a textual analysis of his works, scholars think that Luke was a Gentile convert who knew Israel's scriptures in their Greek Septuagint translation. His rather sketchy knowledge of Palestinian geography and Jewish customs indicates that he was not a Palestinian native.

Who Was Luke's Audience?

Luke writes for a primarily Gentile community probably located in Antioch, Syria, the birthplace of the Gentile mission whose main proponent was the apostle Paul. As Acts relates, starting in the forties Paul began a world-wide missionary effort that changed the Church forever. Not limiting his preaching to Jews, he sought to include Gentiles who did not have a great knowledge of the Jewish heritage that grounded the earliest community and so needed to be instructed in the Israelite scriptures in order to help them to understand their identity and role in God's plan for universal salvation.

Luke's community was struggling with its role in a Gentile world and facing serious questions about why Gentiles should follow a religion based largely on Judaism. How could the words spoken to a Jewish audience by an obscure rabbi who was crucified as a criminal a half century earlier be relevant for a modern Gentile audience? Luke wants his readers to know that they share a connection with Jesus and the early Jewish-Christian community, and that Gentiles were included in God's plan from the beginning even though the Jews were historically the first to hear the message.

Moreover, by the early eighties, the Jewish attitude toward Christians had hardened under the leadership of the Pharisees and they began to expel Christians from their synagogues. How were Christians to interpret the meaning of the Jewish rejection of the message of salvation in and through God's messiah Jesus? Luke also struggles with this issue. It is clear that the Jews have rejected God's plan for salvation through Jesus God's messiah, and consequently have rejected the God who sent him. So Luke's central concern is what exactly is God's plan for salvation.

"Human society perpetuates structures of injustice and exclusion, but God intervenes on the side of the oppressed. The disruptive effect of this intervention is often presented in Luke as a reversal of the structures of society: those with power, status and riches are put down and those without them are exalted. This reversal was proclaimed in the Magnificat (1:51-53)."

—ROBERT C. TANNEHILL
The Narrative Unity of Luke-Acts, Vol. 1 (1986)

By his own long and prayerful mediation on the Old Testament, Luke discovered that the God revealed in the Old Testament began a plan of salvation and carried it out despite human obstacles. As Luke poured over the Jewish scriptures, he discovered that God's plan for salvation is never halted when humans refuse to cooperate. When the Jews reject God's messengers —the prophets, the holy priests and wisdom teachers whom God sends— God uses the rejection to further the divine plan. Luke is really interested in God's journey to appear in our history in Jesus of Nazareth to establish God's kingdom rule and a community that would embody it. This is the story that he sets out to tell. Thus Luke provides a comprehensive salvation history in the form of a journey to the kingdom under the guidance of the Holy Spirit, which is composed of three distinct periods:

1) **the time of promise** (Israel's preparation to receive Jesus as messiah)

2) **the time of Jesus** (his earthly ministry, ending with the ascension)

3) **the time of the Church** (the continuation of Jesus' ministry by the community's mission of witness to the ends of the world).

Luke's Gospel: Structure & Style

Like Matthew, Luke adopts Mark's basic framework—from Jesus' baptism through his Galilean ministry, his journey to Jerusalem for his passion, death and resurrection. But also like Matthew, he modifies this framework using his own community traditions (the "L" source) to begin with an infancy narrative that shows how Jesus' divine sonship begins from birth, long before his baptism. He also adds resurrection appearances at the end that closely reflect his theological vision. He groups most of his supplementary quotes from Jesus (the "Q" source he shares with Matthew but not Mark) in two long sections of Jesus' teaching, the "sermon on the Plain" (6:17-49, similar to Matthew's more famous "Sermon on the Mount") and Jesus' instructions to his disciples on the journey to Jerusalem (chapters 9–19).

Luke's Aim: A Two Volume Work

Of course, Luke's greatest structural innovation was adding a second volume, the Acts of the Apostles, which parallels the Gospel structure and reveals that Jesus' earthly ministry and mission to the world now continue in the community of his followers, which also means us.

In Acts, Luke tells the story of the growth and development of Christian community first through the ministry of Peter and the first disciples in Jerusalem and then through the apostle Paul and his companions on their missions to the Gentile world. Their journey and missions mirror the journey and mission of Jesus to bring God's Good News to everyone so that each person would have the opportunity to respond to it and be drawn into the new community of those saved through Jesus' death and resurrection.

"Acts narrates the conflict that surrounds its presentation of an alternative way of life as a result of certain practices, or a pattern of life."

—*C. KAVIN ROWE*
World Upside Down: Reading Acts in the Greco-Roman Age (2009)

Luke addressed both the Gospel and Acts to "Theophilus" (Gk: "beloved of God," Lk 1:3; Acts 1:1), who may have been a recent convert to Christianity or perhaps the patron who sponsored the writing and circulation of Luke's work. The two volumes, however, had a much wider audience in mind. Luke clearly directed his work to Gentile Christians, who were separated from Jesus by time, geography and culture. Both volumes proclaim the Good News of God's salvation in Jesus. Together they form an integral whole and cannot be understood without reference to one another.

Luke's Literary Style

Luke demonstrates literary excellence and a thorough understanding of Greek literary structure. His Gospel is very well written and exhibits a rich vocabulary (considered as representing perhaps the best Greek in the New Testament). Luke-Acts should be seen as one work (they were in fact joined in the Christian scriptures until John's Gospel was inserted between them).

Luke's Gospel & the Other Gospels

Luke's community is struggling to understand its role in a Gentile world. He wants his readers to understand that they share a Jewish heritage with Jesus and the more Jewish earliest Christian community, and also that Gentiles were always envisioned as part of God's plan for a new community.

Luke Revises Mark for a New Community Situation

Luke's community did not confront the stark challenge of Christian identity faced by Mark's persecuted community. Luke needed to show his Gentile converts how their Christian identity in God's kingdom community was rooted in Old Testament traditions, began in the life, death and resurrection of Jesus, and must be brought to completion through their witness as part of a worldwide mission. To do this, he portrayed Jesus as a compassionate prophet whose witness both in word and suffering gathered everyone, in particular the poor and marginal, into a community of universal table fellowship and service.

Luke Revises Mark to Include New Materials

Luke also wanted to revise Mark because he had new material that Mark did not use. One source was the "Q" collection of mostly "Quotes" of Jesus that he shared with Matthew. Luke also has some unique community traditions that are not found in the other Gospels (the "L" material, see the list and its distribution in the Gospel on the following page). These include the story of the announcement and births of John the Baptist and of Jesus, Jesus' trip to Jerusalem at age 12, many parables and healings, several accounts of the appearances of the risen Christ and his ascension to God.

Passages Found Only in Luke's Gospel ("L" Material)

1:5–2:52	The infancy narrative
3:10-14	Preaching of John the Baptizer
3:23-38	The genealogy of Jesus
4:17–21,23,25-30	Jesus' visit to Nazareth
5:4-9	The catch of fish
5:39	Old wine and new wine
7:12-17	Raising the son of the widow of Nain
8:1-3	Galilean women as followers of Jesus

Luke's Major Addition to Mark: The Journey Section

9:52-55	Jesus' departs for Jerusalem, Samaritan inhospitality
9:61-62	Farewell of a would-be follower
10:17-20	Return of the 72 disciples
10:25-28	Commandment for eternal life
10:29-37	Parable of the good Samaritan
10:38-42	Martha and Mary
11:1	Setting for the "Our Father" prayer
11:5-8	Parable of the persistent friend
11:27-28	Those who are truly blessed
12:1	The leaven of the Pharisees
12:13-15	Warning against greed
12:16-21	Parable of the rich fool
12:35-38	Vigilance
12:47-48	The servant's reward
12:49	Jesus' mission
12:54-56	Signs of the times
13:1-9	Timely reform; parable of the barren fig tree
13:10-17	Cure of the crippled woman on the Sabbath
13:31-33	Herod's desire to kill Jesus; his departure from Galilee
14:1-6	Cure of the man with dropsy
14:7-14	Sayings on the proper conduct at dinners
14:28-32	Conditions of discipleship
15:8-10	Parable of the lost coin
15:11-32	Parable of the lost son [the prodigal]

16:1-8a	Parable of the dishonest manager
16:8b-12	Two applications of the parable
16:14-15	Reproof of the greedy Pharisees
16:19-31	Parable of the rich man and Lazarus
17:7-10	Unprofitable servants
17:12-19	Cleansing of the ten lepers
17:20-21	Coming of God's kingdom
17:28-32	Days of the son of man
18:1-8	Parable of the dishonest judge
18:9-14	Parable of the Pharisee and the toll-collector
19:1-10	Zacchaeus

Jesus in Jerusalem

19:39-40	Answer to the Pharisees
19:41-44	Lament over Jerusalem
20:18	Strength of stone
21:18, 21b, 22,24	Destruction of Jerusalem
21:34-36	Vigilance
21:37-38	Jesus' final ministry in Jerusalem
22:15-18, 19c-20	The last supper
22:27	Who is greater, the one who dines or who serves?
22:31-32	Peter's denial foretold
22:35-38	The two swords
22:63-71	Mistreatment and interrogation of Jesus
23:6-12	Jesus sent to Herod (Herod's judgment)
23:13-16	Pilate's judgment
23:27-32	On the road to the cross
23:35a, 36-37	Witnesses at the crucifixion
23:39b-43	Jesus dialogue with the good thief
23:46, 47b-49	The death of Jesus
23:56	Women preparing spices before the Sabbath
24:13-35	Jesus' appearance on the road to Emmaus
24:36-43	Jesus' appearance to the disciples in Jerusalem
24:44-49	Jesus' final commission

The Good News in Four Versions

Luke Revises Mark to Include a New Perspective

Employing sound scholarship and the sources available, Luke attempted to give an accurate, ordered and reliable account of Jesus' saving ministry and of how the Holy Spirit established and worked through the Church, beginning in Jerusalem and on to Rome, the capital of the empire. (See Lk 4:16-30 and Acts 1:8, the programmatic verses for the two volumes respectively.)

"Luke's Gospel is a 'partial' account—partial both in the sense of being incomplete and in the sense of being committed to a perspective. He has included this material, excluded other; 'ordered' his account in this way, not in that. This is not a neutral, disinterested chronicle but a partisan narrative shaping of the story of Jesus. His aim is communicative in the sense of his purpose to engage his audience in discourse and so to shape them by his work."

—JOEL B. GREEN
The Theology of the Gospel of Luke (1995)

In addition to this overall purpose, Luke wanted to show that the formation and spread of the Church was the natural outgrowth of Jesus' life and ministry. He was also careful to present Christianity as the continuation of Judaism. Not only did he see in the Church the fulfillment of God's promise of salvation found in the Old Testament, but he also wished to argue that Christianity should enjoy the same privilege of official religious recognition in the Roman empire as did Judaism. With the ever-present possibility of persecution, Luke wrote positively of Roman officials and attempted to make the case that Christianity and Christians were not politically dangerous to the Roman authorities.

Yet another purpose of Luke's double work was to proclaim that Jesus' salvation is meant for all, Jew and Gentile alike. The theme of the universality of salvation flows through both the Gospel and Acts. In dealing with the delay of Jesus' second coming, Luke shifted the emphasis away from the end times to the present. He wanted to encourage the Christians of his day because he understood the time period of the Church to be an integral part of God's plan of salvation—a valuable time of prayer, fellowship and wholehearted discipleship for all Christians.

Also uniting both volumes is the activity of the Holy Spirit. More than any of the other Gospel authors, Luke emphasized the importance and work of the Spirit. In both books, the Holy Spirit is the One who initiates each major period in Luke's salvation history. The Spirit's influence is particularly seen in the infancy narrative, at the beginning of Jesus' ministry, and in the early life of the Church.

Luke's Major Additions to Mark

Luke's major insertion of new material occurs when he discontinues his generally close following of Mark's order to elaborate on Jesus' journey to Jerusalem (chapters 9–19) in which Jesus the teaching prophet sets his face toward Jerusalem, the "killer of prophets" (Luke 13:34). On the way, Jesus reveals to his disciples the meaning of God's dream for a kingdom community of disciples living as God wants them to be.

When borrowing from Mark, Luke usually intensifies Mark's emphasis on the rich and poor. He also introduces many new passages that mention the poor that are not found in the other Gospels—Mary's jubilant song before Jesus' birth, (her *Magnificat*, 1:39-54), Jesus' first sermon at Nazareth (4:16-30), the Good Samaritan who uses his wealth to help another (10:29-37), the great supper (14:16-24), the rich fool (12:16-21), the rich man and Lazarus (16:19-26), and Zacchaeus (19:1-10)—who represents the right response of a wealthy person to Jesus' presence and preaching.

Luke's Portrait of Jesus

Each of the Gospels proclaims that Jesus is God's son, but how Jesus is God's son receives different explanations. For Mark, Jesus is adopted as God's son at baptism. For Luke and Matthew, he is God's unique son by God's special procreative action in union with Mary. For John, he is divine (God's eternal Word) before the creation and his incarnation on earth.

Jesus, God's Natural Born Son

Recall that Mark's Gospel contains no infancy narratives but begins with Jesus as an adult. At his baptism a voice from heaven, which of course can be none other than God, uses the customary terminology of an adoption formula to affirm Jesus as God's beloved son (Mark 1:11). Both Matthew and Luke revise Mark's Gospel by adding narratives about the circumstances of Jesus' birth that change the claim of sonship from adult adoption at his baptism to natural generation. Thus, although in the eyes of the Nazareth community Jesus was the son of Joseph and Mary, Luke indicates in both his birth account and in his genealogy (3:23-38) that Joseph was not Jesus' natural father. Through the power of the Holy Spirit (the divine principle of life), God alone, not Joseph, supplied the "seed" for Jesus that was nurtured in Mary's womb. At the time of this unique conception, Mary was a virgin and had not had sexual relations with Joseph (1:26–38).

Jesus the Healing Prophet

Luke also emphasizes that Jesus is a prophet, "mighty in word and deed" (24:19, see also 4:24; 7:16; 7:39). His job description (4:16-30; 7:22-23) is adopted from the prophet Isaiah. As a spokesman for God, his prophetic message is an invitation to see the world from God's perspective rather than from a human viewpoint. Luke emphasizes Jesus' compassion for the suffering and outcast and his eagerness to accept the repentant sinner.

Luke's portrait of Jesus the prophet focuses on his activity of healing-saving. Born "a savior" (2:11), he comes "to seek and to save what is lost" (19:10). The ambiguity of the Greek word for *save* that can also mean *heal* allows Luke to stress the interconnectedness of our bodily and spiritual health. When Jesus tells those he cures, "Go, your faith has saved you," this could also mean "your faith has healed you" (7:50; 8:48; 17:19; 18:42).

"Each scene remains discrete, but comments on the scene before and after it by an almost infinite series of juxtapositions of words, images, phrases, and concepts. Thus everything Luke does to make his story coherent and realistic is done to convince all his readers beginning with Theophilus that his ordered narrative presents a trustworthy guide to the understanding of the real Jesus."

—JAN WOJCIK
The Road To Emmaus (1989)

Jesus' ministry of healing brings God's salvation and so breaks through all our humanly created boundries. Jesus reaches out to draw the poor, the outcasts, the sick, women, and foreigners to himself for healing. His parables about the lost coin, the lost son and the lost sheep (15:1-32) challenge us also to reach out beyond our narrow borders to seek and save the lost.

Jesus the Prophet of Justice & Friend of the Poor

Like the prophets of old, Jesus boldly proclaims God's demand for justice. At the start of his ministry, Jesus associates his work with that of the spirit-filled prophet Isaiah (4:16-30). During his ministry he will reach out to the poor, the blind, the downtrodden, prisoners and those who need to experience God's reversal of the human value system. In the beatitudes and woes (6:20-26) Jesus describes God's values and God's ways as the guidelines for our lives as disciples. Quite unexpectedly, God's blessing is not bestowed on the rich but on the poor, the hungry, the sorrowing, the hated, the persecuted and the rejected. Jesus also harshly criticizes those who, by their selfish use of power or by their indifference, cause injustice to powerless men and women. Jesus' special concern for the poor is revealed in Luke's many sayings and stories that deal with the issues of rich and poor.

Jesus the Prayerful Prophet

Luke also emphasizes the important truth that prayer is the touchstone of Jesus' life. Before making critical decisions or encounters, Luke pictures Jesus going off by himself to pray and commune with the Father. Solitary prayer is augmented by corporate prayer in the community of God's people. The Gospel is also structured so that it begins and ends in the Temple, moving from the faithful prayers of Zechariah and Elizabeth, whose child John the Baptist would herald the messiah, to the praise of the community of the first disciples "continually in the Temple blessing God" (24:53).

"The picture of Jesus at prayer calls attention to both God and Jesus: to God, because in guiding the course of Jesus' ministry God guides the history of salvation; and to Jesus, because in submitting to God's guidance, he attests to his utter dependence upon God and perfect obedience to him. In relation to the disciples, Jesus, the master who prays, becomes both the teacher who instructs them in prayer and the exemplar they are to emulate (11:1-13)."

—*JACK DEAN KINGSBURY*
Conflict In Luke: Jesus, Authorities, Disciples (1991)

Jesus the Suffering Prophet

Jesus' advocacy for justice inevitably led to a confrontation with the Jewish and Roman authorities who conspired to bring about his murder. Luke understands this suffering as an essential part of the prophet's role (13:33-34). In his version of Christ's passion, Luke portrays Jesus as an innocent martyr. Pilate (23:4, 14, 22), Herod (23:15) and the Roman centurion at the foot of the cross all declare Jesus innocent (23:47). Jesus dies as he lived— forgiving his persecutors and saving a repentant criminal.

THE GOOD NEWS IN FOUR VERSIONS

Luke's Portrait of Discipleship

Luke's example of a willing disciple is illustrated in the call of Peter and the other fishermen (5:1-11). While fishing, Peter experiences a wondrous catch of fish and recognizes that this is related to Jesus' mysterious power. When he submits himself to Jesus as a "sinner," Jesus invites him to follow, and in the process changes his name and his mission as a sign of the transformation that is occurring within him. Cephas the sinner becomes Peter the rock, and the fisherman becomes a fisher who will be sent to catch people into the network of Jesus' kingdom community.

Luke highlights the way of discipleship most clearly in the Acts of the Apostles. The risen Christ reveals to the disciples that the kingdom will come through their Spirit-filled witness (1:8) to the ends of the earth. Being a Christian disciple demands fearless witness with their words and with their lives and a shattering of the borders between Jew and Gentile in order to build the new inclusive kingdom community in Christ.

"For Luke Christian discipleship is portrayed not only as the acceptance of a master's teaching, but as the identification of oneself with the master's way of life and destiny in an intimate, personal following of him. Because of the geographical perspective in the Gospel, the 'following' has a pronounced spatial nuance: the disciple must walk in the footsteps of Jesus."

—*JOSEPH A. FITZMYER, SJ*
The Gospel According To Luke, I-IX (1981)

Mary the Model Disciple

For Luke, Mary stands out as the model of genuine discipleship. Like the prophets of old, she is characterized as a person who responds wholeheartedly to God's call whether it comes from an angel or through the words and deeds of her son. Her "let it be" starts God's work to bring forth Jesus both in her body and in her life (1:26-38). She keeps all these things in her heart and ponders them (2:19). In Jesus' ministry, she is identified as one who "hears the word and acts on it" (8:21). And after the resurrection she is found praying with the community of disciples as they await the Pentecostal empowerment of the Holy Spirit for their mission (Acts 1:14). Thus Mary illustrates what we are called upon to be and she does what we are called upon to do. She is the model of what we yearn for in our relation to God.

A Brief Reading Guide to Luke's Story of Jesus

The Preface: An Orderly Account for You (1:1-4)

Luke's preface (1:1-4) provides an introduction to the entire double volume work and is a statement of Luke's own intention for his writing. He wants to confirm for his readers the truth of their faith that in Jesus God has accomplished the divine purposes for history.

The Prologue: Jesus in His Origins & in His Destiny (1:5–2:52)

Annunciation, the Conceptions of Jesus & John the Baptist (1:5-56)

Luke's Gospel begins in the hills of Galilee with the announcement and births of John the Baptist and Jesus, whose unique relation to God is revealed in the circumstances surrounding his birth. God alone was responsible for this child's life in a way that went beyond God's normal role of giving life to a child in connection with the sexual intercourse of the parents.

Manifestation, the Births of Jesus & John the Baptist (1:57–2:40)

Luke also relates Joseph and Mary's journey from Nazareth to Jerusalem for a census, Jesus' birth in an "inn," and the recognition first by the visiting shepherds and then by Simeon and Anna in the Temple that Jesus is the promised lord and messiah who will save God's people.

Jesus at 12, Foreshadowing Jesus' Adult Ministry (2:41-52)

Only Luke tells of the journey of Jesus to Jerusalem at age 12—the time a boy became a man and a full member of the Israelite religious community. Jesus offers a preview of his later life, which will be dedicated to the work of God his father by proclaiming the coming of God's kingdom rule over our world. But for now he returns to an obscure life in Nazareth with his family.

Background & Preparation Jesus in History (3:1–4:13)

Jesus & John the Baptist's Ministry; God's Son Confirmed (3:1-22)

Luke sets his account of John's preaching and the beginning of Jesus' ministry firmly into the context of world history. Into this world comes God's Word manifesting God's active power, as revealed to the prophet John. For

Luke, John is the last of the Old Testament prophets, summing up the time of promise in salvation history and preparing for its fulfillment in Jesus.

Even though Luke added the infancy narrative to explain Jesus' special status as God's son, he retained Mark's adoption formula at Jesus' baptism. But because Luke shifted his explanation of Jesus' divine sonship to his birth, God's identification of Jesus as a beloved and chosen son (3:22) no longer serves as an adoption formula but rather as a public confirmation of the divine paternity and of Jesus' special filial relationship to God.

Jesus' Genealogy: His Place in the History of Israel & of Humanity (3:23-38)

Luke traces Jesus' ancestry as God's son by working his way backwards from son to father. But he notes that what people thought did not conform to the reality. Jesus "was the son (as was thought) of Joseph" (3:23), which brings the genealogy into conformity with the first two chapters of his Gospel that maintained that Jesus was not the natural son of Joseph but the unique son of God, born from the virginal womb of Mary.

Jesus & the Struggle of Humanity: Temptations of Sonship (4:1-13)

After Jesus' confirmation as God's son at his baptism, the Spirit leads him into the wilderness to fast for 40 days, as did Moses and Elijah, reliving the 40 years in which the Israelites' covenant loyalty was tested. Jesus must decide what kind of son he will be. Will he give up the exclusive loyalty and service that he owes God as a son and redirect them to the devil? Will he satisfy his own hungers, seek his own glory, expect special treatment from God? Or will he be a son who spends his life doing what his father wants?

His victory at this time anticipates his later triumph in Jerusalem over the power of evil. Although the present world belongs to the devil who can give it to whom he chooses (4:4-8), Jesus' messianic ministry will directly oppose this evil power and this clash of these two kingdoms will determine finally who will be the lord *(dominus)* who rules over us and our world.

The Ministry & Message of the Son of God (4:14–9:50)

As Jesus went about Galilee, he taught about God's kingdom, demonstraed its reality through his healing, celebrated it through sharing meals and encouraging people to respond. He used parables to teach people to discover God's presence in their ordinary lives. He used the common meal to teach

185

people how to celebrate God's presence. And he used his deeds of power (miracles) to teach people how to reorder their lives around God's presence.

Introduction: Jesus, His Mission & His Journey (4:14-44)

After the temptations, Jesus journeys from the wilderness back to the Galilean hills to begin his ministry of announcing God's promised kingdom rule. His teaching in the Nazareth synagogue and the public's reaction to it foreshadows what will happen as the Gospel unfolds: his ministry for God's kingdom, its rejection by Israel and then the mission to the Gentile world.

Jesus & His First Disciples (5:1–6:11)

Jesus calls followers to share his way of seeing the world and living as God intends. His first followers are Galilean fisherman who are invited adapt their fishing skills to catching people for the kingdom. Jesus also reveals the conditions for following him. First, "Do not be afraid" (5:10). Fear is the opposite of the basic trust or faith in another person that serves as the bond (Lat: *fides*) of a relationship. Because of that bond, we are willing to change our lives (Gk: *metanoia*). Second, Jesus indicates how Peter's life will change. Instead of luring fish into a net, his new job will be "fishing" for people to bring them into the net of Jesus' kingdom community. Following Jesus always opens up a new way of relating to God and to others.

Jesus then widens his ministry by healing a leper (5:11-16) and a paralyzed man (5:17-26) whose sins are also forgiven. He calls a tax collector, Levi, as a disciple and dines with him, which angers the Pharisees (5:27-39), who object to the way he and the disciples keep the Sabbath (6:1-11).

Jesus & the New Israel (6:12–7:50)

After spending all night on a mountain to pray (a common theme in Luke), Jesus chooses the 12 apostles from among all the disciples and instructs them in the basic vision and values of life in God's kingdom.

The Sermon on the Plain

Luke's Sermon on the Plain (6:20-49), like Matthew's Sermon on the Mount (Mt 5:1–7:28), begins with a group of statements called the Beatitudes (Lat: *beatus*, blessed). Luke gives four beatitudes, matching each with an opposite statement, the "woes." Unlike Matthew's wording that reflects the Old Testament wisdom tradition of impersonal description

("Blessed are the poor"), Luke's echoes the prophetic tradition of direct address ("Blessed are you who are poor.")

After these instructions, Jesus resumes his kingdom ministry by healing the sick son of a Roman centurion who showed great faith in Jesus (7:1-10) and by bringing back to life the dead son of an Israelite widow (7:11-17). Jesus acts purely out of compassion for the widow as no mention is made of faith. The account echoes the parallel stories about Elijah (1 Kgs 17:17-24) and Elisha (2 Kgs 4:32-37). Thus the people hail Jesus as "a great prophet." For Luke, being a prophet is one of the primary ways in which Jesus understands himself (4:21; 13:33) and is understood (or misunderstood 4:24-29) by others (9:19; 24:19). Here Luke begins to use the title "the lord" for Jesus. It was usually reserved for direct address (translated "master") or as a substitute for God's personal name, Yahweh, which because of the sacredness of the name, Israelites did not speak out loud.

"The people in Luke are a rogues' gallery of tax collectors, innkeepers, fallen women, shrewd bourgeois owners, thieves, Pharisees, and assorted unclean Gentiles. Jesus saves them willy-nilly; they need not, and do not, utter creeds first. Salvation in Luke, for the followers of Christ, consists in a life of prayer, repentance, and mercy; it is a life in the world with God."

—*ANNIE DILLARD*
in *Incarnation*, ed. Alfred Corn (1990)

There follows a section in which Jesus gives testimony about himself to the disciples of John the Baptist (7:18-35), and declares how important John was for the coming of God's kingdom. Luke places next the account of the woman crashing a Pharisee's dinner party to anoint Jesus (7:36–50), perhaps to let the story confirm the accusation that Jesus was a friend of sinners (7:34) and to show that Jesus provoked the same spectrum of hostile responses from Pharisees and sinners as did John the Baptist.

Jesus & the Formation of the New Israel (8:1-56)

As Jesus moves about the villages of Galilee, Luke stresses how Jesus now begins to teach the Good News in parables, revealing how different persons respond to his message (8:4-18, "the Sower") which is confirmed in the behavior of his own family (8:19-21). He also continues to drive out demons (8:26-39) and to heal (8:40-56).

Jesus & the Mission of the New Israel (9:1-50)

Jesus now enlists the help of the twelve in the kingdom ministry (9:1-6) and their fate will be linked to his (9:7-11). He wishes to withdraw with his disciples in order to give them deeper instruction (9:10-50) but is interrupted by the persistence of the hungry crowd of 5,000 whom he feeds with abundant food, as God also did during the exodus from Egypt.

Luke then reports Jesus' question to the disciples about his identity, which is based on Mk 8:27-33, but with additions and omissions that tailor its message for the needs of his community. Luke omits the location at Caesarea Philippi, but puts the question in the context of Jesus' prayer.

Peter, as spokesman for the disciples, recognizes Jesus as "the christ of God," a title that was previously given to Jesus at his birth (2:11, 26), known to the demons (4:41) and claimed by Jesus himself only implicitly (7:22). Though Peter uses the title correctly, Jesus offers a deeper understanding when he connects it with the mysterious Old Testament figures of the son of man (Dan 7:13-14) who will usher in the fulfillment of history and the suffering servant who gives his life for many (Is 52:13–53:12).

As if to balance the disciples' sadness and fear resulting from Jesus' revelation of his necessary suffering, Jesus anticipates his glory in the transfiguration. Luke's account (9:28-36) points back to Old Testament parallels and forward to Jesus' death, resurrection and ascension. Luke predictably sets the account in the context of Jesus at prayer. Moses and Elijah, who represent the law and the prophets—both now fulfilled by Jesus—speak with Jesus "of his departure," literally his *exodus,* the new exodus he will lead through his death. God's voice again confirms what it proclaimed at Jesus' baptism: Jesus is the son, the chosen, who as messiah/Christ fulfills the roles of Moses, the Davidic king and the suffering servant. The disciples are to "listen to him" as they now journey with him to Jerusalem.

The Journey: Jesus & the Destiny of the Church (9:51–24:53)

Jesus' announcement of God's rule challenges people to respond. Some accept and follow, others resist and reject. Jesus knows that his ministry cannot be complete until he proclaims the message of God's kingdom to the hostile Judean leaders in Jerusalem and elicits their response which will also determine their fate in relationship with God. So Jesus sets out on the

THE GOOD NEWS IN FOUR VERSIONS

journey to Jerusalem and on the way as a prophet speaks God's word and teaches his followers about what discipleship and life in the kingdom community demands—even to the point of sharing in Jesus' rejection and suffering. Note how Luke alternates the audiences—the disciples, the crowds and the hostile opponents—to highlight varied responses to Jesus' teaching.

Ministry in Galilee: Orientation for the Christian Journey (9:51–13:21)

Introduction: the Missionary Journey (9:51–10:24)

Only Luke records the mission of the 70 disciples, which foreshadows the Church's later mission to the world. Going out two by two as witnesses, they are to rely upon God to protect and provide for them. They proclaim Jesus' message, "the kingdom of God has come near to you" (10:9, 11; 11:20), rather than the Christian post-Easter proclamation about Jesus as the crucified messiah and lord (Acts 2:36). The final defeat of Satan that will characterize God's final triumph is anticipated by their success.

Basic Dispositions for Disciples (10:25–11:54)

A hostile lawyer challenges Jesus with a question about the greatest commandment and the definition of a neighbor, to which Jesus responds with the stunning parable of the "good" Samaritan (10:25-37). Then Martha and Mary offer Jesus hospitality (10:38-42), which Jesus reminds them must be characterized by attention to the guest. Jesus then teaches his disciples to pray the Lord's Prayer, which in Luke is similar to Matthew's version but less elaborate. Jesus uses parables to indicate the proper attitudes for praying (11:1-13) and an exorcism provides Jesus with a chance to remind the crowds of the deeper and very serious conflict between God's kingdom and Satan's (11:14-26). Then follows a series of prophetic warnings (11:27-36) and a dinner at which Jesus attacks the Scribes and the Pharisees for their hypocritical behavior, which just increases their hostility (11:37-54).

Toward the Final Crisis: Persecutions & Discipleship (12:1–13:21)

As if to allay the anxiety from all the increasing hostility, Jesus encourages the disciples not to fear because God will be with them in all difficult circumstances (12:1-2). This is followed by a parable and encouragement not to fear for their lives and even less for the loss of their possessions (12:13-34), another parable about watchfulness and service (12:35-48) and a call for conversion before it is too late (12:49-59). Then the healing of a bent woman in the synagogue enrages Jesus' opponents (13:10-17).

From Galilee to Jerusalem: Advice for the Christian Journey (13:22–19:27)

Introduction: the Journey of Salvation (13:22-35)

Luke now weaves together many separate passages that also occur in Matthew but puts them in different contexts. The result is a new teaching about the call to personal conversion and right relationships. The central theme is the attitude of those who will enter the kingdom and those who will be excluded (13:22-30). Jesus turns the crowd's attention from speculation about the fate of others to their own need for conversion. He offers a message of salvation that is meant for all. Yet mere acquaintance with Jesus will not suffice. Although all are invited to the messianic banquet, many who expect to attend might not be allowed to enter.

Discipleship, Wealth & Reconciliation in God's Kingdom (14:1–16:31)

The particular sequence in Luke 14:1-24 of Jesus' healing, teaching and using a parable at a supper in the home of a Pharisee addresses again the themes of healing on the Sabbath and Jesus' inclusive invitation to join the kingdom community (14:15-35). The three parables in chapter 15:1-32 of the lost sheep, the lost coin and the lost (prodigal) son, illustrate God's relentless search so that no one will be lost. Jesus then uses the parables of the wicked but shrewd manager (16:1-13) and of the rich man and Lazarus (16:14-31) to consider right use of possessions and of wealth.

More Teaching & the Arrival at Jerusalem (17:1–19:27)

Jesus then heals ten lepers (17:11-19) and continues to teach about the kingdom, including two parables on prayer (18:1-14), one positive about a widow and an unjust judge and one negative about a Pharisee and a tax agent, and what is necessary for entering the kingdom (18:15-34). The right kind of response is illustrated by the healed blind man (18:35-43) and the reformed tax collector Zacchaeus (19:1-10). Before entering Jerusalem (19:28-48), Jesus tells the parable about a master's successful establishment of a kingdom and the reward for trustworthy servants (19:11-27), which anticipates what is about to unfold for Jesus in Jerusalem.

THE GOOD NEWS IN FOUR VERSIONS

In Jerusalem: Rejection & Victory on the Christian Journey (19:28–21:38)

The increasingly hostile conflict between Jesus and his opponents over his identity, mission and ministry now climaxes during the Passover in Jerusalem, which provides the framework for Luke's passion narrative.

Entry into Jerusalem (19:28-48)

Jesus' final week began with a great public demonstration indicating the popularity of Jesus the prophet, who mocks the pomp of a military messiah by riding in a "triumphal" entry into Jerusalem on a donkey while people joyously celebrated by spreading palm branches on his path.

Jesus in Dialogue with the Leaders of Israel (20:1–21:4)

Jesus teaches in the Temple, reaching out for the final time to his opponents and offering an invitation to conversion. He also performs another prophetic sign by disrupting the Temple business to call attention to God's judgment upon it that will bring its destruction.

Vision of the Destruction of Jerusalem Temple & the End Time (21:5-38)

Luke arranges this discourse in temporal sequence: a description of the time of persecution facing the disciples (21:5-11, including what must precede these events, 21:12-19), a description of the fall of Jerusalem (21:20-24) and a preview of the time of liberation through the son of man (21:25-38).

From Jerusalem to God: Jesus' Passion, Resurrection & Ascension (22:1–24:53)

Although Luke follows the general outline of Mark's passion rather closely, he makes several significant additions to Jesus' way of the cross to emphasize that Jesus continues the saving/healing activity that had characterized his ministry in Galilee. Luke stresses that Jesus is an innocent martyr and carefully notes that Pilate (23:14), Herod Antipas (23:15) and the Roman centurion at the cross (23:47) all declare him innocent. Jesus dies as he lived—forgiving his persecutors (23:34) and saving a good thief (23:39-43).

Introduction: Conspiracy, Betrayal & Preparation (22:1-13)

Jesus proclamation of God's kingdom and his advocacy for justice inevitably led to a confrontation with the Jewish authorities who conspired with the Roman occupation force to bring about his murder. Luke understands this suffering to be an essential part of the prophet's role.

LUKE'S GOSPEL & ACTS OF THE APOSTLES

Passover Supper, Prayer & Arrest (22:11:14–22:53)

Luke follows Mark closely here in the sequence of events, making minor changes. He describes Jesus eagerness to share the supper (22:15-20) and emphasizes in the consecrating words that Jesus' body is "given for you" and his blood "poured out for you" and that the action should be repeated "as a remembrance of me" (22:19-20). He also prays that the disciples will "eat and drink at my table in the kingdom" (22:29-30). Though Jesus knows Peter will betray him, he prays for Peter's faith and expects him afterwards to strengthen others (22:31-34), reminding the disciples not to rely on human power or their "two swords" but on God for their needs (22:35-38).

Peter's Denial, Jewish Trial & Roman Trial before Pilate (22:54–23:25)

At the time of Jesus' arrest by the Judean leaders and the crowd with Judas, only Luke has him heal the man whose ear has been cut off. At the Jewish trial, Luke introduces the accusations that Jesus is "perverting our nation, forbidding us to pay taxes to the emperor, and saying that he himself is the messiah, a king" and "stirring up the people" by his teaching in Judea and Galilee (23:2-5). When Pilate learns he is a Galilean, he sends him to Herod Antipas, the ruler of Galilee, whose soldiers (not the Romans) mistreat Jesus. He finds no merit to the charges and returns Jesus to Pilate (23:6-12). Then though Pilate finds Jesus innocent, he succumbs to the pressure of the mob, frees Barabbas and sends Jesus to the cross.

Jesus' Crucifixion, Death & Burial (23:26–23:56)

On the way to Golgotha, only Luke has Jesus meet the women of Jerusalem (23:26-32) who were sorrowful because of what was happening to him. Jesus comforts them, at least indirectly, by indicating that those who are now doing this violence to him will have their day of judgment. But his prophetic warning is also alarming because he recognizes that innocent women and children will always be victims in acts of violence.

When Jesus is crucified between two criminals, Luke adds the dialogue (23:39-43) between Jesus and the good criminal who recognizes Jesus' innocence and refuses to revile him. Jesus responds to the criminal's request to be with him in his kingdom by promising that this will happen that very day. Even on the cross, Jesus offers forgiveness to all who desire to enter the kingdom. We are also the recipients of this promise when we begin to follow the kingdom guidelines that Jesus outlined for us.

The Message of Luke's Passion Narrative

1. Jesus is the Savior and liberating Messiah, whose death for others brings the power of God's forgiveness into the world.
2. Jesus is the Son of God who trusts completely in God and is faithful to God through death; he is the Just One whom even death itself cannot separate from God.
3. Jesus is the prophet-martyr who fearlessly proclaims God's justice, giving faithful witness even in the face of rejection and death.
4. In the passion of Jesus, the ultimate drama of good and evil, of life and death is enacted. Through his death and resurrection Jesus, the representative human being, defines human destiny.
5. In the experience of the passion, the meaning and challenge of authentic discipleship are revealed.
6. Death is a struggle and a test leading to a profound experience of liberation and life.
7. Death is the culmination point of a life-long journey to God.
8. Death is an opportunity for witness.

—DONALD SENIOR, CP
The Passion of Jesus in the Gospel of Luke (1989)

With Luke's version of Jesus' dying words, he gives his Spirit back to God (23:46), trusting that God will now accomplish what Jesus had only begun but could not complete. Whatever was left to do in order to bring God's kingdom on earth was now handed over to God and the disciples. In Acts, when the Holy Spirit descends on the community of disciples at Pentecost, they will indeed take up Jesus' mission and ministry to bring the kingdom on earth. This responsibility has continued down to our own time.

Visits to the Empty Tomb, Recognition & the Disciples' Mission (24:1-53)
After Jesus died he was taken down from the cross and hastily buried, the disciples then had to wait until Sunday morning when the Sabbath was over to prepare his body according to the traditional burial customs. When Mary Magdalene and other women disciples came to the tomb bringing spices to anoint his body, they discovered that the tomb was empty and his body gone. Their perplexity gave way to joy when they experienced Jesus suddenly alive again and, through a series of appearances to the disciples, he confirmed his identity and revealed his enduring presence with them on their journey both in scripture and in their eucharistic sharing.

A Brief Reading Guide to Luke's Acts of the Apostles

A new era of sacred history now begins. The whole world is now to be evangelized beginning from Jerusalem. Verse 8 is a preview of the worldwide geographical expansion described in Acts: the disciples' mission will develop and spread from Jerusalem, chapters 1–7, to Judea and Samaria, chapters. 8–9, and finally to the whole Roman empire, chapters 10–28.

The Early Christian Community (1:1-26)

Commission of Witnesses & Jesus' Farewell (1:1-14)

The Acts of the Apostles begins with Luke's second account of Christ's ascension. Only Luke describes the ascension, and he provides two accounts, as if to stress that Jesus' presence with the disciples in his embodied way now comes to a definitive end. A briefer account comes at the end of his Gospel (24:50-53) on Easter evening. This more familiar version in Acts (1:6-12) occurs 40 days after Easter, during which time Jesus has been instructing the disciples about the kingdom of God.

Jesus tells them that after he is gone, they are to await the empowerment of the Holy Spirit before embarking on their mission to continue his ministry. Aware of his glory, the disciples ask if the kingdom is now to be restored, for the promise of the Spirit implies that the last days are imminent. Jesus discourages such speculation and redirects their attention to God's unfolding plan in which they will now play an important role.

After Jesus' vanishes from their sight into the clouds, the apostles return to Jerusalem where Luke describes the whole expectant assembly including the 11 apostles, the women who had attended Jesus and Jesus' family (apparently now reconciled and believing in him) all devoting themselves to prayer in expectation of the descent of the Spirit.

Reconstitution of the Twelve (1:15-26)

Luke describes the choice of another apostle to replace the traitor Judas. The early Church sought confirmation in the Old Testament for what Christians experienced, hence the application of the generalized descriptions in Psalm 69:25 and 109:8 to the specific case of Judas. The choosing

THE ACTS OF THE APOSTLES

1:1-26 THE EARLY CHRISTIAN COMMUNITY
1:1-14	Commission of witnesses & Jesus' farewell
1:15-26	Reconstitution of the Twelve

2:1–8:4 THE MISSION OF WITNESS IN JERUSALEM
2:1–3:26	Appeal to all Israel: Pentecost & Peter's ministry
2:42-47	First major summary: unified community life
4:1–8:4	Life & trials of the primitive Jerusalem community
4:32-35	Second major summary: a sharing community
5:12-16	Third major summary: a caring community
6:8–8:1	Stephen's discourse, response & martyrdom

8:5-40 THE MISSION OF WITNESS IN JUDEA & SAMARIA
8:5-25	Philip in Samaria
8:26-40	Philip & the Ethiopian eunuch on the Gaza road

9:1–14:28 THE WORD IS CARRIED FURTHER: WITNESS EVEN TO GENTILES
9:1-31	Saul the persecutor becomes Paul the Christian witness
9:32–11:18	Peter initiates the mission to Gentiles
9:32-43	Peter's miracles in Lydda & Joppa
10:1–11:18	Conversion of Cornelius & his household in Caesarea
11:19–12:25	Spread of the word to Gentiles elsewhere
13:1–14:28	Paul's first missionary journey to Gentiles in Asia Minor *[Cyprus (13:4-12); Pisidian Antioch, Iconium (14:1-7); Lystra & Derbe (14:8-20)]*

15:1-35 THE JERUSALEM MEETING: DECISION ABOUT GENTILE CHRISTIANS
15:1-21	Peter & James's concerns for the Gentile churches
15:22-35	The Jerusalem letter

15:36–22:21 PAUL'S UNIVERSAL MISSION & WITNESS
15:41–18:22	Paul's second missionary journey *[Derbe & Lystra (15:41–16:5); Asia Minor (16:6-10); Philippi (16:11-40); Thessalonica & Beroea (17:1-15); Athens (17:16-34); Corinth; to Antioch (18:18-22)]*
18:23–20:38	Paul's third missionary journey *[Ephesus (19:1-41); Macedonia, Achaia, & Syria (20:1-6); Troas (20:7-12); Miletus (20:13-138)]*
21:1–22:21	Paul in Jerusalem: arrest & extradition

22:22–28:31 PAUL IMPRISONED FOR THE SAKE OF WITNESS TO THE WORLD
22:22–23:22	Prisoner in Jerusalem & Paul's testimony
23:23–26:32	Prisoner in Caesarea & Paul's testimony
27:1–28:31	Prisoner in Rome & Paul's testimony & ministry

LUKE'S GOSPEL & ACTS OF THE APOSTLES

of 12 disciples as a special group seems to have been a sign of the coming age and of the new Israel so their number needs to be restored after Judas's defection. Two candidates are thought suitable and the group casts lots to decide—an Old Testament custom to submit their choice to God's will (see Prov 16:33). Matthias is selected to share in ministry as the servant of the community and in apostleship as the missionary envoy of Christ. The 11 apostles welcome Matthias as a witness of Jesus' resurrection.

The Mission of Witness in Jerusalem (2:1–8:4)

Appeal to All Israel: Pentecost & Peter's Ministry (2:1–3:26)
One of the major features of Acts is Luke's use of speeches by the principal figures to provide not so much their actual words but rather an insight into the meaning of events and a way to discover how the preaching of the Christian message (Gk: *kērygma)* is adapted first to Jewish and then to Gentile audiences as the witness to God's Good News spreads. The first of these speeches is Peter's address to the Jerusalem crowds on Pentecost.

Peter stresses God's guidance in the events of Jesus' death and resurrection. The fate of the messiah reveals how the mystery of human freedom and divine necessity are intertwined. Humanity's rejection is countered by God's affirmation. Then, because Peter is speaking to Israelites who are familiar with the Old Testament, he relies on quotes to show that Jesus is indeed the promised messiah. Of these events foretold in the scriptures, the disciples themselves were eyewitnesses.

Peter concludes with the proclamation that the crucified Jesus has been now exalted as lord and messiah. Right relationship with God (salvation) now is found through Jesus the Christ. Peter then outlines the way of salvation. The first step is repentance (Gk: *metanoia,* a complete change of mind and heart, conversion). The second step is baptism "in the name" (2:38) that brings salvation. Those who submit to conversion and baptism receive forgiveness and the gift of the Holy Spirit, who provides the fundamental principle of life in the Christian community.

First Major Summary: Unified Community Life (2:42-47)
This is the first of three overviews tracing the Church's life and growth. There are four aspects of that life. The "apostles' teaching" was carried

THE GOOD NEWS IN FOUR VERSIONS

on both in public and within the community. Likewise the community continued to offer "the prayers" both at the Temple and in the community. The "fellowship" (Gk: *koinōnia*) was shown especially in the sharing of resources. This probably was not a giving up of all possessions, but the placing of one's assets at the community's disposal to be used as needed. The "breaking of the bread" was a common meal that included the memorial of the Lord's Supper and the eucharistic presence of the risen Lord.

Peter's Ministry

In Acts 3–4, Peter and John witness to God's power by healing a lame man (3:1-10) who begged for money as they went to the Temple to pray. But instead of money, they offered a healing. The story stresses that the apostles do not do this on their own—they haven't the power—but by invoking the name and thus the power of Jesus Christ, Luke shows that Jesus' healing ministry continues through the apostles.

The lame man is "raised up" (3:7) by Peter. The Greek word here is the same one used to describe Jesus' resurrection by God's power (Lk 9:23; 24:6; Acts 3:15). Luke hints that the healing is not just physical but is also a sign of the spiritual healing now available through the risen lord. The lame man jumps up, stands, walks, leaps and praises God because he recognizes where this healing power came from. Just as in Luke's Gospel when experiencing Jesus' miracles (Lk 4:36; 5:9; 5:26), the onlookers here are "filled with wonder and amazement" (3:10). Peter then explains the basic Christian message about the meaning of Jesus' death and resurrection by associating Jesus with various Old Testament figures.

Life & Trials of the Primitive Jerusalem Community (4:1–8:4)

Instigated by the Sadducees who unlike the Pharisees did not believe in the resurrection of the dead, the Judean authorities arrest Peter and John because they proclaim Christ's resurrection as a present and life-giving reality. The appearance of the apostles before the Sanhedrin, the supreme Jewish court responsible for internal affairs, echoes Jesus' examination by the Sanhedrin (Lk 22:66). As Jesus had promised, the Holy Spirit empowers the apostles to speak boldly.

After their release from prison, Peter and John gather the Christian community for discussion and prayer. The Church follows in Jesus' footsteps. He is the "servant" (or child) of God (4:27, 30), and they are the "servants" (or slaves) of God (4:29). The empowering of Pentecost is renewed as the place is "shaken" (4:31), signifying the Spirit's presence with them.

Second Major Summary: A Sharing Community (4:32-35)

Luke summarizes the life of the early Church in Jerusalem with two descriptions of their common life: complete community sharing of goods and their distribution to the needy. The sharing of goods practiced by the Jerusalem community does not seem to have been repeated elsewhere as is evident from Paul's letters. Although the care of the needy was always a feature of Christian communities, the important issue was not an economic principle, but the expression of the community's unity in love. The believers had one source and center of life, and were united in their outwardly visible lifestyle.

Third Major Summary: A Caring Community (5:12-16)

This summary section has as its theme the powerful signs and wonders of the apostles, who continue Jesus' healing ministry as the sign of God's power to save. They meet in the Temple and attract a growing crowd. Many of these believers are from outside the Jerusalem area and take their new faith with them when they return to their homes, thus sending the Christian message throughout the Mediterranean world. Peter's healing of the sick demonstrates the fulfillment of the apostolic prayer in Acts 4:30.

Chapter 6 describes how as the community grew, the sharing among members became increasingly complicated and created tension between the "Hellenists" (Greek-speaking) and the "Hebrews" (Aramaic-speaking) members. The community's solution was to choose men to assist the apostles with the tasks related to the service (Gk: *diakonia*, hence "deacons") to the community, which introduces the witness and work of Stephen and Philip, which Luke describes in detail in chapters 6-8.

Stephen's Discourse, Response & Martyrdom (6:8–8:1)

The deacon Stephen's miraculous works and persuasive arguments draw the attention of certain Hellenistic (Greek-speaking) Jews, who bring false charges against him. Stephen comes before the Sanhedrin, the Jewish court, to make his defense, which enrages the Jewish leaders.

Stephen's words echo Jesus' words (Lk 22:69). Like Jesus, Stephen is charged and led before the Jewish council for trial. Like Jesus, Stephen forgives his murderers even as his life ebbs away. Saul (later to be Paul, who will become the Church's greatest missionary apostle) first appears here as a silent witness to Stephen's death. His approval of this violence later gives way to his recognition of guilt and his confession of faith (22:20).

The Mission of Witness in Judea & Samaria (8:5-40)

Philip in Samaria (8:5-25)

As Jesus' predicted (1:8) the gospel now spreads beyond Jerusalem to the rest of Judea and Samaria as Philip, one of the seven ministers (deacons) chosen in 6:1-6, flees the persecution resulting from Stephen's martyrdom, taking refuge in a Samaritan village and proclaiming the Good News there. Luke describes Philip as a man graced with the gift of evangelism, whose message was accompanied with "signs" of power and healing.

Philip & the Ethiopian Eunuch on the Gaza Road (8:26-40)

After witnessing to the despised Samaritans, Philip is sent to another outsider. Ethiopia in the first century referred to southern Egypt (now the Sudan). The eunuch may have been a Gentile proselyte or a "God-fearer," who accepted much but not all of the Jewish law. As a eunuch, he would also have been barred from Jewish worship.

The eunuch is reading the prophet Isaiah's fourth servant song (Is 52:13–53:12), which was a central Old Testament passage used by the early Church to understand the meaning of Jesus' death and resurrection. Like Jesus with the disciples going to Emmaus (Lk 24:27), Philip begins from the eunuch's question and "starting with this scripture, he proclaimed to him the good news about Jesus" (8:35).

The Word Is Carried Further: Witness Even to Gentiles (9:1–14:28)

Saul the Persecutor Becomes Paul the Christian Witness (9:1-31)

The story of Paul's experience of the risen Jesus on the road to Damascus is repeated twice more with minor variations in 22:4-16 and 26:9-18, indicating Luke's sense of the importance of this event for the history of the early Church. This account not only serves to authenticate Paul's apostleship, but also shows that the Gentile mission was essential to God's plan.

Luke uses a number of terms to describe Christians: here they are called "disciples," those "who belonged to the Way" (an Old Testament term indicating the moral demands of the covenant), "saints," and those "who invoke your name."

Paul's persecution of Christians is persecution of Jesus himself because they are now his body on earth. Blinded by the light, Paul is led helpless to Damascus and revealed to the community there as God's "chosen instrument." But because of Saul's earlier zealous and cruel persecution of the Christian communities, the believers are suspect of his sudden change in behavior and are reluctant to embrace him as one of them.

But Barnabas, from the Antioch Christian community, trusted Saul's conversion experience and introduced him to the leaders of the community in Jerusalem. Then because of a plot on Saul's life, the disciples sent him back to his hometown of Tarsus in Cilicia (southeastern Turkey today) until Barnabas again drew him into active ministry, this time to the Gentiles. Luke briefly reports on the steady growth of the Church (9:31), which enjoyed a respite from persecution since Saul had become a Christian.

Peter Initiates the Mission to Gentiles (9:32–11:18)

Peter's miracles in Lydda and Joppa (9:32-43) again show that the disciples now continue Jesus' healing work. The story of Tabitha's restoration to the community is reminiscent of the resuscitation of Jairus's daughter by Jesus (Lk 8:49-56). Peter repeats Jesus' actions: responding to the request for help, sending the crowd out of the room and speaking to the dead woman. The only difference is that Peter pauses to kneel and pray, thereby illustrating that the authority to raise the dead is not his own like it was for Jesus, but is only provided with the help of the Holy Spirit.

Conversion of Cornelius & His Household in Caesarea (10:1–11:18)

Peter's dealings with the Roman centurion Cornelius marks an important turning point in the outreach of the early Christian community. Many Jewish Christians feared and resisted the possible inclusion of Gentiles, but Luke makes clear that Peter himself (even before Paul) began the mission to the Gentiles under the direction of the Holy Spirit. Cornelius was a "God-fearing" Roman, who accepted Israel's God but not all its religious practices. From Peter he receives baptism, but not before he and his gathered household receive the gift of the Holy Spirit.

This event marks a new Pentecost now for the Gentiles. The circle of Christian faith has now broadened to include the inhabitants of "the ends of the earth" (1:8). The Spirit first came to the Jews (2:1-4), then to the despised Samaritans (8:14-17), and now to the Gentiles. Note that in each major stage of expansion (8:14-17; 10:44-48; 19:1-6), Church leaders are closely involved, which may indicate the Church's responsibility to receive new members and integrate them into the community of faith.

Peter then defends his unprecedented decision to baptize the Gentile Cornelius. His critics illustrate the early Christian opinion that Jesus was for the Jews alone, and that faith must be accompanied by a strict adherence to the Mosaic law. Peter explains the baptism as a God-inspired act since God led Peter to recognize that believing Gentiles' were included in God's kingdom because God granted them the same gifts of the Spirit as the Israelite believers had received (2:1-11). To withhold baptism would have been to oppose God. With this bold act, the Church understood that God's impartiality demands the unity of Jews and Gentiles in one community.

Spread of the Word to Gentiles Elsewhere (11:19–12:25)

The founding of the community in Syrian Antioch, the third largest city in the Roman empire after Rome and Alexandria, represents for Luke the culminating stage of the early mission period. The gospel has been preached to pilgrim Jews and proselytes, to the Samaritans, to the legally outcast eunuch, to sympathetic "God-fearers" and now to Gentiles. The rest of Acts will focus on Paul's world-wide mission to the Gentiles.

Luke also emphasizes the role of anonymous believers in the spread of the gospel. They proclaim "the lord Jesus" because the term *messiah* (Gk: *christos*) would mean little if anything to Gentiles. But the term *lord* (Gk: *kyrios*) for a deity was common in many religions of the time. Indeed, *Christ* seems to have been understood by outsiders almost as a proper name connected with Jesus. Hence the name *Christians* (that is, followers of Christ, 11:26) was first used somewhat derogatorily by non-Christians to distinguish them from the Jewish community.

Paul's First Missionary Journey to Gentiles in Asia Minor (13:1–14:28)
[Cyprus (13:4-12); Pisidian Antioch, Iconium (14:1-7); Lystra and Derbe (14:8-20)]

Paul and Barnabas, having been chosen by the Holy Spirit for missionary work, travel through Cyprus and come to Antioch of Pisidia in central Asia Minor (Turkey today). As was to be his custom, Paul goes first to the local synagogue to proclaim that the salvation history of Israel is fulfilled in Jesus. His speech (13:16-41) shows how Paul proclaimed the Good News to a mixed audience of Jews and sympathetic "God fearing" Gentiles. He follows the general outline of Peter's speeches in chapters 2–3 and Stephen's speech in chapter 7, thus demonstrating the essential unity of his message with that of the other apostles. God's promise of a deliverer from David's line has now been fulfilled by sending Jesus, anointing him with the Spirit at his baptism and raising him from the dead.

Presumably attracted by reports of his speech in the synagogue "almost the whole city," that is, a crowd that also included Gentiles, comes to hear Paul who affirms on the one hand the priority of preaching to Jews and on the other hand his own commitment to reaching Gentiles. The commission given to God's servant Israel and fulfilled in Jesus is now carried out by Christian missionaries. God's impartiality (10:34) now extends the gifts of salvation and a new covenant relationship to non-Jews as well as Jews.

Then Paul's healing of a man unable to walk since birth causes the local populace to worship him and Barnabas, who do not at first understand the people's intentions. Paul as chief speaker is taken as the Greek god Hermes, the messenger, rather than as the leader Zeus. Speaking to this Gentile audience, Paul appeals to what they ought to know from observing the natural world. Although he could not assume their familiarity with Jewish history or a monotheistic belief, his appeal is couched in the general Old Testament descriptions of God as creator and provider.

Paul and Barnabas then reverse their course, courageously revisiting the communities in Iconium, Lystra and Antioch of Pisidia, cities from which they had been violently expelled on their first missionary journey through the area. Their eagerness to encourage these newly planted communities outweighs their concern for their personal safety. "The faith" was a commonly used term for the Christian beliefs that provided the bond of unity (Lat: *fides*) for the new Christian community. Paul and Barnabas encourage and reassure the new disciples by explaining that opposition and trials are to be expected if they are to follow Christ's way faithfully and carry on his mission in the world.

"Luke-Acts does more than share a grand vision. It tells a story from which we are able to learn. It can help us precisely because the mission it narrates was not as successful as early Christians hoped. The vision of God's purpose, to be realized through the mission, had to encounter hard reality, especially in the form of Jewish resistance to the new movement. Rejection and resistance are major factors in the unfolding story, and rejection by Jews is most keenly felt."

—*ROBERT C. TANNEHILL*
The Narrative Unity of Luke-Acts, Vol. 2 (1990)

The Jerusalem Meeting: Decision about Gentile Christians (15:1-35)

Peter & James's Concerns for the Gentile Churches (15:1-21)

Despite its rapid growth, the Christian community was not without its squabbles and theological controversies. The dispute recorded here resulted from Christians of Jewish background insisting that Gentile Christians follow the Mosaic law and be circumcised. Paul stands firmly against such a demand. Sent to the Jerusalem meeting by their community, Paul and Barnabas advocate for their position with the assembled apostles and elders.

The Jerusalem Letter (15:22-35)

Guided by the Holy Spirit, the result of the meeting is a compromise, in which converted Gentiles are not required to be circumcised, but they must "abstain from what has been sacrificed to idols and from blood and from what is strangled and from fornication." (15:29). Paul and Barnabas return to Antioch with a letter assuring the community that circumcision was not to be required of Gentiles.

Paul's Universal Mission & Witness (15:36–22:21)

Paul's Second Missionary Journey (15:41–18:22)

[Derbe & Lystra (15:41–16:5); Phrygia, Galatia & Troas (16:6-10); Philippi (16:11-40); Thessalonica & Beroea (17:1-15); Athens (17:16-34); Corinth; Antioch (18:18-22)]

After a dispute with Barnabas over who should accompany them, Paul joins with Silas for his second missionary journey. Starting in 16:10 Luke's account now becomes more of a travel diary than a news report using the first person plural "we," indicating that the author is perhaps traveling with the missionaries or more likely using an eyewitness account (as many scholars conclude because curiously enough Luke does not seem to have any real knowledge of Paul's theology or of his several letters which were most likely compiled and became popular only after Acts had told Paul's story).

After reconnecting with many of his earlier communities in Asia, Paul, led by a vision of the Holy Spirit (16:9-10), crosses for the first time into Europe from Troas and comes to Philippi, a frontier town with few Jews. Paul looked for a Jewish community but instead found Lydia, a Gentile who worshiped God but had not converted to Judaism. She was also a prominent businesswoman. After her conversion, she opens her home as a base for Paul's ministry and the meeting place for the Christian community.

Paul also encounters a slave girl possessed by a spirit of divination associated with the Greek god Apollo (as at the famous oracle at Delphi). She identifies the missionaries as servants of "the most high God," a term used by non-Israelites for Israel's God (Is 14:14; Dan 3:26; Lk 8:28) and in the Greek world as a title for Zeus. Paul proclaims the message of "salvation," deliverance from subjection to the world and its powers, which was eagerly sought by Greeks through their mystery religions.

But fearing for the loss of their livelihood, the girl's owners charge Paul and Silas with violating the law forbidding Jews to proselytize Romans. This is the first of two attacks on the apostles instigated by Gentiles who were motivated by fear of the gospel's threat to their property rights (see 19:23-41 for problems with Ephesian silversmiths). Paul and Silas are stripped, beaten and jailed. But like Peter's earlier deliverance by God's intervention (12:3-9), they are set free this time by an earthquake. They do not flee but restrain the jailer from suicide and so convert the jailer and his family. This illustrates Luke's view that Christian suffering is brief and for a purpose.

Paul's Third Missionary Journey (18:23–20:38)
[Ephesus (19:1-41); Macedonia, Achaia &Syria (20:1-6); Troas (20:7-12); Miletus (20:13-38)]

Luke describes how a previously founded Christian community in Ephesus is now integrated into Paul's apostolic mission (19:1-7), which echoes important themes from Luke's version of Jesus' baptism and the Pentecost foundation of the early Church. John's baptism only foreshadows "baptism with the Holy Spirit" (Lk 3:16). Just as God's Holy Spirit descended upon Jesus (Lk 3:22; 4:18; Acts 10:38) and upon the Pentecost community (Acts 2) to empower them for ministry, so now the Spirit falls on those prepared by John's baptism, creating a new community and empowering them with gifts for ministry: tongues for praise and prophecy for witness. In Paul's "farewell discourse" to the Ephesus community before leaving for Jerusalem (20:17-38) and so completing his mission in the eastern Mediterranean by bringing the money collected for the Jerusalem community, he reviews his life and ministry and outlines how the group ought to act in his absence.

21:1–22:21 Paul in Jerusalem: Arrest & Extradition

Once in Jerusalem, an agitated crowd thinks Paul has desecrated the Temple by bringing in a Gentile. They begin beating him until the Romans intervene to arrest him thinking that he is an Egyptian revolutionary. Paul is allowed to defend himself and explains his identity by describing his experience with the risen Christ and how it changed his life.

Paul Imprisoned for the Sake of Witness to the World (22:22–28:31)

Prisoner in Jerusalem & Paul's Testimony (22:22–23:22)

The Jerusalem mob refuses to accept Paul's explanation, and demands a flogging. But Paul informs his Roman guards that he is a Roman citizen and so cannot be punished until he is convicted on formal charges. The final chapters describe the next four years of Paul's life as a prisoner and the several ways he witnesses about Christ even as a prisoner, first before the Jewish council or Sanhedrin and then before the civil magistrates.

Prisoner in Caesarea & Paul's Testimony (23:23–26:32)

When the Judeans plot to kill Paul, the Romans put him in protective custody and move him to the jurisdiction of the Roman governor Felix at Caeasrea by the Mediterranean Sea. When the Judeans come to accuse Paul, he once again defends himself (24:1-23) arguing that the real issue is not about disturbing the Temple but about the resurrection of the dead.

For two years Felix successfully postpones any verdict hoping that the Roman tribune Lysias will come to help handle the case. But when Felix's successor Festus arrives, the Judeans revive their attempts to convict Paul. When Festus suggests a Jerusalem trial, Paul invokes his rights as a Roman citizen to be tried in Rome. But before he embarks, Paul once again defends himself before the Roman appointed King Agrippa who was visiting Festus (26:2-23). Paul again describes his conversion and mission to the Gentiles.

Prisoner in Rome & Paul's Testimony & Ministry (27:1–28:31)

Paul is sent by sea to Rome, but is shipwrecked without any loss of life because God wants him to witness openly in Rome. Three months later he finally arrives, and Acts ends recounting that two years later Paul was "welcoming all and proclaiming the kingdom of God and teaching about the Lord Jesus Christ with all boldness and without hindrance" (28:31), a sign of the fulfillment of the worldwide proclamation of God's Good News for all nations.

"The transition from Jewish traditions to specifically Christian traditions did not come without a struggle. Many would not let go of the old. Where change did occur, many wanted to return to the old. Had their attitude prevailed, Christianity could not have developed into the inclusive community called for by the death and resurrection of Jesus Christ. It could not have embarked on its historical mission to the ends of the earth."

—*EUGENE LAVERDIERE, SSS*
The Beginning of the Gospel: Introducing the Gospel of Mark, Vol. 1 (1999)

Luke's Gospel & Us

One way to discover Luke's theology of the transformative journey of Christian discipleship is to consider the many meals he describes in his Gospel. Since meals are all about relationships, Jesus' meals reveal his idea of right relationships with God and with others that are the core challenge of our discipleship. His actions at meals reveal the community relationships that he encourages and the values that characterize life in God's kingdom. So when we consider where, how, when and with whom Jesus eats, we will know what the kingdom of God is like.

Jesus' meals announced that the gift of God's presence transformed ordinary life into something extraordinary and evoked the demand for thanksgiving (Gk: *eucharistia*). His table companions express the diversity of the kingdom: men and women, friends and foes, rich and poor, Pharisees and priests of the religious establishment, tax collectors and "sinners." By examining these meals—where they take place, who is present with Jesus, and what happens when Jesus interacts with those present—we discover various aspects of ourselves that are still being challenged today because of our desire to share the eucharistic meal with Christ.

Following the example of Jesus, we take, bless, break and share the bread and cup. But simultaneously through God's mysterious power we are taken, blessed, broken and shared with others as Jesus was. Our everyday lives become a truly eucharistic experience. God's new table is all-inclusive and demands a heightened sense of inner readiness. To share the kingdom meal is to be in solidarity with Jesus and with his mission to build the kingdom community today.

Jesus' Meals in Luke's Gospel

1. Luke 5:27-39   In the house of Levi, the tax collector
2. Luke 7: 36-50   In the house of Simon the Pharisee
3. Luke 9:10-17   In the wilderness near Bethsaida
4. Luke 10: 38-42   In the house of Martha and Mary
5. Luke 11:37-54   In the house of a Pharisee
6. Luke 14:1-24   In the house of a Pharisee on a Sabbath
7. Luke 19:1-10   In the house of Zacchaeus
8. Luke 22:14-38   Jesus' Last Supper with the Disciples
9. Luke 24:13-35   With the risen lord at Emmaus
10. Luke 24:36-53   With the risen lord at Jerusalem

Like the two disciples going to Emmaus on that first Easter, we want to recognize that Jesus is our constant companion on the journey. He is always present to open the scriptures to us in our reading, reflection and prayer. He is present to in our household and at eucharistic meals. His daily presence with us transforms us into witnesses of the resurrection (for more on this see pp. 243-247). And how our lives will be changed when we are able to say with these journeyers, "were not our heart burning within us as he spoke to us on the way and opened the scriptures to us" (24:32)?

The Gospel according to John

Introduction: The Revelation of God's Word in our World 1:1-51

Part One: The Book of Signs 2:1–12:50

2:1–4:54 First to Second Signs at Cana: revelations & responses to Jesus

5:1–10:42 Old Testament Feasts & Their Replacement

11:1–12:50 The Raising of Lazarus & Its Aftermath

Part Two: The Book of Glory 13:1–21:25

13:1–17:27 Jesus' Farewells to His Disciples

18:1–21:25 Jesus' "Hour": Suffering, Death & Resurrection

21:1-25 Epilogue: Peter & the Beloved Disciple

CHAPTER EIGHT

John's Gospel
God's Son Sent for Salvation

John's Gospel demonstrates how different a gospel life of Jesus can be. Although not directly based on Mark or any of the other Gospels, nevertheless John's way of telling the Good News of Jesus is rooted in the same Christian traditions. It offers a unique perspective on Jesus' divinity and on the non-hierarchical character of the community of disciples as Jesus' friends. Jesus is the divine revealer who has been sent from God to come down to earth to reveal who God is and what God wants in our relationships with God and others. He teaches in long speeches and performs distinctive signs which help us understand his message. Before he returns to God, he gives us the Holy Spirit to abide with us in his place and sends us out to continue his mission.

"As Jesus says to each one of us, 'Come and follow me,' as he calls us by our name with that incredible voice of tenderness calling us to freedom, he will reveal his own self, his own person. His body is the temple of the Spirit of God. He is that place where God resides. He is the resting place of God. He is God on earth. He is the Word made flesh."

—*JEAN VANIER*
Images of Love, Words of Hope (1991)

John & His Community

Who Was John?

The external tradition of the early Church from the second century (e.g., Irenaeus, Polycrates of Ephesus, Clement of Alexandria, etc.) is that the fourth Gospel was written by John, described as a "disciple of the Lord." Papyrus fragments of John's Gospel dating from the first third of the second century have been found in Egypt, which suggests a composition date around the turn of the first century (AD 90–100).

The clearest designation of the author within the Gospel itself is in the expression "the disciple whom Jesus loved" (see especially 21:20, 24 where the editor of this epilogue indicates that the Beloved Disciple is now dead and also that he was the source of the gospel witness for the community). Thus the Beloved Disciple not only refers to an important individual in the history of the community but also exemplifies the ideal disciple for each member of the community to imitate.

Most modern scholars conclude that the Gospel we have was not written by the apostle named John, i.e., the Galilean fisherman and son of Zebedee. To reconcile tradition and modern scholarship, some scholars identify the apostle John as the Beloved Disciple, who was responsible for the earlier oral foundation for the written Gospel. But the Gospel would have finally been edited by his devoted disciples. Other scholars hold that the Beloved Disciple was not one of the apostles (or why wouldn't this honored title be prominent!) but one from the wider circle of disciples who knew and followed Jesus. Although the exact identity of the Beloved Disciple remains unclear, all scholars agree that this person was someone who knew Jesus firsthand and whose eyewitness was central to the faith-life of the community that cherished John's Gospel.

Who Was John's Audience?
John's community was a mixed group of Jewish and Gentile Christian converts. Many scholars argue that the early chapters of the Gospel reflect the stages of growth in the community from an original group of Jews, among whom were followers of John the Baptist, who accepted Jesus as the Davidic messiah, who were then joined by a second group of Jews who stressed the Mosaic aspect of Jesus and who made converts in Samaria, and then finally came Gentiles whose inclusion would reveal God's plan of fulfillment for all the nations. Although there is no absolute certainty, there is practically unanimous agreement that the community was located in the area of Ephesus, the largest city on the central western coast of Asia Minor.

The community situation can best be described as full of tension. They are in conflict with their Jewish neighbors who consider them no longer Jews. By the last decade of the first century the tension between Jews and Christians had exploded into open hostility. Angry denunciations, fruitless arguments and mutual condemnations had wedged the communities far-

THE GOOD NEWS IN FOUR VERSIONS

ther and farther apart. As the story of the man born blind (9:1-41) indicates, coming to "see" (= believe) that "the man called Jesus" (9:11) is a wonder-working "prophet" (9:17) and the expected "messiah" creates such tension with one's neighbors, one's parents and the Jewish authorities that he would be "expelled from the synagogue" (9:22; 12:42). By about AD 85 the Jews had expelled Christians from worship in their synagogues and from their community life. John's Gospel reflects this painfully divisive situation. Although somewhat embittered by their rejection, John's community now struggled to discover its own Christian identity as no longer Jewish.

"The Fourth gospel apparently presumes that much of the story about Jesus, its persons and places, is already familiar to the readers. They would also apparently be familiar with such Christian beliefs as those represented by the christological titles, baptism, the Lord's Supper, and the Spirit. The Johannine reader, then, must be envisaged as a Christian. Perhaps the readers of the gospel are envisaged as falling into one or more of the misunderstandings represented by characters in the story."

—*PHEME PERKINS*
"The Gospel According to John" in *The New Jerome Biblical Commentary* (1990), 61:19

They are also in tension with their Gentile neighbors because their Christian life and practices are different. But their Christian identity must be developed amidst the pluralism of the Hellenistic culture, whose practices and religious outlook have not yet been influenced by Christianity. And, finally, to a certain extent, they are in tension with other Christian communities over issues of theology (e.g., Christ as pre-existent or the idea that the end-time has already been "realized" with the coming of the Holy Spirit) and community organization (e.g., a less hierarchical and more egalitarian understanding of community organization with no stress on specific offices or assigned leadership roles).

John's Gospel: Structure & Style

John's Gospel is carefully organized and shows deep theological reflection both about Jesus' identity—the incarnate Word of God "made flesh" (1:14) and God's son who has been sent for our salvation—and on the significance of the things Jesus said and did, which are "signs" revealing the person and plan of God for our salvation. Most commentators divide John's Gospel roughly into two halves, chapters 1–12 and 13–21, which form an overall arc of Jesus mission from heaven to earth and then his return back to the Father through his death and resurrection.

The Book of Signs: 2:1–12:50

Chapters 2–12 describe Jesus' public ministry as the manifestation of God's salvation clustered around seven signs that Jesus performs to show that he was indeed the promised messiah/Christ. John's emphasis is not so much on the wondrous sign itself but rather on the need of the audience to understand its deeper meaning and respond to it. His Gospel helps us learn to read the meaning of these signs.

"The theological understanding of miracle regards miracles in the way they are described in John's Gospel, as being 'signs,' that is, events that manifest with specific clarity some particular aspect of the divine will and nature that is normally veiled from clear sight. Miracles are not arbitrary divine actions but events of deep disclosure."

—*JOHN POLKINGHORNE*
Science and Religion in Quest of Truth (2011)

The signs are essential to the revelatory work that Jesus, the Word of God (1:1), does on behalf of the Father (1:18) while dwelling with us. These epiphany stories manifest God's power and presence in Jesus' acts, which will culminate in the ultimate sign—Jesus' death and resurrection. The signs are meant to evoke a faith response that can be either positive (belief, acceptance) or negative (unbelief, rejection). The response places the responder either within the believing community or outside of it. Thus the response to the sign and to Jesus who performs it constitutes a "judgment" (5:22; 9:39; 12:31) that remains binding on the responder (12:44-50).

John's signs are complemented by his emphasis on Jesus himself as the focal point of the individual's faith response. Unlike the other evangelists who focus on Jesus' Good News of God's saving presence in our world using the image of "God's kingdom," John stresses that the Good News is Jesus himself. Since Jesus is the definitive disclosure of God, John has Jesus assert that "Whoever has seen me has seen the Father" (14:9).

The Book of Glory: 13:1–20:31

Chapters 13–20 is often called "the book of glory" because Jesus' glory will be fully revealed in his passion, death and resurrection (12:23-36; 13:31-32) and his return home to the Father for his glorification in heaven. In these events the Father gives glory to Jesus, demonstrating that Jesus is what he claims to be (8:54; 17:1-5), and his followers can "see his glory" (1:14; 17:20-26) and proclaim it to the world.

John's Style

John's writing style is dramatic, repetitive and characterized by such stylistic devices as inclusion, chiasm (inverted parallelism, A-B-B-A), irony (a two-fold or double meaning) and the editor's explanatory notes. He prefers to involve Jesus in dialogues with other characters which then introduce long monologues in which Jesus clarifies the truths of his message from God.

Many words also have two levels of meaning. For example, usually "the world" (Gk: *kosmos*) would indicate the ordered character of God's creation. But since John also sees a spiritual dimension to all of our existence, he uses "the world" to describe the forces that we often experience resisting God's ordering power and standing in opposition to Jesus and the Christian community. Though "the world" is hostile to God, God is not hostile to the world but sends Jesus "into the world" for its salvation (1:9-10; 3:16-17).

John's Gospel & the Other Gospels

Although not directly based on the synoptic Gospels, John seemed familiar with them (perhaps from hearing one or more read aloud rather than reading them in written form) but did not rely on their accounts for much more than the general overview of Jesus' life and ministry. Thus John's way of telling the Good News of Jesus is rooted in similar Christian traditions and on Mark's idea of a narrative framework for Jesus' life (although John differs both on the chronology of Jesus life—a three year ministry rather than a single year—and includes several incidents not found in the other Gospels). He agrees in many instances with Mark and Luke, somewhat less with Matthew, but his viewpoint is noticeably different.

John's Aim

John himself states that he has written "so that you may believe that Jesus is the Christ, the son of God, and that believing you may have life in his name" (20:31). His Gospel is meant to strengthen the faith of the Christian community as it tries to live out its commitment to Christ amidst the many tensions both within the community and with outsiders. Reading this Gospel invites us to "see" beyond Jesus' "signs" and discover Jesus as God's unique revelation of "the way, and the truth, and the life" (14:6).

John's Sources—Traditions of a Beloved Disciple

John seems to be based mostly on an independent source of community traditions about Jesus. Many scholars surmise that these traditions are rooted in the oral traditions of his community and perhaps might be the teaching of the community leader, the Beloved Disciple, who although not one of the twelve apostles, was personally familiar with Jesus and his ministry from eyewitness experience and offers a direct connection to Jesus' words and deeds. "This is the disciple who is testifying to these things and wrote these things, and we know that his testimony is true" (21:24).

Why Write It This Way

In the 30 years after Mark wrote his Gospel, Christian communities continued to deepen their understanding of who Jesus was and what he accomplished through his death and resurrection. These more developed conclusions were then expressed in the various Gospels. In comparing John to the synoptic Gospels, several differences both in his presentation and in his theological emphases can be briefly noted.

"John and the other three gospels, in their different ways, all intend to tell the story, not of how Jesus died so that we could go to heaven, but of how Jesus died so that he might become the true king of Israel and of the whole world."

—*N. T. WRIGHT*
"Kingdom, Power and Truth," St. Mary's College Lecture (9/14/2010)

In John there is no story of Jesus' birth, since Jesus' presence was understood as the incarnation of the divine Word in human flesh, the perfect revelation of God to humanity. Likewise since John has no need for the divine confirmation of Jesus' sonship, there is no baptism but only the human witness of John the Baptist and no temptation in the wilderness. In Jesus' ministry, he casts out no demons nor teaches in parables (although there are some parabolic actions or signs). Instead of short parables, he teaches in long rambling discourses that reveal the profound truths of his message.

At the Last Supper, there is no blessing and sharing of bread and wine

THE GOOD NEWS IN FOUR VERSIONS

but a footwashing (13:1-16). Thus although John omits any mention of the institution of the sacraments, he nevertheless reveals a deep understanding of the meaning and purpose of baptism and eucharist.

John often uses the phrase *eternal life* where the synoptics use *the kingdom of God*. Life eternal not only as possibility but as reality has now burst into human life in the person and work of Jesus.

The controversies that erupt between Jesus and the Judean authorities are no longer concerned with Jewish legal interpretations as in the synoptics but rather with Jesus' identity as divine and the repercussions of this for both Christians and Jews. The Jews could not accept Jesus as divine because for them this meant there were two Gods. John struggles to hold that there is one God, but this divinity is shared by a "father" and "son" (John's favorite identification of Jesus). John used the relational concepts of father/son in new ways to accentuate both Jesus' equality with the Father as divine and his subordination to the Father as son.

John's Portrait of Jesus

Jesus is God's revelatory medium, his "Word" who reveals the mystery of God's being and perform "signs" which when rightly understood lead us to faith. Only John stresses that Jesus is divine prior to his earthly existence and has been sent from God into our world for our salvation. Jesus is not only the messenger of God's salvation but also salvation incarnate. Jesus is presented both as fully human (he became tired and thirsty, and he wept), and as the Christ in whom dwells the fullness of God.

John focuses on the intimate relationship of Jesus the son to God the father. Jesus is the Word of God, the revealer of the mystery of God in our midst. He has been sent from God to show us who God is and what God wants. He can do this because of his personal experience and special relationship with God. He teaches in long speeches and performs distinctive signs that help us understand his message. Before he returns, he gives us the Holy Spirit to carry on his work and to abide with us always in his place.

God's Son Sent for Salvation

More than any other Gospel author, John stressed Jesus' divine sonship. John moved beyond the explanation of Jesus as son of God by adoption

(Mark) and natural generation through the power of God's Holy Spirit (Matthew, Luke) to claim the pre-existence of the divine Word (Gk: *logos*, thought, word or idea) who subsequently was sent into our world and became flesh as Jesus of Nazareth. (For more about this development see my *Who Do You Say that I Am? The Catechist's Guide to Jesus in the Gospels* [Faith Alive Books, 2015], chapter 7.)

John pushed the divine sonship claim back to the time before Jesus' birth: he was a divine being, with God at creation, who was sent into the world to save us from sin and bring us into the right relationship with God. Thus Jesus, God's pre-existent Word who is with God and is God and agent of all that is created and so can legitimately claim the divine name "I AM."

JOHN'S "I AM" STATEMENTS

A notable feature of John's Gospel is the *I am* (Gk: *ego eimi*) statements. These words echo God's sacred personal name (4 consonant letters, in English YHWH, usually translated as *Yahweh*) whose meaning was closely related to the verb "I am" (see Ex 3:14, "I am who I am"). John uses these statements to draw attention both to Jesus' divinity when used without a predicate (6:20; 8:24, 28, 58; 13:19; 18:5, 18, 23) and with a predicate to reveal the many dimensions of his relationship to humankind, for example:

"I am he [the messiah]" (4:26)
"I am the bread of life" (6:35)
"I am the living bread" (6:51)
"I am the light of the world" (8:12; 9:5)
"I am from above" (8:23)
"I am the gate for the sheep" (10:7, 9)
"I am the good shepherd" (10:11, 14)
"I am the resurrection and the life" (11:25)
"I am the way, the truth, and the life" (14:6)
"I am the true vine" (15:1, 5)

Thus John's understanding of Jesus' pre-existent divine sonship makes his Gospel very different from the others. As God's son who has been sent into our world for salvation, Jesus is messiah/Christ and true revealer of God's divine self. But he is also the son of man who comes down to suffer, be glorified and judge. He replaces the function of the Jewish feasts with himself and fulfills the religious longings of all humanity. Although the pre-existent son of the Father, Jesus takes on "flesh," i.e., becomes genuinely human. He speaks what he hears the Father saying and does what the Father

THE GOOD NEWS IN FOUR VERSIONS

sent him to do. This speaking and doing invites persons to believe in him and so to receive eternal life. He can do this because he and the Father are one—sharing divinity and life which in turn is shared with believers.

John's special emphasis on Jesus' identity can be summarized in his oft-repeated idea that Jesus was God's son sent for salvation. While it has echoes in the synoptics concerning Jesus as "sent," (e.g., Mt 10:40; Mk 9:37; Lk 4:43; 9:48; 10:16), John uses it as the backbone of his distinctive portrait of Jesus. John stresses in an unprecedented way that Jesus was sent from God (Jn 4:34; 5:23-24, 30, 36-38; 6:29, 38-39, 44, 57; 7:16, 18, 28-29, 33; 8:16, 18, 26, 29, 42; 9:4; 10:36; 11:42-44; 12:45, 49; 13:20; 14:24; 15:2, 21; 16:5; 17:3, 8, 18, 21, 23, 25; 20:21). As son, Jesus was under the authority of the Father and was recognized as sent into the world for judgment and salvation. This mission was closely linked with his divine status as God's son. John's emphasis on the sender/sent, father/son categories is his unique contribution to our understanding of Jesus.

John's Portrait of Discipleship

Jesus calls disciples (John is careful not to use the word "apostles") into intimacy with him and so with God. John's community is a group conscious of this intimate relationship to Jesus, as Jesus' words at the Last Supper make clear—his disciples are no longer merely pupils, but "friends" (15:15). As Jesus' friends they share Jesus' life because they share the Holy Spirit. They are characterized by their love for one another, loving as Jesus has loved them—a love that is not only intimate but which is willing to give everything for the beloved. Jesus' death is the ultimate sign of his love.

Jesus invites them into a deep and tender experience of intimacy with him and consequently with the Father. A disciple is one who comes to see where the Lord dwells and dwells with him (1:38-39), and who invites the Lord to dwell with him or her. Disciples share an intimate, loving relationship with Jesus and hence with the Father and the Holy Spirit. Finally, disciples are also sons and daughters sent to continue Jesus' work in the world.

The Beloved Disciple Is the Model Disciple

A mysterious figure appears in John's Gospel. This "Beloved Disciple" represents John's ideal disciple, who is so intimate with Jesus that he can rest his head on Jesus at the last supper (13:23). In contrast to Peter, he faithfully follows Jesus during the passion, even getting Peter into the courtyard of the high priest (18:15). Although Peter denies Jesus and runs away, the Beloved Disciple stands at the foot of the cross (19:26). Jesus tells the Beloved Disciple to care for his mother. After the resurrection, the Beloved Disciple more quickly believes in the resurrection (20:8) and recognizes the mysterious risen Lord (21:7) on the seashore. He is the model of loving friendship for John's congregation.

John's Characters
Examples of the Challenge of Believing

John uses the persons presented in his Gospel to further his task of proclamation. In general. the characters are models of belief or unbelief. Jesus' opponents serve as models of what it means to reject God's revelation in Christ, while the disciples are models of acceptance.

Examples of the Beginning Stages of Believing
Believers are, however, representations of faith at many different levels of maturation. Some characters are examples of the transition from unbelief to the beginning stages of faith, for example:
- Nicodemus (3:1-13; 7:50-51; 19:39)
- the Samaritan woman (4:1-30)
- the blind man (9:1-41)

Examples of the Failure of Believing
Other characters exemplify the failure to believe, for example:
- the man with the thirty-eight year illness (5:1-18)
- "many disciples" (6:60-71)

Examples of Other Aspects of Believing
- The royal official (4:43-54) represents a profound faith that believes on the basis of Jesus' word without evidence of the success of the wondrous healing of his son
- Martha models the growth in faith (11:1-44), and Mary the gratitude and love of faith (12:1-8)
- In the discovery of the empty tomb, Mary Magdalene, Peter and the Beloved Disciple (20:1-10) represent three different kinds of faith
- Thomas demonstrates the way in which faith is born from doubt (20:24-28)

An Invitation to Identify with Their Example
Some persons are passed over with little or no interest (Annas, 18:19-24, Joseph of Arimathea, 19:38-42), while others are more developed (Pilate, 18:28–19:16). So by inviting his readers to contemplate the response of each of the characters depicted in his Gospel, John encourages them to examine and compare their own faith response to Jesus with that of the Gospel characters.

The Good News in Four Versions

A Brief Reading Guide to John's Story of Jesus

Introduction: The Revelation of God's Word in our World (1:1-51)

Prologue: God's Word Made Flesh in Our World (1:1-18)

John's prologue is a poetic introduction to and summary of the career of the incarnate Word, who exists before and is active in creation, revealing himself to the world and to Israel, who do not accept him. So he takes the surprising step of becoming human ("flesh") in Jesus, God's son sent for salvation.

"John's prologue serves as an overture to his Gospel. It is written in stately and solemn prose and summarizes the Gospel's quintessential message. It testifies to the Johannine community's belief in Jesus' divinity, his pre-existence, his function in the creation of the world, and his function in the Father's plan for the salvation of humanity."

—*PETER F. ELLIS*
The Genius of John (1984)

John the Baptist's Witness about Himself & Jesus (1:19-34)

The evangelist adds further understanding of Jesus' identity through a sequence of titles in 1:29-51 culminating in John the Baptist's witness to Jesus as "the lamb of God" (1:29), associating him with Isaiah's suffering servant and the Passover lamb as a symbol for the atoning death Jesus would suffer. Jesus receives and retains the Spirit for his ministry, and then gives it to others so they too may share that abiding relationship of life with God.

Call of the First Disciples (1:35-51)

Through the Baptist's witness, two of his disciples begin to follow after Jesus, who invites them to stay with him (1:39), an invitation to a new relationship. They do stay with him and then begin to act as apostles, bringing their family and friends to discover Jesus too.

Part One: The Book of Signs (2:1–12:50)

First to Second Signs at Cana: Revelations & Responses to Jesus (2:1–4:54)

The Wedding at Cana—1ˢᵗ Sign (2:1-12)

Like much in John's Gospel, the Cana wedding story hints at multiple meanings. The event echoes the Old Testament themes of the marriage bond between God and Israel and the messianic banquet at the end of time. Jesus' "hour," set by the divine plan, is the final revelation of his glory in his passion and crucifixion. He reminds his mother that his mission is not to fulfill human desires but to do God's will. Though he does respond to her request, he does so only in cooperation with the purposes of his ministry.

Disrupting Temple Business (2:13-25)

Jesus then travels to Jerusalem at Passover time. In the Temple courtyard, he sees unblemished animals being sold for sacrifice and the money changers busy at their tables. He disrupts these money-making practices and attacks not only the dishonesty of the Temple trade but its very existence.

When challenged about his actions, Jesus' ambiguous reply, as so often in John's Gospel, is interpreted in two different ways. The Judean leaders think he is talking about the Temple building but his followers realize (only later) that he was talking of his own body, which will be raised from the dead. Jesus himself, not the Temple building, is now the primary place where God dwells among us and so the true source of sanctification, forgiveness and eternal life. This incident initiates the hostility between Jesus and the Judean leaders that will eventually end with his murder.

Jesus & Nicodemus at Night (3:1-21)

This is the first of John's lengthy expositions of Jesus' teachings. Two characteristic techniques are employed: a question asked on the physical level is answered on the spiritual level, and the focus on the questioner's misunderstanding. Nicodemus's misunderstanding centers on the word translated "from above," which, in Greek, has two meanings. The first is "anew, again," which is what Nicodemus understands; the second is "from above," which is what Jesus seems to intend. Jesus contrasts the realm of the Spirit, which is eternal and heavenly, with the realm of the flesh, which is earthly, weak and mortal (but not necessarily sinful). Both flesh and spirit make up human life, but the Spirit is life itself.

Jesus & the Samaritan Woman at Noon (4:1-42)

The Samaritans were descendants of the peoples settled by the Assyrians in the kingdom of Israel after its conquest (721 BCE) who worshiped other gods as well as Yahweh. After the Judeans returned from exile, enmity with

THE GOOD NEWS IN FOUR VERSIONS

the Samaritans developed and persisted. Though the Samaritans worshiped Yahweh, their center of worship was on Mount Gerizim not in Jerusalem.

In response to the woman's questioning, Jesus challenges her to recognize him as "the gift of God," the "living water" (4:10) and the messiah (4:26). The woman first recognizes Jesus as the prophet like Moses, on whom the Samaritans centered their messianic expectations. She brings up the dispute over the proper place of worship, but Jesus' answer focuses on the most important issue—the response to God's gift of life. Jesus' reply finally invites the woman to acknowledge him as the messiah and she shares this experience with her neighbors.

Jesus Heals the Official's Son—2nd Sign (4:43-54)

Returning to Cana, Jesus meets a royal official whose son was ill in the town of Capernaum. Jesus assures the father that his son will live and the healing occurs at a distance and exactly when Jesus announced the cure. Thus the father believed. This is a further instance of how seeing beyond the sign leads to the positive response of faith.

Old Testament Feasts & Their Replacement (5:1–10:42)

Once John's community no longer thought of themselves as Jews, they would no longer celebrate the Jewish feasts. To reassure them that their new Christian forms of worship were acceptable, in chapters 5–10 John identifies Jesus himself with the symbols and themes associated with the major Jewish feasts. Jesus continues God's life-giving work on the Sabbath (5:1-47). He is the "bread of life" (6:35, 51) replacing the manna given during the Exodus, the source of "living water" and "light of the world" (8:12; 9:5), and specially consecrated as was the Temple (10:36).

"Expulsion had cut the Johannine Christians off from the rich Jewish liturgical life, and to compensate for that the Johannine tradition emphasized a strong motif of replacement: Jesus takes the place of many of the institutions of Judaism."

—*RAYMOND E. BROWN, SS*
An Introduction to the Gospel of John (2003)

Jesus & the Sabbath: Curing a Paralytic—3rd Sign (5:1-47)

In this sign, Jesus cures a paralytic on the Sabbath. The Judean bystanders first accuse the man and then Jesus of breaking the Sabbath, but Jesus defends his actions as merely an extension of God's healing power at work. But the hostility toward Jesus increases and his opponents want to kill him.

Feeding of the Five Thousand—4th Sign (6:1-15)

The feeding of the 5,000 is the only miracle of Jesus' ministry recorded in all four Gospels. John's account seems to come from a tradition independent of, but similar to, the other accounts. As so often in John, Jesus takes the initiative, even before the people arrive. This event echoes the eucharistic practice of John's community since he does not describe a eucharistic ritual at the Last Supper. In response to the sign, the people acclaim Jesus as "the prophet" and want to make him a king. But Jesus withdraws for he does not seek this kind of political leadership.

Walking on Water—5th Sign (6:16-25)

Nature wonders like walking on water and changing of water to wine at Cana are signs of God's powerful presence breaking into our world to reorder it forever. Jesus' self-identification here, "It is I" (Gk: *ego eimi*) echoes the Greek translation of the unutterable name of God ("I am who I am," Ex 3:14). John thus draws attention to the manifestation of Jesus' divinity.

Jesus & Passover: the Bread of Life Discourse (6:26-71)

Jesus proclaims that he is the real bread of life, thus replacing the Passover festival. As usual, John's narrative moves on two levels at once: the audience focuses on the physical and Jesus on the spiritual. Just as God drew people to the *Torah* to give them life, so now God draws them to Jesus to bestow eternal life. Jesus' relationship to humanity is one of nourishment and those who eat this bread and unite themselves intimately with him will have eternal life in the present and participate in the resurrection "on the last day."

Jesus & the Feast of Tabernacles (7:1-52)

Jesus affirms once again, as with the Samaritan woman, that he is indeed the source of the "living water" that will nourish us for eternal life. This water is the Holy Spirit that will pour forth when the disciples will receive it after Jesus has departed.

The Woman Taken in Adultery (7:53–8:11)

Most scholars consider this passage to be a non-Johannine story inserted into his original Gospel by a later editor. The scribes and Pharisees test Jesus about the proper punishment for a woman caught in the act of adultery, hoping that Jesus' response would either incite the crowd to stone the woman (a violation of the Roman prohibition of capital punishment, 18:3) or else appear to condone the sin (a violation of the Mosaic law). In either case, they were attempting to dishonor and discredit Jesus as a teacher in front of the people. Jesus tells the accusers to go ahead and stone the woman, but only if they have never sinned. As they drift away, Jesus links his compassion for the woman with an exhortation to change her behavior.

Light of the World (8:12-20)
The prologue already connected the themes of life and light in relation to the divine Word through whom all reality was created (1:4-9). Chapters 8–11 now elaborate in detail what the prologue hinted at: Jesus is the light (for both the blind man in chapter 9 and for the world) and provides the life (both for Lazarus in chapter 11 and all humanity). He has been sent into our world of darkness and sin to illuminate us with divine light so that we might live in a new and richer way.

Statements, Misunderstandings, Corrections (8:21-59)
Jesus engages with the Pharisees concerning the validity of his testimony about God's ways because he speaks of spiritual things that he knows. But they cannot bring themselves to believe in him and persist in their darkness and want to stone him.

The Man Born Blind—6th Sign (9:1-41)
This healing story is an enactment of the triumph of light over darkness. The belief in a causal relationship between sin and suffering was widespread, but Jesus turns the attention from cause to purpose—not why but for what reason—God is being revealed through Jesus' ministry.

The increasing insight of the blind man who learns to "see" because of Jesus' sign contrasts with the persistent blindness of the Pharisees who think they see quite well (9:40-41). The blind man progresses from seeing Jesus as just a man to seeing him as a prophet, then asserting that Jesus must be from God, and finally worshiping him as the son of man, through whom God would usher in the final era of judgment and salvation.

The Good Shepherd (10:1-21)

Chapter 10 continues the dialogue from chapter 9 between Jesus and the Pharisees. In the Old Testament, God is called *the shepherd of Israel* (Ps 80:1). Now Jesus is "the good shepherd." In the Greek, the word for "good" more literally means "fitting," as in an ideal of perfection or model. Jesus is the ideal or model shepherd, both because of his willingness to lay down his life and also because of his intimate knowledge of his flock.

Jesus & Hanukkah (10:22-42)

But despite Jesus' teaching, the Pharisees do not understand. Then there is a shift to Jesus' presence at the feast of Dedication *(Hanukkah)*. The theme of light is again emphasized (10:22-39), ending with a note about Jesus' return to the area where John the Baptizer's work had begun (10:40-41).

The Raising of Lazarus & Its Aftermath (11:1–12:50)

The Raising of Lazarus—7ᵗʰ Sign (11:1-44)

John here combines both a sign narrative and a teaching dialogue. Jesus reacts to the death of Lazarus with intense emotion, mingling grief, compassion and anger. He prays for the bystanders, that they may perceive the truth of this sign. As God's word gave life and light in creation, so now the incarnate Word gives light and life as signs of the eternal life he now offers.

The Plot against Jesus (11:45-57)

Although bringing Lazarus back to life was the cause for many to believe in and follow Jesus, it also intensified the hostility of the authorities toward Jesus for they now feared Rome's involvement. Therefore they decided to find a way to arrest and kill Jesus.

Anointing at Bethany & Entry into Jerusalem (12:1-19)

Jesus stops at Bethany on his way to Jerusalem for the Passover festival. Lazarus's sister Mary anoints Jesus for burial, expressing her deep love and devotion with an extravagant gift of perfumed oil with which she anoints his feet. John contrasts Mary's simple, selfless act with Judas's protest, which might seem sensible but perhaps masks his greed.

The End of Jesus' Public Ministry (12:20-50)

The appearance of "some Greeks" (12:20, probably "God-fearers"—those who were attracted to Judaism but for various reasons did not fully join) indicates that Jesus' public ministry is now complete. He announces that his "hour has come" (12:23), the time for his glorification in death, resurrection and ascension. The victory over Satan will be won through Jesus' "lifting up" (12:32, a term indicating both his crucifixion and his exaltation).

Part Two: The Book of Glory (13:1–21:25)
Jesus' Farewells to His Disciples (13:1–17:27)

Like the other Gospels, John describes Jesus' final meal with his disciples. Although much is the same, John follows a slightly different calendar that puts the Passover one day later, thus making the meal a farewell supper not a Passover meal (13:1-38). So he shifts the meaning of this meal from the eucharistic memorial that focuses on the bread and wine (which John does in chapter 6 on the Bread of Life) to an enacted sign of service: washing the feet of the disciples.

"In the second part of the gospel (chs. 13–17), the disciples find themselves in the historical situation of the final gathering and the approaching farewell, but at the same time they clearly represent the Church after Jesus' glorification. They are the representatives of all believers who have never seen Christ. 'If you love Me, keep my commandments' (14:15). And what are these commandments? Faith in Jesus and fraternal charity!"

—*W. K. GROSSOUW*
"Christian Spirituality in John," in *A Companion to John,* ed. Michael J. Taylor, SJ (1979)

The Footwashing at the Last Supper (13:1-20)

Footwashing was not part of the Passover ritual but a common gesture that for John exemplifies the deepest meaning of eucharist—giving oneself in loving service for others. In the biblical world, sandals protected the bottom of the foot but did not keep dirt away. So a customary sign of hospitality upon entering a house was for a servant to wash the guest's feet. Thus, when Jesus assumes the servant's role instead of the master's, what would normally be considered undignified and humiliating becomes a positive sign of his love for his disciples and a lesson for them to imitate.

Prophecies of Betrayal & the New Commandment (13:21-38)

As in the synoptics, Jesus predicts Judas's betrayal and Peter's denial. Then he reminds the disciples that their lives are to be shaped by a new commandment to love one another as he has loved them. The commandment is new, not as a commandment, but because Jesus' love now becomes the model for all love: an unconditional love poured out to everyone.

Assurances & Promises (14:1-31)

The meaning of Jesus' departure is now clarified. It mysteriously brings not separation but a deeper fellowship as the disciples abide with him always, in the body of Christ, the Christian community. To those who keep his commandments, Jesus promises a new indwelling presence described variously as being of both the Father and Jesus, of the Holy Spirit or of Jesus himself. The Father will send "another Advocate" (14:15), who will remain with believers. "Advocate" (Gk: *paraklētos,* paraclete) may also be translated *counselor* or *helper.* The presence of the absent Jesus after his return to the Father will be continued in and through the Holy Spirit.

Love & Hate (15:1–16:4)

Chapter 15 contains the last of the great "I am" discourses in John's Gospel, on the vine and the branches. Jesus uses the relationship of the vine and branches to explore the disciples' relationships with Jesus and with one another. Jesus' relationship of mutual indwelling with the Father is now extended to all Christians who are to love one another with a love characterized by self-sacrifice. Thus while Christians are still "servants" (15:15, literally "slaves") of Christ in terms of ministry (see 12:26; 13:14-16), they are "friends" (15:15) of Christ in terms of intimacy with God.

"John teaches how we live in Christ and Christ lives in us. Just as the trunk of the vine gives its natural properties to each of the branches, so, by bestowing the Holy Spirit, Christ gives Christians a certain kinship with himself."

—*ST. CYRIL OF ALEXANDRIA*
Commentary of the Gospel of John

Jesus' Departure & Return (16:5-33)

In chapter 16, Jesus warns the disciples of his impending death and of the persecution to come. Death is for him a return home to the Father (the Christian theological understanding of death as a return home to God is rooted in this Johannine perspective) and thus it is to their advantage for only then can he send the Spirit to them—the Spirit of truth, who will lead the disciples into an ever-deeper understanding of Jesus' revelation and help them with their mission. Just as Jesus was the presence of the invisible Father, so the Holy Spirit will be the presence of the absent Jesus. Jesus must "go away" for that to be accomplished.

The Prayer of God's Son (17:1-26)

Jesus' prayer is one of union or communion between the Father and the son, given to the disciples so that they may share that union. Their unity is based not upon their own effort but upon the act of God who loves them as God loves the son. Jesus prays for himself (17:1), for the disciples (17:9), for future believers (17:20) but not directly for the world because the unity of believers will witness to the Father's love for the world.

"Eternal life consists in knowing the true God—as distinguished from the false gods and mental constructs we invent to elude God—and in knowing Jesus as Christ, that is, as messiah. John 17:3 is really the summary of the entire message of John and of the New Testament. Eternal life depends on this knowledge and will come to be throughout the world through this knowledge."

—*JOSE MIRANDA*
Being and the Messiah: The Message of St. John (2006)

In his ministry Jesus revealed God's nature and character (literally, "God's name") to the disciples, who know his works are those of the Father. He prays that they may be kept safe from the world by the power of God's name and experience eternal life, which is "to know the only true God, and Jesus Christ" (17:3). The disciples, and all Christians, "do not belong to the world" (17:14) but to God for they have been reborn and are now consecrated, set apart, as Jesus was by his incarnation and empowerment by the Holy Spirit, not merely for self-purification but for their mission into the world, which continues Jesus' presence and brings the world to judgment.

Jesus' "Hour": Suffering, Death & Resurrection (18:1–21:25)

For John, the cross is the revelation of God's plan for salvation. Jesus' "hour," the final revelation of God's presence in his suffering and death, has come. In the completion of the work of redemption, the Father and the son reveal one another in mutual "glory," which means a visible revelation of God's presence and holiness. Thus the cross is not a humiliation but a glorification of Jesus, who is not a victim but a victor over sin and death.

"The Jesus who comes at last to his hour (Jn 13:1) in the Fourth Gospel is a different dramatic character from the Jesus of the Synoptic passion narratives. He is a Jesus conscious of his pre-existence. Through death, therefore, he is returning to a state he has temporarily left during his stay in this world (17:5). He is not a victim at the mercy of his opponent since he has freely chosen to lay down his life with the utter certitude that he will take it up again (10:17-18)."

—*FR. RAYMOND E. BROWN, SS*
A Crucified Christ in Holy Week: Essays on the Four Gospel Passion Narratives (1986)

The Arrest of Jesus (18:1-27)

Jesus and the disciples depart for a garden to pray. Judas brings the soldiers of the Judean authorities to arrest Jesus, whose "I am he" again suggests his divinity and strikes fear into the soldiers. But Jesus submits and is taken off for a hearing before the High Priest and the Judean leaders. Peter and another disciple follow Jesus, but Peter then denies Jesus three times.

The Trial before Pilate (18:28–19:16)

Convinced of Jesus' guilt but unable to put him to death, the Judean authorities take him to Pilate, the Roman governor. Jesus' dialogue with Pilate reveals how all the main characters—Jesus, Pilate and the Judean leaders and crowds—are challenged to reveal where their loyalties lie (see chapter 3, pp. 82-86). Having lost control of the situation and trying to find a way out of the loyalty dilemma brought on by the threats of the Judean leaders and the crowd, Pilate then hands Jesus over to be crucified.

The Death of Jesus (19:17-42)

Much of John's account of Jesus' final moments is similar to the synoptic accounts, but John introduces certain elements that reflect his theology and important themes. Jesus carries his own cross to Golgotha where he is crucified. The soldiers cast lots for his seamless outer garment. He gives his mother to the care of the Beloved Disciple and the Disciple to his mother, indicating that both family and non-family are now to be joined in his new community. Jesus' dying words on the cross, "It is finished" (19:30) show his control over events to the end. He does not die until the mission for which he had been sent by the Father has been fully accomplished.

THE GOOD NEWS IN FOUR VERSIONS

Only John reports Pilate's decision to break the legs of the crucified so they would not remain on the cross for the Sabbath. When the soldiers found Jesus already dead, to make sure they pierced his side with a spear and from his side flowed blood and water—his life-giving fluids that would continue to nourish the Christian community's life through the eucharist and baptism.

JOHN'S PASSION MESSAGE

1. Through the passion John's Gospel proclaims that the death of Jesus, as an act of total self-donation, is God's ultimate revelation of redemptive love for the world.
2. Jesus' death is the victorious culmination of his mission, the "hour of glory" triumphantly leading him back to God.
3. From his cross, Jesus stands in judgment over the powers of darkness and death and defeats them; at the same time the power of the cross becomes a norm of judgment on all other expressions of power.
4. Jesus' death has redemptive value and from the crucified Jesus new life streams into the world.
5. The crisis of the passion reveals the meaning of faith and the cost of discipleship.
6. Jesus' cross gives new meaning to the Christian encounter with death.
7. The passion is the summit of the deadly hostility of Jesus' opponents and reveals the tragedy of their failure.

—DONALD SENIOR, CP
The Passion of Jesus in the Gospel of John (1991)

Easter Faith (20:1-31)

In his resurrection accounts, John stresses how Jesus fulfills the promises that he made in his farewell address at the Last Supper: his return and the gift of the Holy Spirit, which will be the presence of the absent Jesus.

The risen lord's first appearance describes the discovery of the empty tomb by Mary Magdalene and the different responses of the disciples. The simple fact of the empty tomb does not produce faith for Mary or for Peter, who did not, as yet, understand the meaning of scripture about the resurrection of the dead (20:9). Only the Beloved Disciple, the model Christian disciple for John and his community, "saw and believed" (20:8). Mary, Peter and the other disciples must depend on subsequent appearances of Jesus or a report of his appearance to trigger and confirm their belief.

Jesus next shows his wounds to the gathered disciples to establish that the crucified Jesus and the risen Christ are one and the same. Then as he had promised, he breathes the Holy Spirit upon the disciples and gives them a mission to mediate divine forgiveness.

Thomas personifies the mixture of doubt and faith found in the other Gospels' resurrection accounts. He will not accept the Good News of the resurrection on the word of others but demands to experience the risen Christ directly. Yet without touching the lord he penetrates the meaning behind the marvel and makes a full affirmation of Christian faith. He then consummates the sequence of titles given to Jesus in the Gospel by calling him *God*. In response, Jesus' blessing reassures believers like us who experience the risen Christ through faith but without seeing him bodily.

Verses 30-31 serve as a fitting conclusion to the Gospel. They reveal the author's intent and invite the reader to understand Jesus' life, death and resurrection and, through belief, to share in a saving relationship with him.

Epilogue: Peter & the Beloved Disciple (21:1-25)

Chapter 21 is regarded by most scholars as an epilogue to the Gospel, added later either by the evangelist himself or more likely by an editor-disciple. The helplessness of the disciples on their own is transformed by the power of the risen lord and their obedience to him. The shared meal is described in terms harking back to the multiplication of loaves (6:11). (Note that the common early pictorial symbol for the eucharist was bread and fish, rather than bread and wine.) Nourished by the eucharist, Christians led by Peter, are to become missionary fishers of people.

John's Gospel & Us

From our perspective as readers, John's Gospel is an exercise in learning to see beyond the signs and interpret the meaning of God's word. He works carefully to lead us to new levels of knowledge and experience through our encounter with his text. Most importantly, John not only identifies Jesus as God's son sent for salvation but he also extends the model of sender/sent to Jesus and the disciples. After greeting the disciples with peace, the risen Lord commissions the disciples, "As the Father has sent me, so I send you" (20:21). Then he breathes on them the Holy Spirit and connects their mission with the forgiveness of sins. John recognizes that the Christian life is caught up in a network or chain of messengers. The Father sends Jesus and the Paraclete. Jesus in turn sends the Paraclete and the disciples (17:8).

The implications of this chain of messengers means that each Christian disciple, through faith in the risen lord and personal contact with the Paraclete, shares directly in Jesus' mission and hence in God's saving work in our world. John's insight is that the church's life now is linked to Jesus' mission and ministry. Through their faith in him and participation in his mission, disciples receive the "life" that Jesus promises. We for whom John's Gospel has become a normative (canonical) statement of the truth of our faith, must also conclude that the church today is still intimately linked with Jesus' life-giving message and mission.

"The relationship between Jesus and the one who sent him into the world is *the* central focus of his whole life and teaching. He urges us to see how he comes to us not on his own but sent and in relationship with God the Creator-Spirit. Following Jesus calls me to believe not only in the full communion between Jesus and the one who sent him but to believe in my communion with the one who sent me into the world."
—*HENRI J. M. NOUWEN*
Home Tonight: Further Reflections on the Parable of the Prodigal Son (2009)

As Christians we are commissioned as Christ's messengers to offer an alternative "word" for our world and provide a way of life different from others. Empowered by the Paraclete, we are called to be "words made flesh" and so bring light and life to our world. Like Jesus whom we must imitate, we are meant to be living parables of God. Though ordinary in every way, we become extraordinary through our faith. We become "signs" that both reveal God and evoke faith. As John demonstrates, true life is centered on Christ and we Christians believe that the key to true life is Jesus. He can teach us what true life is all about through his example of love and sacrifice.

We must also recognize that giving life does not simply happen by spouting abstract ideas and complicated theological principles. John recognized that God's mission will be accomplished first of all through a life lived in witness to God. Jesus enters fully into the everyday life of the people of his time. He performs his signs in the ordinary circumstances of wedding receptions, amid the crowds of sick at the pool of Bethesda, in the open fields of the countryside, on a boat trip across the Sea of Galilee, on the road where a blind beggar sat, and in the home of friends Martha and Mary and Lazarus. His signs, though extraordinary, occurred in familiar places. In fact, the signs were often missed by those who were closest to them because the bystanders perceived only the superficial results but did not really "see" what the sign pointed to.

Amidst the ordinariness of our lives, we are called upon as missionary disciples to point beyond the way the world is now to the way it could be through Jesus' influence. John stresses that we must work as Jesus did to bring about the abundance of life. This means that we must work to ensure that whatever is necessary for material life—security, food, water, shelter—is available for all. But as Christians we believe that the material is not all there is to life. There are further dimensions to genuine human life that must also be recognized and fostered—education, moral values, beauty, truth, love and the life of faith.

"We must find the effects of Jesus' cross and resurrection in the world, not just in our inner lives, nor in the Church. The way in which Jesus both declared the kingdom and lived in the freedom of the kingdom provides the model of what the Church is created to be. The Church is not the kingdom but, through the Spirit indwelling their fellowship, Christians live the kingdom life as men and women of the world. The mission of the Church, therefore, is to live the ordinary life of human beings in that extraordinary awareness of the other and self-sacrifice for the other which the Spirit gives."

—*JOHN V. TAYLOR*
The Go-Between God (2004)

The chain of messengers initiated by Jesus has not been broken during the long history of Christianity. We continue to struggle with our identity as Christians who have been sent into our world to offer an alternative to the false life we have created for ourselves. In our consumer society where life is measured by greed and self-indulgence, we offer another way. In our violent society where life is cheapened by depersonalization and indifference, we offer another way. Like Jesus we have been sent to proclaim God's message of self-sacrificing love in order to have life, and so have it more abundantly.

THE GOOD NEWS IN FOUR VERSIONS

Part 3
Good News
that Stays News

"The Gospel is the power which can transform the world! How can we profess faith in God's word, and then refuse to let it inspire and direct our thinking, our activity, our decisions, and our responsibilities to one another? Openness to the Lord—a willingness to let the Lord transform our lives—should produce a renewed spiritual and missionary vitality among Catholics. Jesus Christ is the answer to the question posed by every human life, and the love of Christ compels us to share that great good news with everyone."

—*POPE ST. JOHN PAUL II*
Make Room for the Mystery of God (1995)

FOLLOWING THE WAY OF DISCIPLESHIP

*Christian discipleship is the way we live out our relationship with God
and with others in the Christian community and in the world.
It follows the same general pattern of all personal relationships.*

1. CALL: Christian discipleship always begins with an experience of God [a free, mysterious divine self-revelation—God's grace poured into our hearts] through Jesus, a personal call or invitation to a relationship that is *our vocation*. Our whole life is lived as our response.

2. COMMITMENT: The absolutely essential foundation of our discipleship is the establishment of the bond (Lat: *fides)* of our personal relationship with God. This entails first our *trusting* acceptance (faith) of the gift of the one who calls and invites us into relationship, and secondly an *entrusting* of ourself to this mysterious other.

3. CO-MISSION: We live out our relationship with God by participation in Jesus' mission to create a community of disciples who would embody in themselves and their lives the right relationships to God and to one another, and thus realize God's dream for a community of justice, love and peace. Our co-mission is grounded in Jesus' commission to continue his earthly ministry by sharing in *the roles and their tasks* he performed to bring about God's kingdom:

- THE PROPHETIC / WITNESSING: to witness both in words and deeds, to announce the Good News of God's mysterious saving presence among us that is transforming all reality.
- THE PRIESTLY / SANCTIFYING: to consecrate the world to God by infusing all our actions and all the situations of our daily lives with God's sanctifying presence.
- THE KINGLY / ORDERING: to order all things and activities according to Jesus' vision and values and so bring about God's dream for a kingdom community based on justice, unified by love to produce peace for all.

4. CONVERSION: [Gk: *metanoia,* to change one's mind, outlook or attitude, Lat: *convertere,* to turn back around, or go in another direction] Our conscious decision to live more responsibly in the light of our faith relationship. This means the complex and dynamic process of *re-forming our self and our life* by turning toward God and away from the evil forces that dominate us and our social systems. It is a life-long challenge to align ourselves and our world with Jesus' kingdom worldview and live out the obligations [Lat: *ob-ligare,* what is done "on account of the bond"] of the new relationship in the community of disciples. The process of conversion follows three general phases:

1. INFORMATION: To follow Jesus, we must learn how he sees the world, understands its workings and evaluates it in relation to God's mysterious presence working for salvation, i.e., the right relationship of all reality to God.
2. CONFORMATION: Simply knowing about Jesus is never enough. We must assimilate and make our own the information that we acquire and want to apply it to our lives.
3. TRANSFORMATION: Information and conformation are incomplete unless these interior changes are translated into action, which gives us a new self-definition as a Christian disciple or follower of Jesus expressed in the practical way we live our lives.

5. COST: Living out our relationship with God and others will always cost us. Being disciples means paying this price in order to be like Jesus and carry on his work of community building and transforming the world into God's new creation.

CHAPTER NINE

Shaping a Gospel Spirituality
Discipleship, Conversion & Evangelization

"Come, follow me!" With this inviting command and commanding invitation, Jesus calls followers to a Christ-like life, to be as he is and to do as he does. The Jesus who invited his first disciples so long ago still extends that same invitation to us today when we encounter him and his world in and through the Gospels. They provide a way to live in a personal relationship with him and "see" the world anew from the viewpoint of God and Jesus. Accepting and living this new vision and vocation will open up a way that will lead us through death to new life with God forever.

"The Christian faith is, above all, conversion to Jesus Christ, full and sincere adherence to his person and the decision to walk in his footsteps. Faith is a personal encounter with Jesus Christ, making of oneself his disciple. This demands a permanent commitment to think like him, judge like him and live as he lived. In this way the believer unites himself or herself to the community of disciples and appropriates the faith of the Church."

—U. S. BISHOPS
General Directory for Catechesis, (1997) #53

Christian Discipleship

Christian discipleship is the way we live out our relationship with God and with others in the Christian community and in our world. Our spiritual lives as *Christ-ians* are patterned after the example of Jesus, *the Christ.* We strive to become like Jesus. As Paul described it, we put on the mind of Christ (Phil 2:5) and then are able to speak and act as he did. Our discipleship—our following Jesus—is a relationship that is based on seeing the world as he did (vision) and being the kind of person he was (vocation).

When Jesus invites us to follow him, he is inviting us into a relationship, which, like all relationships, has five basic stages. It begins with our response to Jesus' **call** or invitation to a relationship with him, which is expressed in our **commitment** both to him and to this relationship. Then we assume with him the **co-mission** of building the relationship together, which he identifies as the kingdom community. This will demand the life-long process of **conversion**, that is, making the necessary changes in our self and our behavior to adopt his vision of reality, his values, his goals, his roles and dedicate ourselves to realizing God's dream of transforming our world into a community of justice, love and peace. Because of the total investment of ourselves in this relationship, there will always be a **cost** for our involvement because of the resistance of our world to God's grace.

"What does it mean to become a Christian? It means at least this: to trust that, empowered, enabled, gifted and commanded by the Christ event of God, I can (because I must) attempt to risk a life like that disclosed in these gospel narratives. The gospel narratives of the message, actions and fate of Jesus of Nazareth are the primary story that the Christian learns to trust: to focus, confirm, correct, challenge, confront and transform my present questions, expectation, reflections on life and all my attempts to live a life worthy of the name 'human.'"

—*DAVID TRACY*
The Analogical Imagination: Christian Theology and the Culture of Pluralism (1981)

Living as a Christian disciple in relation to God is always a challenge. The discipleship relationship we commit ourselves to and the decision to live our life more responsibly in the light of that decision demand that we grow or transform ourselves into Christ. But growth as a disciple does not happen automatically but rather slowly, almost imperceptibly, through the power of God's Holy Spirit working in and through us.

Although we enter whole-heartedly into this relationship, nevertheless it is a challenge because when we adopt Jesus' worldview, then many things about who we are, how we have learned to think and act from our family, from our society, and even from the Church that we have grown up with, might have to be changed if we are going to live the Jesus way. As Jesus so aptly put it "unless a grain of wheat falls to the ground and dies, it remains just a grain of wheat; but if it dies, it produces much fruit" (Jn 12:24).

Physically, we begin to die from the moment we are born. Spiritually, we begin to die from the moment we make our faith commitment to be in a discipleship relationship with Christ and our conversion decision to live more responsibly. Being a disciple means being willing to die to our self,

GOOD NEWS THAT STAYS NEWS

our own "ego," our old vision of reality, our old values, our old behaviors in order to be transformed into Christ. To see the world the way Jesus does, to value it as Jesus does and to act in it as Jesus does will lead us inevitably to the cross as it does Jesus. But like Jesus, we must trust ourselves to God and believe that through our cross comes the new life of resurrection.

Spirituality: Faith Seeking Embodiment

To consider what is necessary to shape a discipleship spirituality, let us briefly consider what we mean by the term *spirituality*. If you are like me, when growing up, spirituality was not something that you created but something that was given or handed to you. Some famous saint or writer had produced it by writing a book about prayer or about how to live a spiritual life. You were expected to read the book, adopt its suggested method and practices of prayer and behavior, and that was your spirituality.

"We are summoned to be disciples, and so to a discipline. A disciple is a learner and his discipline is the training whereby one learns. To learn the way of the cross is the hardest thing of all, and the training by which we are to advance in this learning is provided for us by the discipline of prayer and worship. Those who disparage prayer and worship and imagine that without these one can achieve some kind of instant Christianity do not know what they are talking about. They understand neither the weakness of our humanity nor the depth of the richness of the spiritual maturity into which Christ is calling us."

—*JOHN MACQUARRIE*
Paths in Spirituality (1992)

But spirituality must be something more. The heart of our Christian reality is our experience of God in Christ through the Holy Spirit. Our personal and communal response to this central experience is faith, which has a theological dimension in which we use our minds to try to get some words (Gk: *logos*) to describe the God (Gk: *theos*) we encounter. In the long Christian tradition, theology has often been described as faith seeking understanding. What it searches for is concepts and ideas that are clear and distinct and as exhaustive and complete as we can achieve.

But we must not confuse theology with spirituality. Spirituality is always more than good ideas and can be described best as *faith seeking embodiment*. We have to practice what we believe, to live in a way that corresponds to what we believe. Thus spirituality requires not just having

237

good ideas about Christ, but also living a Christ-like life. It is our personal attempt to adopt the Christian worldview and put it into a lifestyle.

Another way of thinking about this is to recall that before the early Christians were known as Christians, they referred to themselves simply as followers of "the Way" (Acts 9:2; 18:25, 26; 19:9, 23; 24:14, 22). The Christian way is the way to God through Christ in the Holy Spirit. So spirituality is all about the way we get from where we first start to where we end. It is a way of seeing the world (our worldview) and a way of being in the world (our actions). We all have a way of seeing things and deciding what the reality of our world is. And from this understanding of the world, we also develop a way of being or lifestyle patterned upon how we understand the world. So spirituality is our own way of "putting on Christ" (Rom 13:14) and thus becoming and being a Christian.

Becoming a Christian Disciple

Becoming a disciple or follower of Jesus is not an inherited characteristic, like a genetic endowment or the capacity for sensation and for language that we are born with. And even though many of us are baptized as infants, becoming a Christian is a long and arduous journey that lasts a lifetime.

"We will never come to know our true vocation in life unless we are willing to grapple with the radical claim the gospel places on us—the call to follow Christ without compromise. Regardless of the particular shape we give to our lives, Jesus' call to discipleship is primal, all-encompassing, all-inclusive, demanding a total commitment. One cannot be a little bit for Christ, give him some attention, or make him just one of many concerns."

—HENRI J. M. NOUWEN
The Selfless Way of Christ (2007)

From the disciple's point of view, discipleship is a learning experience with three distinct stages: information, conformation and transformation. Attending to these stages as they are revealed in the biblical texts gives us both "clues" about who God is and how God is present in power to create a covenant community of friends, and "cues" about how we are to act in response to God's mysterious presence once we have discovered it.

Becoming a Christian disciple depends on assimilating Jesus' genuine Good News and the worldview it embodies. For this reason, it is necessary to consider carefully what Jesus' Good News is (information) so that we can assimilate it and make it our own (conformation) so that it can change us, our communities and our world (transformation).

1. Information

To follow Jesus by responding to his Good News message, we must learn how he sees the world, understands its workings and evaluates it in relation to God's mysterious presence working for salvation, i.e., the right relationship of all reality to God. We do this by our continual encounter with the Gospels, in which most of everything we know about Jesus is found.

This first stage requires attentiveness to both Jesus and his message. We must listen, observe, experience and understand reality the way Jesus does. Very often what Jesus says and does is puzzling and requires much effort to understand. His words seem to have too many meanings and his behavior can be strange and puzzling. But through continued effort we slowly become aware of a whole new way of understanding the meaning of our world and how our social relationships must be reconfigured.

2. Conformation

Simply knowing about Jesus from the Gospels is never enough. We must make our own the information we learn so we can see reality, evaluate it and act the way Jesus does. His vision and values and the behavior that follows from them must become our own.

This second stage of discipleship is characterized by the assimilation of a whole new outlook that depends upon our eagerness to imitate Jesus. When this new understanding of the world and his place in it becomes our own, when we are conformed to Jesus' worldview and adopt his values, then we will really be changed, which is the heart of the process of conversion.

3. Transformation

The phases of information and conformation are incomplete unless they are translated into action. This third stage of discipleship follows naturally upon the successful assimilation of our knowledge of Jesus' worldview. Since actions and behavior result from our attitudes and beliefs, this new worldview will lead naturally to new forms of behavior. The Gospels were written to evoke this response that leads us to a new way of life.

SHAPING A GOSPEL SPIRITUALITY

Changed by this new internal experience, we reenter the mainstream of everyday life. We find that our old patterns of living and relating that used to motivate our behavior are no longer relevant. Our job, our family, our neighborhood are still the same. It is us who are now radically changed. The ordinary is no longer ordinary because we now recognize that God is an integral and important part of our world. Our new perception generates a revised understanding, which in turn leads to new behaviors and alternative relationships and communities. The ordinary now becomes extraordinary. Reality indeed is more than meets the eye.

"When the story of Jesus is truly our story, when we have caught his fire, when his good news shapes our lives individually, as families and as a church, his influence will be felt far beyond our church."

—*U. S. BISHOPS*
"Go and Make Disciples" (1992)

Responding to Jesus' call and our faith commitment to him and to our relationship, though they may occasionally offer difficulties, are usually not the hardest challenges that we have to face. The main challenges arise from our attempt first to align our minds and hearts with Jesus' vision and values through life-long conversion, and secondly to share in the co-mission to continue his work of bringing mercy and justice to our world. Thus we must now explore further what is involved in the key discipleship challenges of conversion and evangelization and then indicate how we can shape our own personal discipleship spirituality using the Gospels as our guide.

The Challenge of Conversion

We live in a time when many people are bothered by God's absence. But the fact is that God's absence is not nearly as challenging or scary as God's presence. When God breaks into our lives we cannot remain in a business-as-usual mode. When, quite literally, all hell breaks lose with God's entry into our lives, we are challenged to change in ways we never dreamed possible. Jesus' Good News is that God's presence is unleashed in our world to do what it always does: transform us and our world.

Responding to God's powerful presence will require realigning our whole being so that we will continue to experience the world but now with

GOOD NEWS THAT STAYS NEWS

God as its center. Though apparently simple, this reordering is, in fact, so extraordinary that it brings about a total transformation of our lives. This constant transformation has been a part of Christianity from its very beginnings and is described as the experience of conversion, changing your mind and therefore reforming your whole life.

"We can only approach the kingdom of Christ by *metanoia*. This is a profound change of the whole person by which one begins to consider, judge and arrange one's life according to the holiness and love of God, made manifest in God's Son."
—The Roman Catholic *Rite of Penance*, #6

So when first confronting God's Good News, the key question is, What should we do? Jesus says "change your life (Gk: *metanoeite)* and believe in the good news" (Mk 1:15). Peter tells the Pentecost crowd, "change your lives (Gk: *metanoēsate),* and be baptized every one of you in the name of Jesus Christ so that your sins may be forgiven; and you will receive the gift of the Holy Spirit" (Acts 2:38). Clearly, then the first challenge is conversion: to reform, reshape and change your life around. How would our lives change if we really begin to hear Jesus message as Good News?

Conversion begins by accepting the truth of Jesus' kingdom message and worldview, then leads to changes in our values and actions. Becoming a Christian disciple demands more than just "knowing the catechism." It requires taking personal and communal responsibility for a whole new way of life that will have consequences for every dimension of our self—intellectual, affective, moral, social and spiritual. Understanding what these responsibilities demand is essential to our whole-life conversion.

Intellectual conversion demands that we take responsibility for the truth or falsity, the adequacy or inadequacy of our beliefs and convictions and their explanations. Because divine mysteries have been revealed to us, we must constantly grope for more suitable descriptions of these mysteries even though we know our human knowledge and theological formulas will never completely explain them. We can never think deeply or thoroughly enough about God's mystery and presence in our lives.

Affective conversion demands that we take responsibility for our emotional health and development. We change our accepted habits of feeling and intuitions. We must overcome the dysfunctions introduced by our previous emotional attitudes. We must reorganize our sensitivities to those who are suffering, oppressed, marginalized or devalued in any way, according to Christ's example. We must constantly discover ways to purge our emotions of anger and other destructive, aggressive and violent behaviors.

Moral conversion demands that we take responsibility for the correctness of our judgments and for the formation of our conscience. Identifying God as the center of our world shifts everything else in our value system. If we see the world as Jesus does, we must also value it as he does. Thus we discover and must embrace such kingdom values as non-domination, non-violence, justice, inclusiveness and service. It takes a lifetime of commitment to put these values into action. And as we all learn, knowing what is right is no guarantee that we will do what is right. Living a God-centered life is always a continual challenge.

Social conversion demands that we take responsibility for the structure and functioning of our communities. Our commitment to right relationships will bring us into conflict with the present systems that define our worlds and regulate our lives. We must realize God's kingdom not only in our individual lives but also in our families, our faith communities, our societies and our global systems, including the environment. Our challenge is to refashion our world in the image of Jesus' dream of God's kingdom.

"The kingdom of God is what life would be like on earth if God were king and the rulers of this world were not. It is about God's justice in contrast to the systemic injustice of the kingdoms and domination systems of this world. The kingdom of God is not about heaven; it is for the earth. To cite one of John Dominic Crossan's memorable serious quips: 'Heaven's in great shape; earth is where the problems are.'"

—*MARCUS J. BORG*
The Heart of Christianity (2009)

Spiritual conversion demands that we take responsibility for our response to God's self-revelation. Not only must we change our mistaken ideas about God, but we must also change our responses to God both in prayer and in our lives. As Christians we adopt a distinctive understanding of God as a trinity of persons in relation to one another and to us. When we live in light of a God-dominated reality, everything we do becomes a pursuit of God's presence and an endeavor to learn how to relate to God's mystery.

Discovering our new identity as Christian disciples changes everything. When we can let go of our old familiar worldview and live in this new reality that finds God's transcendent presence everywhere, life is forever changed. But although this reality reorders our lives, there is always a risk because we will have to change our perceptions of who we are, what we think and how we act. These do not change easily because they have become part of us and remain as remnants of our previous worldview through which we understood our world and guided our behavior.

The Challenge of Evangelization

For most of us, *evangelization* is a scary word that we usually associate with TV "evangelists" or foreign missionaries, not recognizing that evangelization or sharing of the gospel message, is an essential task for every Christian that is rooted in our fundamental Christian experience of the risen lord and the relationship that it creates. We cannot be Christians unless we accept our deepest Christian call or vocation to participate in the Christian mission of evangelization by sharing God's Good News with others.

"Evangelization happens when the word of Jesus speaks to people's hearts and minds. Needing no trickery or manipulation, evangelization can happen only when people accept the Gospel freely as the "good news" it is meant to be, because of the power of the Gospel message and the accompanying grace of God."

—*U. S. BISHOPS'*
"Go and Make Disciples" (1992)

Evangelization Begins with the Resurrection

If we look to the Gospels for some help in understanding our Christian vocation to share the Good News, we find that it is directly connected to the disciples' Easter experience of the risen Christ. The resurrection narratives in the Gospels illustrate the relationship between the risen Christ and the community of disciples. The disciples in these accounts continue to serve as examples for us. We are like them because we also live between the experience of the resurrection and Jesus' promised return in glory. Like them, we are called to continue the mission and ministry that Jesus began.

Each Gospel author has his own perspective on the events of the resurrection. They select and present those events to offer examples to their communities of how Christians ought to respond to their own experience of the risen Christ. As we study these passages, we discover the basic pattern guiding our Christian discipleship as the disciples move from an experience of the risen Christ to an understanding of its meaning and then to a response that expresses this meaning in their everyday lives.

> "We must stand before the world as a witness to the resurrection and life of the Lord Jesus and as a sign that God lives. As a body and individually, the laity must do their part to nourish the world with spiritual fruits and to spread abroad in it that spirit by which are animated those poor, meek, and peacemaking persons whom the Lord in the gospel calls blessed."
>
> —*VATICAN COUNCIL II*
> *Dogmatic Constitution on the Church (Lumen Gentium)* (1964), #38

Experiencing the Risen One

Every Christian is a Christian because in some way or other he or she has experienced the risen Christ. As the various resurrection narratives indicate, some experience Christ in a special bodily form. Others experience him through the witness in words and in the lives of others. Still others experience him in the sharing of a meal. But for each person, the experience of the risen Christ is always the essential starting point of Christian belief.

The resurrection narratives also reveal how hard it is to detect the risen one. Mary Magdalene mistakes him for a gardener (Jn 20:15). When Jesus appears to all the gathered disciples on Easter evening, they are alarmed and think he is a ghost (Lk 24:37). The two disciples on their way to Emmaus fail to recognize Jesus while he walks with them and only recognize him in the breaking of the bread at their meal (Lk 24:30-31).

Experience Demands Understanding

As the resurrection accounts in all the Gospels, especially Luke's, emphasize, the experience of the risen Christ as alive and active in our lives demands an interpretation. The "news" of the fact of the resurrection needs to be understood in order for its meaning or significance to become "good news" for us. Unless we discover its meaning, the resurrection remains simply a fact without any relevance for our lives.

Luke (24:1-9) describes how hard the first disciples had to struggle to understand what was happening. Their first experience was of the empty tomb. But since there might be many possible reasons why the tomb might be empty, the empty tomb itself proved nothing to them. The "what" was clear, the "why" was the real problem. It was just a fact until they could understand its significance.

"No one was an eyewitness to Christ's resurrection and no evangelist describes it. No one can say how it came about physically. Still less was its innermost essence, his passing over to another life, perceptible to the senses. Although the resurrection was an historical event that could be verified by the sign of the empty tomb and by the reality of the apostles' encounters with the risen Christ, still it remains at the very heart of the mystery of faith as something that transcends and surpasses history."
—*Catechism of the Catholic Church* (2000), #647

The women who discovered the empty tomb were completely puzzled. They received guidance for their interpretation from two men in brilliant clothes who announced that their quest for Jesus in the tomb was misguided. They should look for him among the living. These messengers then recall Jesus' statements about his crucifixion and resurrection. With this clue to the meaning of the empty tomb, the women understand Jesus' words and rush off to announce their Good News to the eleven disciples.

But Luke indicates that the empty tomb continued to be more a puzzle than a clue. When the women tell Peter and the other disciples about finding it empty, they then run to the tomb. Peter experiences the tomb, but does not understand what it means. There are no angels helping him and the women's testimony is not convincing enough. He is utterly baffled. There is nothing to the empty tomb except emptiness. It does not immediately lead Peter to faith (Lk 24:12; Jn 20:6-9) because he does not yet have the eyes of faith to see beyond the signs. Only with an experience of the risen Christ will he understand and see more than the emptiness.

Or take the case of the two despondent disciples traveling to Emmaus who also have a problem understanding the meaning of all the events that they had witnessed. They tried to use their knowledge of Scriptures to supply some context to make sense out of the nonsense of Jesus' death. But like so many others then and since, they have the words of Scripture, but they fail to understand their meaning.

So Jesus, the mysterious unrecognized stranger who walks with them,

SHAPING A GOSPEL SPIRITUALITY

teaches how to read and interpret the meaning of the Scriptures. He goes back through the whole Old Testament and explains the meaning of all the passages about the messiah. When understood correctly, they show that he had to suffer, i.e., that this was God's own plan for bringing about the right relationship with God and others that had begun with Abraham.

Like those disciples, we too must learn to read and interpret the meaning of the Scripture so that we can discover and recognize God's plan now working in our lives. Reading and studying the Scriptures does not simply give us an experience of the risen Christ but gives us clues about how God has broken into our world in the past and how we might expect God to do it again. Without the guidance of Scripture, it can be extremely difficult to detect the presence and activity of God at work in our world.

Understanding Leads to Action

The resurrection narratives also show us that our Christian lives never just stop when we have understood the significance of our experience of the risen Christ. Curiously enough, whenever we try to hold on to Christ like Mary Magdalene did (Jn 20:17) or delight in the enjoyment of his presence (like the disciples at the ascension, Acts 1:9-11), he reminds us (as God did in the initial covenant-defining call and vocation of Abraham, Gen 12:1-3) that we must let go and go forth and become witnesses to what we have experienced so that we can bring God's blessing and new life to all nations.

"Evangelism is an activity of transformed consciousness that results in an altered perception of world, neighbor, and self, and an authorization to live differently in that world. The news that God has triumphed means that a transformed life, i.e., one changed by hearing of the news, works to bring more and more of life, personal and public, under the rule of this world-transforming, slave-liberating, covenant-making, promise-keeping, justice-commanding God."

—*WALTER BRUEGGEMANN*
Biblical Perspectives on Evangelism (1993)

The disciples journeying to Emmaus also discover this. After their heart-warming conversation with the mysterious stranger, they finally recognize his identity in the breaking of the bread. Then suddenly, "he vanished from their sight" (Lk 24:31). Despite their astonishment, they immediately set out to share their experience with the other disciples, only to

GOOD NEWS THAT STAYS NEWS

find out that Christ has already appeared to the other disciples too.

The emerging pattern is clear. When we understand our experience of the risen Christ, sharing this Good News—evangelization—follows. Christian discipleship is incomplete until we share our belief and become, as Pope Francis likes to say, "missionary disciples."

"The disciple, founded upon the rock of God's word, feels driven to bring the Good News of salvation to his brothers and sisters. Discipleship and mission are like the two sides of a single coin: when the disciple is in love with Christ, he cannot stop proclaiming to the world that only in him do we find salvation (cf. Acts 4:12). In effect, the disciple knows that without Christ there is no light, no hope, no love, no future."

—POPE BENEDICT XVI
Inaugural Address to Latin American Bishops, (May 13, 2007), #3

Both Matthew and Luke recognized this by portraying the risen Jesus as officially commissioning the disciples with the task of evangelization. Matthew ends his Gospel with Jesus sending the disciples to *"disciplize* all nations" (Mt 28:18-20). Luke describes how on the first Easter evening, the risen Christ declares to the gathered community of disciples that the Good News of the forgiveness of sins is "to be preached to all the nations, beginning in Jerusalem. You are witnesses to this" (Lk 24:47-48). In Acts, Luke then shows how the early community of disciples carried out this task.

The Task Remains the Same Today

As we read the resurrection narratives and Acts of the Apostles, we discover that their story and our story connect. Since we are the continuation of that community of disciples, we also are commissioned to spread the Good News. Without evangelization, our Christian experience is incomplete.

Good news is always for sharing. When the risen Christ becomes a deeper reality in our self and our community, no one really has to tell us to share it. As individuals, we are so filled Christ that we begin to see the world the way he did and act in it as he would. We become Christ's presence to our world. Our evangelization starts with our own example. As St. Francis of Assisi said, "We must preach with our lives, and use words if we have to."

But this is not simply an individual task. We can be Christians only if we are joined to the whole community of believers who share the experience and understanding of the risen Christ. Our baptism is the public sign of belonging to this community of disciples and fulfilling Jesus' commission to share his mission and ministry. As communities, we begin to live as the kingdom community that Christ envisioned. We must dare to create communities based on justice and right relationships, based on love and respect for each person as a beloved child of God, which leads to harmony and peace. A community like this will stand as a witness against the communities of our world that are based on unjust dominations of one group over another, held together by violence and in constant conflict.

"In calling his own to follow him, Jesus gives them a very precise mandate: to proclaim the gospel of the kingdom to all nations. Hence, every disciple is missionary, for Jesus makes him participate in his mission, while also binding him to himself as friend and brother. Thus, as he is witness to the mystery of the Father, so the disciples are witnesses to the Lord's death and resurrection until he returns. Fulfilling this duty is not an optional task, but an integral part of Christian identity, because it is the witnessing extension of the calling itself."

—*LATIN AMERICAN BISHOPS (CELAM)*
Fifth General Conference (Aparecida, Brazil, 2007), #144

So our evangelization begins when we are changed by our contact with the risen Christ. The power of the resurrection is that Christ transforms us through the power of the Holy Spirit into himself. As individuals and communities, we become the body of Christ, to be taken, blessed, broken and shared so that a world might live. We become Christs for others and our selves and our lives become the gospel that people can most easily read.

Resources for a Discipleship Spirituality: Four Ways to Follow Jesus

As we have learned in our examination of the four Gospels, they were invented to help Christians find and shape their own identity and to know what it meant to be a Christian in a world that was not yet influenced by Christian beliefs or values. They portrayed Jesus in such a way that his words and deeds became the primary example of Christian living and so indicated ways for their communities to faithfully follow Jesus in the daily situations in which they found themselves.

Because each author wrote his Gospel to respond to the challenges and needs of his own community, we have four different portraits of Jesus. But like every portrait, how Jesus is presented is shaped by both the author's perception and audience's needs. Just as a portrait artist chooses certain details to express the inner character and personality of the person being painted, so each evangelist emphasized different aspects of Jesus' personality. Just as their portraits of Jesus shaped the contours of their ways of discipleship, so our understanding of Jesus will guide our way of discipleship. Luckily for us, there are four portraits of Jesus to choose from. Since we can shape our way of discipleship using all these portraits, our personal style will probably include some aspects from each one.

So if we want to know what is necessary to be followers of Jesus in our world with all its modern complexity, we must first examine the Gospels to discover the basics of our Christian faith—who Jesus was, what he said and did, and how we can build a relationship with him in a community of those who accept his message and try to live by it.

"The study of the sacred Scriptures must be a door opened to every believer. It is essential that the revealed word radically enrich our catechesis and all our efforts to pass on the faith. Evangelization demands familiarity with God's word which calls for a serious, ongoing study of the Bible, while encouraging its prayerful individual and communal reading. Let us receive the sublime treasure of the revealed word."

—*POPE FRANCIS*
The Joy of the Gospel (2013), #175

Moreover, our way of discipleship must relate to our experience of being a Christian in today's world. Although the world has changed greatly since the time of Jesus and the early Christians, the fundamental challenges they experienced still exist for us today as we face the challenge of proclaiming God's Good News. In a changing world of powerful domination and exploitation, Mark challenges us to a way of service and self-denial that will always cost us dearly. In a world of indifference and unconcern, Matthew challenges us to a way of compassionate instruction that discovers God as our mysterious companion—"when did we see you hungry, thirsty, a stranger, naked or in prison?" (Mt 25:37-40). In a world of political, racial, economic, social, geographical and religious divisions, Luke challenges us to a way of reconciling witness that breaks through the boundaries we find. In a world of hatred and lonely isolation, John challenges us to a way of familiar friendship in community with God and others.

Following Mark's "Suffering Servant"

Recall that Mark portrays Jesus as the suffering messiah. Mark's model of discipleship is one of suffering service, which has been especially prominent in times of religious anxiety and persecution. We should think of those who are willing to give their lives for others and for the cause of justice. In our own lives, suffering service is an essential part of family life and parenting.

> "Jesus' choice of suffering servanthood rather than violent lordship, of love to the point of death rather than righteousness backed by power was the fundamental direction of his life."
>
> —*JOHN HOWARD YODER*
> *The Politics of Jesus* (1994)

The demand of constant care is the sacrifice parents must make. In the first few years of life, mothers especially sacrifice sleep, time, energy and their own health so that their child might grow. Parents continue to sacrifice to provide what their children need. For any family to make it through the years, not only the parents but each member must be ready to make sacrifices, to give in sometimes, and to help one another.

Following Matthew's "Compassionate Teacher"

Matthew presents Jesus as the master, a teacher and compassionate healer who guides us step by step through a course in Christian discipleship. The risen Christ tells the disciples that their task in the world is to "*disciplize* all nations" (Mt 28:18-20) and they can use this Gospel to teach the way of discipleship as Jesus had taught them. Being a disciple means carrying on Jesus' ministry, becoming a master of the Christian Way and sharing what we learn with others so that they can also become Jesus' followers.

> "Christ is the Teacher who reveals God to us and us to ourselves, the Teacher who saves, sanctifies and guides, who lives, who speaks, rouses, moves, redresses, judges, forgives, and goes with us day by day on the path of history, the Teacher who comes and will come in glory."
>
> —*POPE JOHN PAUL II*
> *Catechesis in Our Time (Catechesi Tradendae)* (1979), #9

Compassionate teaching makes the Church's doctrines understandable so that others can grow in faith. It is also an essential part of parenting. The

GOOD NEWS THAT STAYS NEWS

Church reminds parents that they are the primary religious educators of their children. Like Matthew's Jesus, their compassionate teaching occurs not only when children ask questions about Catholic beliefs, but also when the parents communicate Christian values by their own behavior. Children assimilate their Christian worldview and its life-sense from their parents.

Following Luke's "Healing Witness"

Luke portrays Jesus as a healing-saving prophet who wants "to seek and to save what is lost" (19:10), thus challenging us as disciples to reach out beyond our narrow and comfortable borders to seek and save those who need help. As is more clear in Acts, God's kingdom will come through the disciples' Spirit-filled witness (1:8) to the ends of the earth. They will witness not only with their words but even more with their lives. Being a Christian demands fearless witness and a shattering of the borders between Jew and Gentile to build a new community in Christ.

"Each of us should find ways to communicate Jesus wherever we are. All of us are called to offer others an explicit witness to the saving love of the Lord, who despite our imperfections offers us his closeness, his word and his strength, and gives meaning to our lives."

—POPE FRANCIS
The Joy of the Gospel (2013), #121

When we think of Lukan discipleship, we ought to think of the many prophetic people who have called our attention to the oppression, hatred and violence that plague our society, and also those who have tried to break the boundaries that separate us. In our families, there are so many things that can go wrong— inadequate parenting, abusive and dysfunctional relationships, divorce, sickness, addictive behaviors, suicide, tragic accidents, the list goes on and on. Healing witness is a constant need. Each of us is challenged to cross the boundaries of our own comfort zone to reconcile and be reconciled with others. To admit our mistakes, to say we are sorry, to forgive and be forgiven are Christian behaviors that have to be part of any family's everyday life.

Following John's "Loving Friend"

John portrays Jesus as God's son sent for salvation, the manifestation of

SHAPING A GOSPEL SPIRITUALITY

God's mysterious presence in our midst, who sends his Spirit to be with us to continue his work. As disciples, we are no longer merely followers, but "friends" (15:15) who share his Holy Spirit, his sonship and his mission. Empowered by the Holy Spirit, we are God's children sent into the world like Jesus was for its salvation. We are to love as Jesus has loved us—a love that is not only intimate but which gives everything for the beloved. Jesus' death is the ultimate sign of his love.

When we think of Johannine discipleship, we find ecumenists who have been inspired by the Johannine view to build a community in which "all might be one" (17:21) and spiritual writers and mystics who have encouraged us to become closer "friends" with Jesus through prayer. John's ideal of loving friendship can help us create renewed experiences of Christian community in which people really know one another, pray together and reach out to others through their witness and concern.

"Love is the only force capable of transforming an enemy into a friend."
—*REV. MARTIN LUTHER KING, JR.*
Strength to Love (1963)

Beginning first with our own families, we need to learn about Jesus, pray together and work for justice. Our family experience of Christian community can then become the basis for a renewed experience of parish community. In particular, our parish life must include not only a prayerful participation in worship but also involvement in the Church's work to evangelize our culture and bring about a more just and peaceful world.

Shaping Our Own Way of Discipleship

If as we discovered, Christianity is "The Way" to God through Jesus Christ in the Holy Spirit, then spirituality must be our own way of becoming and being a Christian. What Matthew, Luke and John did to Mark's Gospel is what we are still doing to the Gospels. We use their message to discover the solutions for our problems today.

Each of us shapes our own gospel by selecting from all four Gospels the words and deeds of Jesus that we find most important because of our situation, our emphases—what we need Jesus to be an example of—and for following his path to God. Thus the Good News in four versions becomes the Good News in many, many more. (For directions on how to create your own Gospel, see below, pp. 274-276.) How providential it is that we have four versions rather than merely one! And how interesting it is to trace the uniqueness of each version and recognize the different theologies and community responses to Jesus that are available to us today.

Reading and studying the Gospels then is a chance to think about our own spirituality by seeing it against the spiritualities offered by the Gospel writers. We can then choose from the Gospels whatever we need to grow and transform our Christian life from our old ways of seeing and old ways of being into Jesus' new way of seeing and being in the world.

"Action on behalf of justice and participation in the transformation of the world fully appear to us as a constitutive dimension of the preaching of the Gospel, or, in other words, of the Church's mission for the redemption of the human race and its liberation from every oppressive situation."

—*THE SYNOD OF CATHOLIC BISHOPS*
"Justice in the World" (1971)

As catechists, we also need to become familiar with these Gospels and what they communicate about Jesus, not just for our teaching and for our students, but even more for ourselves. As Pope John Paul II reminded us, following Christ requires "learning more and more within the Church to think like him, to judge like him, to act in conformity with his commandments, and to hope as he invites us to" *(Catechesis in Our Time, #20)*.

Faithful Following Today

Encountering the Gospels helps us discover that God is always present in our life and eager to enter a relationship. God has called us so that we can live a fuller and more spiritual life. Although following this spiritual path can often make us anxious, it is essential if we are to meet God.

Through our encounter with the Gospels we will be transformed in a way that will certainly surprise us and probably scare us too. To see the world the way Jesus does, to value it as he does and to act in it as he does will lead us into a new relationship with God. This is the risk we all face when we say "yes" to God. Living in a relationship with God is always a challenge. Engaging with the Gospels invites us to encounter a divinely charged reality that always involves more than we can imagine or comfort-

SHAPING A GOSPEL SPIRITUALITY

ably manage in our present circumstances. Touching the divine transforms us forever. Can we let ourself be drawn in directions we would never choose and be transformed by our journey? There is no way to meet Jesus and ever be the same again.

The bottom line is that there is not just one way and certainly no easy way to follow Jesus. We often want our discipleship to be characterized by our keeping control over our lives, by comfortable service, by fixed boundaries and by easy access to God. But Jesus reminds us that his way is often difficult and hard (Mt 7:14). Any way we choose to follow Jesus will demand suffering service, compassionate disciplizing, healing witness and loving friendship that we can be sure will be tested daily.

"All evangelization is based on the Word of God—listened to, meditated upon, lived, celebrated and witnessed to. The sacred Scriptures are the very source of evangelization. Consequently, we need to be constantly trained in hearing the word. The Church does not evangelize unless she constantly lets herself be evangelized. It is indispensable that the word of God be ever more fully at the heart of every ecclesial activity."

—*POPE FRANCIS*
The Joy of the Gospel (2013), #174

As Christian missionary disciples, our challenge is to refashion our world in the image of Jesus' dream of the kingdom of God. When Jesus' kingdom worldview is adopted and lived, "all things will be made new" (Rev 21:5). Domination will become service, sovereignty will become compassion, weakness will become strength, foolishness will become wisdom, suffering will become well-being, despair will become hope, vulnerability will become power and death will become new life.

CHAPTER TEN

Working on God's Word
Reading & Studying the Gospels

In all my years of teaching the Bible to adults, the one constant certainty was this: As we work on God's Word, God's Word works on us. For the catechist who wants to continue his or her understanding and appropriation of the Gospels, here are some suggestions of further resources that might be helpful. My criteria is that they be user-friendly, blending solid and accurate scholarship with readability. Of course there are many other books and resources that you will discover for yourself, and even these recommendations will lead you to other new and exciting discoveries. [For a large and extremely fine collection of materials available online see Electronic New Testament Educational Resources (E.N.T.E.R.) provided by Fr. Felix Just, SJ, at *catholic-resources.org/Bible/index.html*].

"Learning to read the gospel, and to connect it to one's life, is a central activity in the Christian life, from beginning to end. It is in a sense the foundation of the entire Church, for this is where we hear of Jesus of Nazareth, of his conversations with his disciples and others, of his life, death and resurrection. We never stop trying to tune ourselves to the gospel, to learn from it. This is a challenge for a whole life."

—JAMES BOYD WHITE
Connecting to the Gospel (2010)

The marvel of the Gospels is that they always outrun our attempts to control the truth they express and our certainty that we know how to discover that truth. Our goal as readers is not to become experts, but to become more competent readers who can read the Gospels carefully and with ever increasing sensitivity. The more you know about the Gospels and how to read them, the better you will understand God's message of Good News and be able to make it the foundation of your Christian life.

Gospel reading, and the personal relationship with God and others that it nourishes, can be the most fascinating, most rewarding and sometimes even the most frustrating experience you will ever have. The Gospels are full of surprises. We can never assume that we have exhausted the divinely revealed mysteries found in them. Whatever you think you know about God and about Christ is never the full answer because being in a relationship with someone else is a never-ending surprise both about the other person and yourself.

When people share with one another what they are discovering in their encounters with the Gospels, it becomes clear that the texts are full of endless meanings and applications. One reason for this is that the Bible's divinely revealed realities can never be fully fathomed by our human minds. The Bible's truth is not the truth of a proposition but the truth of a person. Thus the Biblical text not only illuminates us, guides us and helps us but it also challenges us and calls into question who we are and how we live in relation to God and others.

Another reason for different interpretations is that meanings change when contexts do. When your reading situation or your personal needs change, your discoveries in the Gospels will change too. Learning to use the Gospels demands the skills of reading, interpretation and application. Moreover, as our lives change, we will need to use these skills to apply the Bible to our relationship to God and to other people.

So enter into the Gospel's world to encounter Jesus and be changed as you respond to his challenges. And when what you read makes you feel uncomfortable, you can be sure that this is a sign from God about where you need to grow in following Jesus and adopting his kingdom worldview.

Reading the Gospels

The Gospels were written to be read, and can be read for many different reasons and in a variety of contexts. New questions about the Gospels are always being asked and new approaches to the text are always being explored. It will take the lifetime of the Church to understand the Gospels completely. As you begin your encounter with the Gospels, your first task is to read the four Gospels themselves. The brief Reading Guides in chapters 5–8 can help with this. Despite various arguments to the contrary, these Gospels are still the most reliable reports about who Jesus was and what he did.

Before any detailed study, you should just read the Gospel right through as though it were a modern short story or a novel. Don't get bogged down in all the details but just appreciate the drama and sweep of the whole story, without stopping to explore puzzling passages or checking out information in the footnotes. In a way this is more like the experience of the original hearers and the readers of the Gospels, many of whom could only listen to the story and even those who could read had no footnotes. Their only commentary came from teachers in the community and shared conversations with other community members about the meaning of what they heard and learned about Jesus.

"First of all, we need to be sure that we understand the meaning of the words we read. I want to insist here on something which may seem obvious, but which is not always taken into account: the biblical text which we study is two or three thousand years old; its language is very different from that which we speak today. Even if we think we understand the words translated into our own language, this does not mean that we correctly understand what the sacred author wished to say."

—*POPE FRANCIS*
The Joy of the Gospel (2013), #147

Which Bible Translation to Use?

The first requirement for reading and studying the Gospels is a good Bible translation. Bible translations come in a great variety not only of bindings, sizes and costs but also of styles of translation. Some try to be very exact in their word for word correspondence, while others attempt to translate the authors' thought rather than their exact words. Some digest certain passages and eliminate others. Many Bibles provide helpful notes to aid the reader, while others have minimal notes or no notes at all.

Probably the most commonly asked question of Bible readers is: which Bible translation is best? But best for what? The answer hinges on why you want to use the Bible. Bibles can be read for a variety of reasons—for personal reading, for study, for private prayer or for public reading during community worship. Your reasons for reading the Bible can help you to determine which translation you might find most suitable.

Remember that since languages never correspond exactly with one another, every translation is to some extent also an interpretation of the

WORKING ON GOD'S WORD

Bible's meaning. Readers should compare one or more translations to recognize the different ways that scholars have attempted to express the original meaning of the Bible in a modern way. You might find it helpful to compare one or two Bibles to determine which one you prefer. (For more about the variety of biblical translations, see my *Catechist's Guide to Reading Your Bible* for information about their history, pp. 67-78, and pp. 89-99 for brief descriptions of several modern translations.)

A SPECTRUM OF BIBLE TRANSLATIONS

One way to get some idea of the variety of biblical versions that result from the different scholarly theories and methods that guide biblical translations is to show the different types on a spectrum that illustrates the translation styles. You can quickly access and compare most of these translations online at *BibleGateway.com*.

Very accurate but not very readable
- *King James Version (KJV)*
- *New King James Version (NKJV)*
- *New American Standard Bible (NASB)*

Accurate and readable
(formal equivalent—a word-for-word emphasis)
- *Revised Standard Version (RSV)*
- *New Revised Standard Version (NRSV)*
- *New American Bible Revised Version (NABRE)*

Accurate and readable
(dynamic equivalent—a thought-for-thought emphasis)
- *The Common English Bible (CEB)*
- *New Jerusalem Bible (NJB)*
- *New International Version (NIV)*
- *The Good News Translation (GNT)*
- *Revised English Bible (REB)*
- *The NET Bible (NET)*
- *The Kingdom New Testament (N. T. Wright)*

Very readable, but not very literal
- *The Message (MSG)*
- *New Living Translation (NLT)*

Paraphrase
- *The Living Bible (TLB)*

The Catholic *New Jerusalem Bible* (NJB, 1985) is not available on Bible Gateway but can be found at Catholic Online *(catholic.org/bible/)*. The *New American Bible Revised Version (NABRE)* is also available at the US Bishops' website *(nccbuscc.org/bible/)*, which also provides the daily scripture readings used at Mass taken from the older NAB because the liturgy readings in the lectionary do not yet use the NABRE translation.

For personal reading, use a translation that is readable and accessible. Beginning to read the Gospels can be a challenge. Often for our personal reading we want to experience the biblical text in a way that grabs us or speaks to us in language that is familiar to us. Using a translation that tries to make the reading easier is often a good way to start. Bibles that are guided by the philosophy of thought-for-thought translation (dynamic equivalence) are in general more suitable for personal reading.

By using popular translations like the *Common English Bible*, the *New Jerusalem Bible, Today's New International Version*, the *Good News Translation*, the *New Living Translation* or the *Revised English Bible*, you will gain an introduction to the story and the message of the Gospels in language that strives to make the text more accessible and reader-friendly.

Two other modern translations try to give a feel for the everyday style of the language of the ancient biblical texts. The first is *The Kingdom New Testament: A Contemporary Translation* (HarperCollins, 2011) by the world-renowned biblical scholar N. T. Wright. This translation is not only contemporary but also very readable. Wright also uses this translation in his excellent and helpful series of introductory commentaries called *The New Testament for Everyone* (18 volumes, Westminster /John Knox Press, 2004–11), which unites high-level scholarship with popular applications as he guides us through each New Testament book passage by passage.

The second translation is *The Message: The Bible in Contemporary Language* (NavPress 1993, 2002) by Eugene Peterson (now available in a Catholic version from ACTA Publications, 2013, that includes all of the books arranged in the Catholic Bible's order). Peterson's earthy and force-ful translation helps us sense the impact that the Gospels and letters might have had on their first century listeners. But the danger in converting "the tone, the rhythm, the events, the ideas, into the way we actually think and speak" is that we no longer get the actual words of the ancient authors. Reading Peterson is a treat, but it is best done in conjunction with a translation that strives for more word for word accuracy (formal equivalence).

For Bible study, use a translation that is reliable and accurate.
The best Bible for study is one that gives verbal accuracy in translation and provides scholarly notes to help with difficult passages. *The New American Bible Revised Version* and the *New Revised Standard Version*, which put more emphasis on the formal-equivalence theory of translation, are most helpful for careful study because they focus on the author's own words.

They also allow the reader to get a flavor of the grammatical syntax and sentence structure of the original text. Since these Bibles strive to represent as accurately as possible what the author said, they can convey the obscurity and the sometimes awkward or complicated expression of the original author. Where the original text is unclear, as in several sections of Paul's letters, this can be conveyed and not simply glossed over by presenting what someone thinks the author was trying to say.

Using a Good Study Bible

To respond to the growing interest in Bible study, many publishers now have special editions of the Bible that include many of the helps that beginners will find helpful. If you are going to purchase a new Bible, you might consider one of these study Bibles as a way to get both a modern translation and some convenient study helps such as maps, historical and literary backgrounds on each book, extensive notes and application helps, and perhaps a glossary or a brief dictionary of important terms.

A very good investment for the serious Bible reader would be one of these two excellent study Bibles: the *Oxford Catholic Study Bible* (rev. ed., 2011) or the *Little Rock Catholic Study Bible* (Liturgical Press, 2011). Both include the *New American Bible Revised Edition* (NABRE) as well as background articles and helpful reading guides for every book of the Bible. Although it costs a bit more, you might consider purchasing the hardbound edition, which will last longer despite abundant use. Another option might be the *HarperCollins Study Bible* (rev. ed., 2006) which includes the *New Revised Standard Version* (NRSV) translation and excellent notes by an ecumenical group of biblical scholars including several Catholics. Many other study Bibles use other Bible translations so check to see which one is used.

Methods & Approaches for Studying the Gospels

Reading the Gospels is just the first step toward making their message your own. But reading always leads to studying the Gospels in greater detail, and your study of the Gospels will take you on your own path, guided mostly by what you want to learn more about. As we noted in considering the three worlds of the text in the introduction, our approach to the Gospels at any time will vary because of what we want to learn. This is also true of scripture scholars, and so many different approaches and corresponding methods have been developed to mine the riches of the Gospels.

"People have been reading the Scriptures for centuries without the benefit of scholarly preparation. There are nevertheless good reasons to study the Bible. We do so to enlarge our imaginations. We are all limited by culture, language, gender and class. Our relationship to others must respect their otherness. We need to be prepared to learn things we did not know, to be surprised in a variety of ways. We study the Bible and its historical and linguistic environment so as to make reading a richer experience or to adjudicate our serious differences of opinion."

—*DONALD H. JUEL*
A Master of Surprise: Mark Interpreted (1994)

Methods for discovering the many different meanings of the Gospels are related to the various questions that curious and competent readers ask. Each method or set of questions arises to solve satisfactorily the specific questions that readers can ask of the text. Usually they are provoked by an awareness of the strangeness or otherness of the text (e.g., texts from 20 to 30 centuries ago, in languages not ours, reflecting historical, social and religious ideas that we are not familiar with). The "gaps" created by these distances of the texts from our situation demand a way to get from "here" to "there"—which is exactly what a "method" is. (For more on how scholars help us close the "gaps" opened by language, history, culture and meaning see my *Catechist's Guide to Reading Your Bible*, pp. 149-156.)

The word *method* comes from the Greek and is a combination of the preposition *meta* meaning across, and the word *hodos* meaning a road or a way. Methods then are the way by which we can traverse or get across the

WORKING ON GOD'S WORD

strangeness which stands in the way of our reading and understanding the scriptures. The many methods we can use are the careful formalization of the ways that readers have found to question the texts they are trying to understand and find the answers they need for their lives.

"Catholic exegesis does not claim any particular scientific method as its own. It recognizes that one of the aspects of biblical texts is that they are the work of human authors, who employed both their own capacities for expression and the means which their age and social context put at their disposal. Consequently, Catholic exegesis freely makes use of the scientific methods and approaches which allow a better grasp of the meaning of texts in their linguistic, literary, socio-cultural, religious and historical contexts, while explaining them as well through studying their sources and attending to the personality of each author."

—*PONTIFICAL BIBLICAL COMMISSION*
The Interpretation of the Bible in the Church (1993), III

In general, the need for methods is related to our beliefs about the character and specific messages that we expect to find in our sacred texts. As sacred, we recognize that God assisted in their production, i.e., the texts arise by inspiration not dictation. We cannot know exactly what happened psychologically in the human authors' minds, but we do know God was at work. (If you find this strange, think for a minute about our belief that God is present in us through the Holy Spirit by actual grace, i.e., enlightening our minds and strengthening our wills to do good and avoid evil. We believe *that* it happens even though we find it very difficult to explain exactly *how* it does.) Our belief in the inspiration of scripture is a theological belief, not a psychological explanation.

The result is that the books we consider normative (canonical) as Catholics, are a thoroughly mysterious amalgamation of both divine and human elements. When we examine them, we will find that the full meaning of scripture will encompass what both of the divine and human authors intended to communicate. This belief stands behind the age-old practice of seeking not only the literal meaning which the human authors intended, but also the mysterious spiritual meaning which God intended for our salvation. Thus a Catholic approach for the interpretation of scripture must attend to both of these dimensions if it is to be successful.

GOOD NEWS THAT STAYS NEWS

(For more on the specifically Catholic approach to interpreting the Bible, see my *Catechist's Guide to Reading Your Bible,* pp. 43-50.) However, specific methods must also be devised to lift out from the text all the various dimensions of meaning that we wish to discover. The Bible is a treasury which has something in it for everyone.

As a written text, the Bible works like any book. It is a human composition by an author for an audience in a particular place and time that somehow satisfies what they want to know. It must be read and interpreted by using the various methods that careful and capable readers have devised. The biblical texts demand that we use all our skill to read and interpret properly the meanings inscribed within them. Reading and interpreting ancient texts also demand special attention to their textual, historical, literary and sociopolitical issues. To read texts adequately, we must consider all of these historical and critical factors.

One good way to familiarize yourself with these various methods and approaches is to read the Catholic Biblical Commission's 1994 *The Interpretation of the Bible in the Church* (which is available online at *catholic-resources.org/ChurchDocs/PBC_Interp-FullText.htm*). See especially, **Section 1: Methods and Approaches for Interpretation,** which explains:

(1) The Principles of the Historical-Critical Method

(2) New Methods of Literary Analysis *(Rhetorical, Narrative, Semiotic)*

(3) Approaches Based on Tradition *(Canonical, Jewish Traditions of Interpretation, and the History of the Influence of the Text)*

(4) Approaches That Use the Human Sciences *(Sociology, Cultural Anthropology, Psychology and Psychoanalysis)*

(5) Contextual Approaches *(Liberationist, Feminist)*

(6) Fundamentalist Interpretation.

We now know that for an adequate reading or interpretation of a text, we need a method to first understand the historical and cultural situation of the original author and his audience. This method, called the historical-critical method, searches for what the text meant in its original situation. Only through using this method can we hope to bridge the chasm that separates the ancient historical and cultural world of the author and the modern technological and cultural world of today's readers.

The historical-critical method is **historical** because it attempts to understand the meaning of ancient texts in their original context, i.e., in relation to the historical, social and literary situation in which they originated. It is **critical** because it compares and analyzes in order to arrive at historical and literary judgments about its results.

The historical-critical method was first devised especially for reading ancient texts. It is based on the principle that any adequate reading demands attention first to historical issues—who (author) addresses whom (audience) in what circumstances (situation)—and then to issues of literary criticism—in what way (form) with what message (content) for what reason (function). These six basic questions structure the historical-critical method and contribute to its primary goal of learning what the text meant to its author and its first readers.

Most scholarly commentaries follow this essential historical-critical method but, as the Catholic Biblical Commission's *The Interpretation of the Bible in the Church* illustrates, there many other methods and ways to approach the study of the Gospels. An interesting example of several of these other approaches in action is found in *Mark & Method: New Approaches in Biblical Studies* edited by Janice Capel Anderson & Stephen D. Moore, (Fortress Press, 2nd ed., 2008). In a series of chapters, several scripture scholars illustrate how approaching Mark using these newer approaches—narrative, reader response, deconstructive, feminist, cultural, social and postcolonial—yields various informative results.

If you are interested in understanding more about the methods of biblical scholarship, you might wish to read Corrine L. Carvalho, *Primer on Biblical Methods* (Anselm Academic, 2009); Daniel J. Harrington, *Interpreting the New Testament: A Practical Guide* (Liturgical Press, rev. ed., 1990); George T. Montague, *Understanding the Bible: A Basic Introduction to Biblical Interpretation.* (Paulist, 2nd ed., 2007). For more scholarly analyses see Raymond E. Brown, *The Critical Meaning of the Bible* (Paulist, 1981), Richard N. Soulen, *Handbook of Biblical Criticism: Revised and Expanded* (Westminster/John Knox, 4th ed., 2011); Gordon D. Fee, *New Testament Exegesis* (Westminster John Knox, 3rd ed., 2002).

GOOD NEWS THAT STAYS NEWS

Studying the Synoptic Gospels

Most of us carry in our heads a curiously mixed-up version of the Gospels. Because we have been variously exposed to four different Gospels, we easily run them together. But as careful Scripture readers discover, the four different Gospels are often difficult or even impossible to harmonize because each Gospel shapes a unique portrait of who Jesus is and what his life, death and resurrection meant for his followers. Scholars have long recognized that three of the four Gospels—Matthew, Mark and Luke—have a remarkable similarity in both wording and structure. They can easily be put into parallel columns and viewed together at one glance. This has led scholars to call them *synoptic* (Gk: "seeing together or at the same time").

Putting the synoptic Gospels in parallel columns illustrates their interdependence. In the history of biblical scholarship, the Synoptic problem addresses their interrelationships, in particular which came first and so was the inspiration and source for the others. Many ingenious solutions have been proposed, but only a few hypotheses have been widely accepted.

From the time of St. Augustine (d. 430) to the 18th century, the accepted view was that the Gospels were written in the order in which they appear in our Bibles—Matthew, Mark, Luke and John—and that each depended on its predecessors. In the 18th century, biblical scholars eliminated John from synoptic consideration, retained the priority of Matthew and identified the order of composition as Matthew, Luke, Mark.

But in mid 19th century, a two-source solution gained prominence, arguing for the priority of Mark as the original Gospel and identifying the second source as a collection of Jesus' sayings not found in Mark but used by both Matthew and Luke (the "Q" source). This two-source solution was expanded in the 20th century to recognize other sources unique to Matthew ("M") and Luke ("L") found in their infancy and resurrection narratives and some sayings of Jesus. Almost all biblical scholars today accept this expanded two-source theory as the basis for their analysis of the interrelationships of the synoptic Gospels.

Working with a Synopsis of the Gospels

The older standard text was Burton Throckmorton's *Gospel Parallels*, whose first edition (1973) used the RSV translation, and revised edition

WORKING ON GOD'S WORD

(1992) used the NRSV text. Other options are Kurt Aland's *A Synopsis of the Four Gospels* (American Bible Society, 1985) or the *Common English Bible Gospel Parallels* (2012). But instead of buying a print edition, one can now more quickly and easily compare the four canonical Gospels using the RSV translation (and even include the non-canonical Gospel of Thomas) online at The Five Gospel Parallels website sponsored by the University of Toronto *(sites.utoronto.ca/religion/synopsis/)*.

A Helpful Method for Studying the Synoptic Gospels

To study the synoptic Gospels, scholars devised a method that focuses on the process of editing called *redaction criticism (redaction* is an older word for editing), which aims to "shed light upon the personal contribution of each evangelist and to uncover the theological tendencies which shaped his editorial work" (see the Pontifical Biblical Commission's *The Interpretation of the Bible in the Church*, 1993, I. A. 1.). Using this method, scholars have been able to recognize and to appreciate the unique literary and theological characteristics of each synoptic Gospel.

We can summarize the basic presuppositions that guide redaction criticism in this way. Both Matthew and Luke knew and used Mark for the general structure and the basic content of their Gospels. But they also added material from other sources at their disposal—the "Q," "M" and "L" materials.

Since Luke and Matthew both had Mark's text, we presume that their changes to Mark are conscious and freely made. By asking why they might have made these changes, we can try to discern their intentions and discover the unique features of their Gospels. Of course there is no guarantee that we can get back into their minds, but still we can recognize the themes and ideas that each one stresses when they change Mark. As we reflect upon the possible reasons for their changes, we discover that they are often linked to each author's understanding of who Jesus is and the special needs facing their communities. New times and new challenges demanded new versions beyond Mark's original version of Jesus' story.

Steps for a Synoptic Examination

As you begin to study the synoptic Gospels more carefully by working with a synopsis of the Gospels that places the text in columns, you can quickly compare the texts of each evangelist and detect more easily the changes among the Gospels. First locate the Gospel passage you wish to examine, then proceed in this general way.

First, since almost all New Testament scholars consider that Mark is the original source, notice the changes that Matthew and Luke make to Mark. These changes can be grammatical, such as the use of different vocabulary or sentence construction, or thematic, such as the introduction or omission of material that the evangelist thinks is necessary to get his point across. Notice that changes can be by addition, omission, change in location or substitution (sometimes Matthew and Luke think that a version of an incident from their own sources is better than that of Mark).

Second, decide which changes are more significant and which might be just stylistic. Luke, for example, is always touching up Mark's rather rough Greek. As the first careful readers of Mark's text, Luke and Matthew often make changes because what Mark wrote was either not clear to them or was not what they wanted to emphasize about Jesus or discipleship.

Third, in light of the significant changes, ask why Matthew and Luke would want to make these changes to Mark's text. Obviously they could have repeated Mark's text word for word, but since they chose to make these changes, they must have had a good reason to edit Mark's text.

The reasons can often be traced to each author's theological themes or emphases, especially his distinctive portrait of Jesus. As we noted in earlier chapters, Mark stresses that Jesus is a suffering messiah opening a new way of relating to God. Matthew emphasizes Jesus as an authoritative teacher who presents the new guidelines for life in relation to God. Luke highlights Jesus' healing and prophetic activity as a witness to God's new action for salvation. Many changes reinforce their own portraits of Jesus.

Another major reason for making changes was the particular challenge that each community faced. All the evangelists believed that Jesus was the solution to their problems. So Jesus' words and deeds hold the key that unlocks the solution to the crises facing their communities. Matthew and Luke change Mark because Mark's Gospel is no longer the way that their communities need to hear the Good News and apply it to their lives.

Consulting a Bible Dictionary or Encyclopedia

For quick information about biblical people, places, things and themes that you encounter in your reading, consult a Bible dictionary or Bible encyclopedia. The best single-volume ones are the *Oxford Dictionary of the Bible* (2nd ed., 2011), *HarperCollins Bible Dictionary* (rev. ed., 2011), *The Mercer Dictionary of the Bible (2001)*, *Eerdmans Dictionary of the Bible* (2000), *Zondervan Illustrated Bible Dictionary* (2011), the Intervarsity Press *Dictionary of Jesus and the Gospels* (1992) and Fr. John L. McKenzie's older but still useful *Dictionary of the Bible* (Macmillan, 1965, 1995), which is distinctive in that it often relates the biblical information to Catholic theology and doctrine.

The most extensive and finest Bible dictionary is still the six-volume *Anchor Bible Dictionary* (Doubleday, 1992), a compendium of biblical scholarship by nearly 1000 scholars from all over the world. It is also available on CD for your home computer or at your local library. A great advantage of the CD version is that you can quickly search through the whole dictionary (which is impossible in the print version) for cross-references to words, topics and themes.

Using a Commentary

After having read the Gospels straight through to get a grasp of the whole story, you can then work through each one more carefully with the aid of a commentary, which helps determine the meanings of the biblical text. Although a commentary is no substitute for engaging with the Gospel texts themselves, they should help you to read the Gospels with more insight and understanding. Commentaries are particularly helpful for explaining ancient terms, customs and references in the Gospels that a modern reader may not understand, reminding us that the Gospels come to us from another time and culture and that the world of the Gospel is not our world. They were not written for modern readers and we are always outsiders and strangers to their thought world. (For more on how we overcome these historical, cultural and social gaps, see my *Catechist's Guide to Reading Your Bible*, pp. 149-56.)

A commentary can also reference other texts that provide a context for our reading of the Gospel such as those from the Old Testament, first-century Jewish writers and historians (Philo, Josephus, the Dead Sea Scrolls), later Jewish writings (the *Mishnah* and *Talmud)*, early Christian writings not included in the Bible (Christian letters, non-canonical gospels, apocrypha, pseudepigrapha and Gnostic texts), writings of the earliest Church Fathers and Greco-Roman writers. These ancient writings provide illuminating insights into the Gospel and its world and times.

Types of Commentaries

Commentaries are numerous and come in various degrees of difficulty. Although it is not possible to list all the various commentaries, the series noted here are representative and usually have a commentary on each of the Gospels and the Acts of the Apostles.

Beginning commentaries take you through larger units of the Gospel text so that you get the general flavor of the book. They provide enough detail to enhance your reading but not so much to bog you down. A very good Catholic commentary on this introductory level is the older *Collegeville Bible Commentary* (Liturgical Press, 1992) or the revised version called the *New Collegeville Bible Commentary* (Liturgical Press, 2005). Covering every book of the Bible, these handy pamphlet size booklets include the NAB text on the top of the page and the running commentary below. Study questions are also included. The complete commentary, without the Bible text, is also published in separate Old and New Testament volumes or in a convenient single-volume edition.

You might also look at N. T. Wright's *The New Testament for Everyone* (18 volumes, Westminster /John Knox Press, 2004–2011) that skillfully weaves together the meaning of the scripture passage and its application to our everyday lives. He reminds us that the ultimate challenge of reading scripture is not just to understand it (the "what" question) but to apply it to our everyday lives as Christians (the "so what" question).

Intermediate-level commentaries cover the Gospel text section by section or even verse by verse offering more detailed information to help understand the Gospel text. They are readable and yet challenging because they start to reveal the greater depths of meaning that the biblical texts can conceal. Examples of this type of commentary include the excellent multi-volume *Sacra Pagina* series (Liturgical Press), the *Interpretation Bible*

Study series for teaching and preaching (Westminster/John Knox Press), and the several *Abingdon New Testament Commentaries* (Abingdon Press).

Advanced commentaries are the kind that scholars use. They deal with the Gospels in great detail and often contain far more information than we ever imagined. However, you can often read these with great profit when you wish to explore specific chapters or verses or some particularly puzzling passage in greater depth. Perhaps the best place to locate these is in a seminary or university library or get them through interlibrary loan.

There are also one-volume Bible commentaries that contain explanations for each Gospel such as *The International Bible Commentary, The Women's Bible Commentary, The Interpreter's One-Volume Commentary on the Bible, Harper's Bible Commentary,* and *The NIV Bible Companion.*

The finest Catholic one-volume Bible commentary is still *The New Jerome Biblical Commentary* (1990), edited by Frs. Raymond Brown, Joseph Fitzmyer and Roland Murphy. Besides thorough introductions and detailed commentary for each Gospel, this volume contains more than twenty topical articles about the Bible that any reader would find helpful. If there were only one book to put in your home reference library, this would be it. There is an abbreviated and somewhat simplified version of this, called *The New Jerome Bible Handbook* (Liturgical Press, 1992). However this digest contains only very brief introductory material and no detailed comment on the biblical books.

Using a Bible Concordance

Another resource for exploring the Gospels is a concordance or alphabetical list of the principal words with citations of their locations and often a brief portion of the sentence in which each is used. Thus tracing themes or finding similar passages is easily done. But since different Bibles might translate the same Greek word differently in English, a concordance must be correlated to the specific translation you are using. Although concordances still come in printed volumes, having a Bible translation on your computer or using one online gives you a much faster and better concordance because most programs allow you to search not only for single words but also for particular phrases or combinations of words.

Learning about the Gospel World

An atlas of biblical lands, with historical and geographical maps, helps situate the Gospels in their world and picture the places where Jesus walked and worked. Some of the many options are: *The Macmillan Bible Atlas* (1977, 1993); *The Harper Atlas of the Bible* (1987, 2008); *The Zondervan Atlas of the Bible* (2010), the *Oxford Bible Atlas* (2009), National Geographic's *The Biblical World: An Illustrated Atlas* (2007) or Jerome Murphy-O'Connor, *The Holy Land: An Oxford Archaeological Guide* (Oxford University Press, 2008). Many Bible computer programs also include maps and you can also find many different maps online.

For general background on the historical, political and social situations of the New Testament world, see Craig A. Evans, *Jesus and His World: The Archaeological Evidence* (Westminster John Knox Press, 2013); John J. Rousseau & Rami Arav, *Jesus and His World: An Archaeological and Cultural Dictionary* (Fortress, 1995); John Dominic Crossan & Jonathan L. Reed, *Excavating Jesus: Beneath the Stones, Behind the Texts* (HarperSanFrancisco, 2001); Warren Carter, *Seven Events That Shaped the New Testament World* (Baker Academic, 2013); K. C. Hanson & Douglas E. Oakman, *Palestine in the Time of Jesus: Social Structures and Social Conflicts* (Fortress Press, 2008); Douglas E. Oakman, *The Political Aims of Jesus* (Fortress Press, 2012); and E. P. Sanders *Judaism: Practice and Belief 63 BCE–66 CE* (SCM/Trinity, 1992), which describes the Judaism familiar to Jesus, his disciples, Paul and the Gospel writers.

To appreciate the social and cultural difference between the Gospel world and ours, see Joel B. Green & Lee Martin McDonald, *The World of the New Testament: Cultural, Social and Historical Contexts* (Baker Academic, 2013). Bruce Malina and Richard Rohrbaugh's *Social Science Commentary on the Synoptic Gospels* (Fortress, 1992) and *Social Science Commentary on the Gospel of John* (Fortress, 1998) explain the social and cultural background needed to understand the Gospels in their first-century Mediterranean milieu. Bruce Malina and John J. Pilch's *Handbook of Biblical Social Values* (Baker, 2009) explains the cultural values, such as honor and shame, that characterized Jesus' first-century culture and underlie the Gospel writers' presentation of his life and ministry.

A Few Other Good Books on Selected Gospel Topics

The number of books on the Gospels is enormous, but here are a few books on selected topics that might lead you to discover other resources that will answer your own questions and respond to your own interests.

On Interpeting the Bible

Corrine L. Carvalho, *Primer on Biblical Methods* (Anselm Academic, 2009).

Michael J. Gorman, *Elements of Biblical Exegesis: A Basic Guide for Ministers & Students* (Baker Academic, 2010).

John H. Hayes & Carl R. Holladay, *Biblical Exegesis: A Beginner's Handbook* (Westmisnter/John Knox Press, 2007).

Daniel J. Harrington, *Interpreting the New Testament: A Practical Guide* (Liturgical Press, rev. ed., 1990).

George T. Montague, *Understanding the Bible: A Basic Introduction to Biblical Interpretation* (Paulist, 2nd ed., 2007).

On Jesus

James D. G. Dunn

(popular) *Jesus, Paul & the Gospels* (Eerdmans, 2011).

(scholarly) *Jesus Remembered* (Eerdmans, 2003).

E. P. Sanders

(popular) *The Historical Figure of Jesus* (Penguin, 1993).

(scholarly) *Jesus and Judaism* (Fortress, 1985).

Gerd Theissen

(popular) *The Shadow of the Galilean: The Quest of the Historical Jesus in Narrative Form* (Fortress, 1987).

(scholarly) With Annette Merz, *The Historical Jesus: A Comprehensive Guide* (Fortress, 1998).

N. T. Wright

(popular) *Simply Jesus: A New Vision of Who He Was, What He Did, and Why He Matters* (HarperOne, 2011).

(scholarly) *Christian Origins and the Question of God* (4 vol., Fortress 1992-2013).

On the Infancy Narratives

(popular) **Pope Benedict XVI,** *Jesus of Nazareth: The Infancy Narratives* (Image Books, 2012).

(scholarly) **Raymond E. Brown,** *The Birth of the Messiah: A Commentary on the Infancy Narratives in the Gospels of Matthew and Luke* (Yale University Press, 1999).

On the Passion

(popular) **Donald Senior,** *The Passion of Jesus* (4 vol., one on each Gospel, Liturgical Press, 1984–91).

(scholarly) **Raymond E. Brown,** *The Death of the Messiah: From Gethsemane to the Grave. A Commentary on the Passion Narratives in the Four Gospels* (Yale University Press, 1998).

On the Resurrection Narratives

Francis J. Moloney, SDB, *The Resurrection of the Messiah: A Narrative Commentary on the Resurrection Accounts in the Four Gospels* (Paulist Press, 2013).

On the Parables

John R. Donahue, SJ, *The Gospel in Parable* (Fortress Press, 1988).

Mary Ann Getty-Sullivan, *Parables of the Kingdom: Jesus and the Use of Parables in the Synoptic Tradition* (Liturgical Press, 2007).

Bernard Brandon Scott, *Hear Then the Parable: A Commentary on the Parables of Jesus* (Fortress, 1989).

On the Gospel Meals

Eugene LaVerdiere, *Dining in the Kingdom of God: The Origins of the Eucharist According to Luke* (Liturgy Training Publications, 1994).

On the Gospels & Catechesis

Maureen Gallagher, *The Art of Catechesis: What You Need to Be, Know & Do* (Paulist Press, 1998), ch. 3.

John Shea *The Spiritual Wisdom of the Gospels for Christian Preachers and Teachers* (3 vol., one for each liturgical cycle, Liturgical Press, 2005).

On Jesus & the Domination Systems

Walter Wink

(popular) *The Powers That Be: Theology For A New Millennium* (Doubleday, 1998).

(scholarly) *Engaging the Powers: Discernment & Resistance in a World of Domination* (Augsburg Fortress, 1992).

On the Evangelists as Authors

Francis J. Moloney, SDB, *Mark: Storyteller, Interpreter, Evangelist* (Baker Academic, 2004).

Warren Carter, *Matthew: Storyteller, Interpreter, Evangelist* (Baker Academic, 2004).

Daniel J. Harrington, SJ, *Meeting St. Luke Today: Understanding the Man, His Mission, and His Message* (Loyola Press, 2009).

Warren Carter, *John: Storyteller, Interpreter, Evangelist* (Baker Academic, 2006).

The Gospel According to You! How to Create Your Own Gospel

As a final way to understand both what a Gospel is and the process of thinking that might have gone on in its composition, and to explore your ideas about how to proclaim the "Good News" of Jesus and his kingdom message today, the following might be an enjoyable project to do.

The task is to "revise" the Gospel as you think it needs to be proclaimed today, using the four canonical Gospels as sources to work from. Recall that Mark did not hesitate to shape his sources into a coherent narrative and then Matthew and Luke did not hesitate to reshape Mark's text to make it more appropriate for the changing needs of their audiences.

Secondly, remember that creativity in their time did not mean writing new materials, but rather taking the already existing materials and reshaping them into a new form that communicated the gospel message to your community in a way that would provide the understanding of who Jesus was, who they were as his followers and what they ought to do to build the kind of community that he revealed to them.

So like the original Gospel authors, your gospel must be a response to the needs of your audience, which are met by using your understanding of who Jesus is (your portrait of Jesus or Christology), and your idea of what is necessary to be his follower/disciple (your portrait of discipleship).

Step 1. Think Through Your Approach

Answer the following questions in order to clarify the overall guidelines of your gospel project:

1. Identify the **audience** for whom you are composing your gospel.
2. What are the three most serious and important problems they face in following Christ today? List three of **their needs** that your gospel will respond to.
3. Identify your primary image or description of Jesus (e.g., Jesus as creator of an inclusive community, champion of the oppressed, reformer of the way to relate to God), together with two secondary or supporting images or roles, which will guide **your portrait of Jesus** (e.g., healer, reconciler, servant, teacher, man for others, etc.) to meet the needs of your audience (#1, 2) for their discipleship (#4).
4. Identify at least three **characteristics of discipleship** that you are trying to encourage in your audience in response to the portrait of Jesus that you are creating (#2) for your audience's needs (#1). This portrait should highlight the important virtues and values that can most help them live better as Christian disciples today.

Step 2. Chose your sources/texts from the four Gospels to illustrate and develop the basic orientation you decided on in Step 1.

Limit your selected passages to the four canonical Gospels. Include a brief reason for each choice and an indication of any significant changes that you would need to make it adapt to your guidelines (Step 1) and flow together with your other texts. Be brief and keep your focus. You cannot include everything so be selective. One way of helping you organize your texts might be to create a page that is divided into three columns, like this.

Passage	Reason for Selection	Significant Changes Needed
Lk 1:1-4	I want a more formal introduction like Luke's	change Theophilus to "my friend"
Jn. 20:30-31	to emphasize why I am writing this gospel	change to "I write this so that..."

Step 3. Compose your gospel by putting the texts together.

Using a computer Bible program (if you do not have your own, you can go online to *BibleGateway.com*), follow your finished outline (Step 2) to copy and paste your chosen texts. Then make the editorial changes necessary to connect your texts and make your gospel flow smoothly.

Step 4. Share your gospel with your household or with a Bible group.

Explain briefly what you were trying to do in composing your gospel and answer any questions that the group might have.

A Final Word

These, then, are just a few recommendations for resources that will help you continue your engagement with the Gospels. Using any of these resources will lead you to other books and authors who can guide you further on your journey into the Gospel world. As with any search, one thing always leads to another, one path opens upon another, one interest yields to a new one and one question answered sparks more questions.

As you continue to read and study the Gospels, you will discover even more God's mysterious presence in your self and in your life. The interesting thing is that the Gospels always just begin a conversation that will continue to grow and deepen as you stay involved with it. As you listen to God's Word, you begin to realize that maybe a lot of what you thought was so clear, especially your presuppositions about God and God's reordering of our world and about Jesus and his kingdom message and how it demands changes in your life, need to be constantly revised in the light of your discovery of new meanings.

Your engagement with the Gospels, both through the questions you ask them and the even more the challenging questions they ask you, will gradually transform you into a more mature follower of Jesus. As you make the kingdom worldview your own, the Good News subtly reorients your life, refocuses your attention and re-describes your understanding of the people and events in your life and their meaning in relation to Christ, the mysterious stranger who has called you and even now walks with you on your journey back to him.

CHAPTER ELEVEN

Sharing the Good News
Resources for Personal Reflection and/or Group Sharing

The gospel message is that God desires to be with us in our world for a relationship intended to bring us into the fullness of life. This relationship will not end with death but will go on forever. Building and nurturing this relationship now is what living with Christ is all about.

> "We cannot be messengers of God's comfort if we do not first feel the joy of being comforted and loved by God. This happens especially when we hear God's Word, the Gospel, which we should carry in our pocket: do not forget this! The Gospel in your pocket or purse, to read regularly."
>
> —*POPE FRANCIS*
> *Angelus,* December 7, 2014

The Gospels, whether read at home or heard at Mass or shared with others, help us deepen our relationship with Jesus and with others. Through the Gospels, we learn who God is, who Jesus is and who we are as his followers. We also discover ways to grow in our relationship with God and with others. Reading, reflecting and discussing the meaning of the Gospels is the key to discovering how to follow Jesus by making his vision and values our own and sharing in his vocation to build God's kingdom.

Growing in Christ
Whether alone, with our family or household members, or with a group of friends, we mature in our imitation of Jesus by using the Gospels as the guide for our Christian living. Through them, Jesus asks us how our lives will change when we take our relationship with God more seriously.

Finding *companions* (Lat: "sharing bread") with whom we can share our encounter with God through the Bible provides new perspectives for growing as a disciple and reminds us that as Christians, our communal sharing of bread is the eucharist, whose pattern can also be the model for personal reflection and for sharing the gospel message with one another.

In our eucharist (Gk: *eucharistia*, thanksgiving) and also in our preparation for the eucharist, we imitate Jesus' actions—take, bless, break, share. Jesus' command to "do this in remembrance of me" (Lk 22:19; 1 Cor 11:24) thus characterizes not just our worship but our lives and our mission as his disciples. Participating in the eucharistic liturgy and living eucharistic lives is our way of "thanking" Jesus and of celebrating and nurturing his continual presence with us not only in church but also in all the moments and situations of our daily lives. Through our ever-deepening experience of Christ in Word and sacrament, we announce and celebrate the Good News of God's transforming presence among us.

A Eucharistic Pattern for Scripture Reflection & Sharing

As a eucharistic people, our Christian lives are stamped by how Jesus gives himself in the form of bread and wine to nourish us. The fourfold pattern that characterizes our eucharistic response is rooted in Jesus' own actions: "He took bread, blessed and broke it, and gave it to them" (Lk 24:30). This dynamic eucharistic pattern—take, bless, break, share—can also provide a pattern for sharing our biblical journey. These four actions translate into four steps for our Gospel sharing. They guide us to take up the Gospel, to bless God and expect a communication for our own lives, to break the Gospel into manageable meanings and to share our understanding of God's Good News with others.

He Took Bread

Just as Jesus took the physical bread, so we must take up the Gospel. Nothing happens until we do. The meanings remain locked up within its covers, inert and useless for our lives. Food on the supermarket shelves looks great and promises nourishment, but it does nothing for us until we buy it, prepare it and eat it. The same is true of the Gospels.

Although there are many helpful books about the Gospels, no amount of knowledge about them can substitute for reading them. By reading the Gospels we become familiar with God's personality and how God prefers to relate to us. When we actually read them, we do more than read words; we encounter a person through that person's self-revelation.

GOOD NEWS THAT STAYS NEWS

He Blessed

Blessing is a biblical idea that needs some explanation. For the ancients, blessing described God's everyday care for us. Besides the spectacular events through which the people learned that God cared for them—creation, the exodus, the giving of the land, the restoration after the exile—there were the ordinary events that also showed God's loving providence. The everyday experiences of health, wealth, children, family, friends, good weather, abundant harvests and all the little things that make our lives satisfying and enjoyable were all recognized as God's blessings.

Through these divine blessings, we live long and happy lives. Since we cannot produce any of these blessings ourselves but must depend on God alone to give them, when we bless we do not cause these blessings to happen but ask God to give them. When Jesus blesses bread, he is asking God to communicate life to us through the bread. This is the spiritual life—God's own life in us—which our material food cannot give.

Just as God communicates life to us through the bread that is Jesus, so God also imparts life to us through the words of the Gospels. Through our reading, our eyes are opened to recognize God's past blessings and those being given in the present. Whenever we read and reflect upon the meaning of the Gospels, we can ask God to empower us to make our everyday lives better. We use the Gospels to discover clues about God's hidden presence in our midst. They also makes us more familiar with God's favorite ways of entering into everyday situations to bless them.

He Broke

Bread is no good for nourishment unless it is broken, chewed, digested and transformed into the nutrients our body can use. Likewise, the bread of God's Word is no good for our spiritual nourishment unless we break it down into meanings that help us to live better Christian lives.

Breaking a text down into intelligible meanings is interpretation, i.e., understanding not only what the text *says* but also what it *means*. When we move beyond reading the words "to understand what God has wished to communicate to us, we must carefully investigate what meaning the biblical writers actually had in mind; that will also be what God chose to manifest through their words" (Vatican II, *On Revelation*, #12).

SHARING THE GOOD NEWS

After we discover what the Gospel meant to its original audience, we can then consider what it means for us now. We believe that God's revealed Word communicates a message that still applies today. God is always working in our world to transform it into the world God wants it to be. Through reading and interpreting the Gospels, we detect God's presence and discover God's vision for a transformed world.

He Shared

We humans are not the only animals that eat, but we are the only ones who cook! And much of our cooking is not merely for sustenance but for showing others that we care for them. Food always means more to us than biological nourishment. It also communicates many symbolic meanings that reveal our social and cultural values.

Eating alone is not much fun. Sharing food signifies our willingness to share our lives. So we tend to be very selective about the people we dine with. We share bread with the people we want to share our lives with. Jesus' inclusive dining was a sign of his universal love. Just as he was willing to share himself with anyone who wanted or needed his company, so we Christians must learn to share ourselves with others.

The word of the Gospel, like the bread that is Jesus, is for everyone. Our discovery of God through the Gospels is an experience that we are expected to share with others. Meanings cannot exist in isolation. Meaning is shared when we speak it. Speaking expresses (pushes out!) our inner experience into the shared realm of public language. Others now hear our words and are expected to respond. So dialogue begins.

"All spiritual growth comes from reading and reflection. By reading we learn what we did not know; by reflection we retain what we have learned."

—*ST. ISIDORE OF SEVILLE*
Book of Maxims

Personal Reading & Reflection: Take Time with Jesus

Our lifetime is a journey on which we mold ourselves into who we are. Self-making occurs in and through relationships with others through whom we discover who we are and what our gifts are. Ultimately, we find our identity in relationship to God, the divine other who calls us into a

GOOD NEWS THAT STAYS NEWS

special relationship. The Gospels are our primary resource for discovering the person and plan of this God for us as revealed in Jesus of Nazareth.

Reading the Gospels opens up the often neglected spiritual depths of ourselves and our world. It can jump-start our personal spiritual life and help us live out our relationship to God much more consciously. Living more consciously helps us to be more aware, to care and to share.

As we learn to notice how and where God is present, we become more spiritually aware and see our familiar world through the eyes of faith. Reading the Gospels reveals that the surface appearances of our self and our everyday world hide the deeper mystery of God's powerful transforming presence that normally escapes our notice.

Pope Francis's Advice for Encountering the Biblical Text

"In God's presence, during a recollected reading of the text, it is good to ask:

- Lord, what does this text say to me?
- What is it about my life that you want to change by this text?
- What troubles me about this text?
- Why am I not interested in this?
- Or perhaps: What do I find pleasant in this text?
- What is it about this word that moves me?
- What attracts me? Why does it attract me?

When we make an effort to listen to the Lord, temptations usually arise. One of them is simply to feel troubled or burdened, and to turn away. Another common temptation is to think about what the text means for other people, and so avoid applying it to our own life. It can also happen that we look for excuses to water down the clear meaning of the text. Or we can wonder if God is demanding too much of us, asking for a decision which we are not yet prepared to make.

This leads many people to stop taking pleasure in the encounter with God's word. But this would mean forgetting that no one is more patient than God our Father, that no one is more understanding and willing to wait. God always invites us to take a step forward, but does not demand a full response if we are not yet ready. God simply asks that we sincerely look at our life and present ourselves honestly before him, and that we be willing to continue to grow, asking from God what we ourselves cannot as yet achieve."

—POPE FRANCIS
The Joy of the Gospel (2013), #152

Using the Eucharistic Pattern for Personal Reflection

A eucharistic format—take, bless, break, share—reminds us that our whole lives are a "thanksgiving" for God's gift of a relationship with us.

We have been called into communion with God and with others. Each day we discover ways to show in our words and actions our love for God and for others. To use this format, find a quiet spot where you can read, reflect and pray. If you want to record your spiritual thoughts and experiences, have your spiritual journal handy.

Take

Take a few moments of quiet to become prayerful and centered.

Bless

Begin your reflection with a prayer. You may wish to use a spontaneous prayer to the Holy Spirit to guide your prayer or the Opening Prayer from the Sunday Mass or another favorite prayer of your choosing.

Break

Read the selected reading from the Gospel. Pause for 1-2 minutes of silence to be attentive to God's message for you today. Reread the passage pausing wherever you are drawn to stop, reflect and pray.

Reflect on the meaning of the reading. Consider *Some Basic Questions for Exploring Any Scripture Reading* (p. 283) to start and guide your reflection.

Share

Respond after your reflection by deciding how you can apply the message of the readings in some concrete way in your household, at work, at school or in other situations during the coming week.

Closing Prayer

After time for reflection and your proposed response, take time to be quiet and attentive to Christ's presence with you—where he wants to dwell now. Then end with a spontaneous prayer, or one from the Mass of the past or coming Sunday, or another one you choose.

The Gospel Is for Sharing

Our relationship with Christ is a personal experience but it is never just a private one. It always involves sharing Christ's companionship with others. Just as the risen Jesus shared his insights about scripture and a meal with his Emmaus companions (Luke 24:13-49), so we follow his example and share our beliefs and practices with members of our household.

Some Basic Questions for
Exploring any Scripture Passage

Here are four basic questions and several follow-up questions you can use to explore a biblical passage and stimulate individual reflection or small group discussion. (Note that not all questions are equally answered in every passage.)

1. What does this text tell me about God? Jesus? the Holy Spirit?

- Does this confirm what I already know and believe?
- Is there something new here that I had not noticed before?
- What does God want me to know or do, change or improve?

2. What does God, Jesus, the Holy Spirit do in relation to us & our world?

- How is the divine presence and power revealed?
- Why does God come to us at this time and in this way?
- What is required of us to do or not to do in response?

3. What does this text tell me about myself?

- How am I like the persons in this scripture passage?
- How would I respond if this happened to me?
- How would I be changed if I did what the text says?
- What surprised me the most about this passage?
- What puzzled me the most?
- What challenged me the most to live out my faith more fully?
- What made me most comfortable? Why?
- What made me most uncomfortable? Why?

4. What does this text tell me about the community that God desires?

- What does this text tell me about how to love God?
- What does this text tell me about how to love others?
- What guidelines for better community living does the passage offer?

Sharing With Your Family or Household

Sharing with those in our household about how we experience the Gospel not only helps us apply its message but also prepares us to share the Gospel with others beyond family or household—loved ones, friends, acquaintances, co-workers and others in our parish, neighborhood and city.

Household members can participate more fully in the Sunday eucharist by sharing about the Sunday readings, especially the Gospel, at home. This also reminds us of the connection between the household table and the eucharistic table, where God's Word is heard and God's presence is shared in a meal. So gather your household and use the Gospel readings when you gather for a meal or, like the early Christians, for a lively exchange after a meal. [You can find the daily lectionary readings online at the US Bishops' website: *www.usccb.org/bible/readings/053116.cfm* or hear them read aloud at *www.usccb.org/bible/readings-audio.cfm.*]

Using the Eucharistic Pattern for Household Sharing

The four moments in the eucharistic pattern can also be used for Bible sharing in your household or a small group.

Take

Each week, choose a convenient time for and gather all the household members around the family table, recalling that when we hear God's Word it is as if God were present at the table talking directly to us.

Bless

After all are gathered, begin with a prayer to the Holy Spirit to guide your sharing or pray the Opening Prayer from the day's Mass or from the coming Sunday or another favorite prayer of your choosing.

Break

Read the Gospel from the Mass for the coming Sunday out loud (and if you have time, also read one or more of the other readings).

Share

After some time for quiet reflection, invite each member of the household or group to share their answers to questions taken from *Some Basic Questions for Exploring Any Scripture Reading* (p. 283). End with ideas about what you might do in the coming week as individuals and as a group to make this Gospel's message more applicable to your lives.

Closing Prayer

End the sharing time by praying together a spontaneous prayer, the Opening Prayer for the coming Sunday, or one of your choosing.

Sharing with a Faith-Sharing Group

A faith-sharing group provides a way to gather with others, read scripture, reflect on its meaning and share our insights with one another. One way that we grow as followers of Jesus is to read and pray the scriptures with others. Faith-sharing gatherings invite us to develop our spiritual lives to their full potential in community with others and to participate more fully in the shared life and mission of the Christian community.

"The secret of the apostles' immense success in preaching the gospel was that they shared Good News about a terrific person who loves each human being with inexhaustible energy. They did more than preach about Jesus. They shared the personal stories of their own development of a love relationship with Christ. They shared their weaknesses, their betrayals, and their abandonments of their best friend. They told of how Christ reached out to them and touched them with the warmth of his heart."
—*FR. ALFRED MCBRIDE, O. PRAEM.*
To Love and Be Loved by Jesus (1992)

To encourage you to get involved in sharing your faith with others, here is what you need to explore the Gospels with a small group. Gathering a group for faith sharing does not require any special permission or elaborate materials. Each week the foundation for sharing is based on Gospel passages or on the Sunday Mass readings. If you choose the Sunday readings as the content, either meet to discuss the readings in advance, which enhances your response to them at Mass, or you might prefer to meet after Mass or on Sunday afternoon or evening and explore more in-depth the readings that were already heard earlier at Mass.

No Need for Experts

Since the goal of your time together is not "study" but just sharing your faith experience, no one needs to be an expert on the Bible or on doctrine. We are each an expert on how we live our Christian faith. So we learn from one another as we share our own unique Christian journey and how our Christian beliefs and values influence our everyday lives. The point is not just to learn about our faith (the "what") but to find ways to make that faith effective in our lives (the "so what"). All of our learning is ultimately for developing a better relationship with Christ and with others with whom we share the journey. The group can be made up of anyone who wishes to grow in faith together and is willing to share their experiences of living with Christ—a group of friends from the neighborhood, the workplace or the parish, fellow catechists, those who attend daily Mass regularly or meet as a Small Christian or Small Church Community, an RCIA group or an adult faith formation group.

Using the Eucharistic Pattern in a Faith-Sharing Gathering

The four moments in the eucharistic pattern provide a helpful model for the practice of small-group Bible sharing that is faithful to the four essentials necessary for building and maintaining a strong faith-sharing group—community building, prayer, scripture sharing and outreach.

As the group gathers in a circle, place the Bible reverently on a small table in the center of the group. A candle can be lighted to remind us that Christ our light is present to guide our path through Scripture.

Take

Take a few moments of silence in which group members can become centered and prayerful. Then invite them to think about their lives since the last meeting and consider what new or renewed demands they have been experiencing in their relationship with Christ. Then briefly share your answers to questions like these:

- Since our last meeting, what has happened to me spiritually?
- How did last meeting's reading make a difference in my attitudes or behavior towards others?
- When did I feel Jesus to be most close or most far from me?

Bless

After everyone has had a chance to share, invite a volunteer from the group to pray for God to **bless** the group with the presence and guidance of the Holy Spirit to open their minds and hearts to hear, heed and apply God's message to their lives.

Break

Invite someone to read the selected Gospel passage or the Sunday readings aloud while the other group members listen. If you wish to have more participation in a reading, invite several volunteers to read dramatically, taking the parts of the narrator, Jesus and the other characters in the story.

After the reading, pause for 1-2 minutes of silence so that the group members can be attentive to what God's Word is trying to say to them today. After the silence, invite the group members to **break** the passage into its meanings by considering first what the author said and what the passage meant to its first readers. See *Some Basic Questions for Exploring Any Scripture Reading* (p. 283). Then consider what this text means now by making connections between it and their lives.

Share

No small group session is complete without considering how the group can go from the meeting and put their belief and learning into action in the coming week. Invite the group to **share** for example:

- What changes in my attitudes or actions might be called for this week because of this reading?

Close the discussion by deciding on a practical activity for group members to do either individually or together before the next meeting.

Closing Prayer

Invite the group to become quiet and attentive to Christ's presence with them. Then close with a spontaneous prayer or another of your choosing. Invite the group to share a sign of peace with one another, then end with a song, a prayer and the commissioning of the members to share what they have heard and learned with their family, friends, co-workers and others with whom they will come into contact until the next gathering.

"Be constant in both prayer and reading. First speak with God: then let God speak with you. Let God instruct you, let God direct you."

—*ST. CYPRIAN OF CARTHAGE*

In this way, God's Word is like the eucharistic bread and wine. When we take, bless, break, and share God's Word, we are simultaneously taken, blessed, broken and shared by God's mysterious and loving presence. We are taken into the community of sisters and brothers identified as Christians by being formed in Jesus' image. His story becomes our story; his example becomes our model for living; his vision and values become our guidelines for consecrating and reordering the world.

Questions for Personal Reflection and/or Group Sharing

These questions can be used by persons of all ages and interests who are exploring the meaning of the Gospels as the foundation for their Christian identity and want to adopt that worldview (vision) and to participate more fully (vocation) in working with God to transform our world.

> "In the face of death, live humanly. In the middle of chaos, celebrate the Word. Amidst babel, speak the truth. Confront the noise and verbiage and falsehood of death with the truth and potency and efficacy of the Word of God. Know the Word, teach the Word, nurture the Word, preach the Word, defend the Word, incarnate the Word, do the Word, live the Word, and more than that, in the Word of God, expose death and all death's works and wiles, rebuke lies, cast out demons, exorcise, cleanse the possessed, raise those who are dead in mind and conscience."
>
> —*WILLIAM STRINGFELLOW*
> *An Ethic for Christians & Other Aliens in a Strange Land* (1973)

Whether you choose to use these questions for personal reflection or as the starting point for a group discussion in your household or with a faith sharing or a Bible study group, they should be helpful for:

- catechists in training or in their catechetical ministries
- adults in families or in faith-sharing or study groups
- those investigating the Christian faith for the first time in RCIA
- inquisitive young adults in high school or college
- individuals or groups who are interested in sharing their faith with others in a small group Bible study who wish to discuss this book chapter by chapter, or in conjunction with a study of the Gospels themselves.

As you continue to grow in your identity as a disciple of Jesus, which will in turn change and shape your life and spirituality, spend some time reflecting, writing and discussing your answers to the following questions that are correlated to the material found in the chapters in this book.

Introduction: The Catechist & the Gospels

- What questions, concerns or needs are now most drawing you to the Gospels and not some other book?

- What personal fears or obstacles most hold you back from reading and studying the Gospels?
- From what source or sources has most of your information and knowledge about the Gospels come?
- Why do you think it is appropriate to identify Jesus' message as "Good News." Why is it "News" and what makes it "Good"?
- Who was the most important messenger of God's Good News for you?
- What questions would you most like to ask the Gospel authors if they sat across from you right now?
- Describe the three worlds of the text for Shakespeare's play *Julius Caesar*.
- What problems can arise if we do not recognize the differences between our world and that of the Gospel authors?

1. The New Testament Social World

- What are the most important characteristics of an agrarian society?
- Why was one's social status rank (honor) so important for them?
- Briefly describe a "domination system" and give an example of how they influence our lives today?
- How do the assumptions of "domination systems" impact our Christian lives today and why are they so hard to overcome?
- Identify and briefly describe the five different groups in first-century Judahism that were trying to direct its beliefs and practices.
- What do they all have in common? About what do they most differ?
- What do you think is the greatest difficulty in trying to read the Gospels through first-century eyes? Why?

2. God's New Rule Is Here!

- Why do you think Jesus chooses "kingdom" language to proclaim his message to his first-century audience?
- What terminology might be more appropriate for today's Christians?
- Briefly summarize Jesus' Good News.
- What is a worldview and how does it shape us and our identity?
- What are the six questions that characterize a worldview?
- How would you answer these questions for Americans today?
- How would you answer these questions for Christians today?

SHARING THE GOOD NEWS

- Why is the Christian worldview so important for creating and maintaining one's Christian identity and the Christian community?

3. If God Rules, then What?

- Briefly describe what is necessary to adopt a new worldview?
- What challenges you most in adopting the Christian worldview?
- Why are worldviews incompatible and exclusive? (Relate this to an instance where worldviews conflict in today's world.)
- Briefly explain why and how the Christian worldview challenged one of the four social realms of their first-century society.
- How is the Christian worldview most in conflict with our American worldview today?
- What most challenges your loyalty and use of power as you try to live according to the Christian worldview?

4. Why the Gospels Were Written

- Briefly explain the three stages of the Gospel formation. Why is it so important not to confuse these stages?
- How is the written Gospel similar and different from other types?
- What reasons were most important for writing down the four Gospels as narratives for the different communities?
- What does it mean to say Mark "invented" the Gospel form?
- Why did Matthew and Luke "revise" Mark's Gospel?
- Why would John try to write a different Gospel from the others?
- Describe the sources used by each of the four evangelists.
- Does the fact that we know so little about the actual Gospel authors bother you? Why or why not?
- What benefit would there to reading the Gospels in the order in which they were written and not as they appear in our Bible?

5. Mark's Gospel

- Briefly describe the structure of Mark's Gospel.
- How would you characterize Mark's portrait of Jesus?
- How would you characterize Mark's portrait of true discipleship?
- How do these portraits challenge you to a new way of being a disciple?
- Briefly explain the most important theme for you in Mark.

- Why might Mark's audience need a messiah who is misunderstood, abandoned and crucified, and disciples who fail in their following?
- How could Mark's proclamation be "Good News" for anyone?
- In chapters 1–4, which of Jesus' personality traits or titles most appeals to you? Why?
- What do you discover about Jesus' identity from the five conflict stories found in 2:1–3:6?
- How does Peter's example help you understand your discipleship?
- What do you learn about what it means to be a disciple from the call stories of 1:14-20, 2:13-17 and 3:13-19?
- How would you summarize in your own words "the mystery of the kingdom of God" as it is expressed in the parables of chapter 4?
- The two miracle stories of 8:22-27 and 10:46-52 frame Mark's passion prediction/journey section and so comment on its meaning. How do they alert us to what is happening on the way to Jerusalem?
- How does Mark's account of Jesus' anointing (14:3-9) go against some common expectations about the messiah ("anointed one")?
- In 12:13-17 Jesus cleverly resolves the legal question of what is owed to Caesar, but does not explain what belongs to God. Based on what he says and does in this story, what do you conclude belongs to God?
- If Mark 14–16:8 (Mark's original ending) were the only Gospel version you had, what would be your personal reaction/response to the passion narrative and to the empty tomb story?
- How would our Christian lives (e.g., emphasis among our beliefs about Jesus and ourselves, practices of prayer, worship, the sacraments, church organization, etc.) be different if Mark were our only Gospel?
- What is the most important thing you have learned about the "Good News" of the kingdom of God from Mark?

6. Matthew's Gospel
- Briefly describe the structure of Matthew's Gospel.
- How would you characterize Matthew's portrait of Jesus?
- How would you characterize Matthew's portrait of true discipleship?
- How do these portraits challenge you to a new way of being a disciple?
- Briefly explain the most important theme for you in Matthew.

- Each Infancy Narrative goes only with the Gospel in which it is found. Summarize the theological message of Matthew's infancy narrative.
- In chapter 1, what titles does Matthew apply to Jesus and what clue does each give about Jesus' identity?
- In chapters 1–2, identify two ways that Matthew expresses continuity with the Jewish tradition and openness to the new Gentile world.
- In chapters 1–4 choose one of the "fulfillment" quotes (introduced by "this was to fulfill…"). Explain the Old Testament context of this quote (i.e., the situation of the original audience) and how it provides a new meaning or clarity when applied to the situation of Jesus' life?
- In 4:1-11, what significant changes does Matthew make to Mark's version of Jesus temptation (Mk 1:12-13) and how do the changes help you to understand the meaning of this event?
- Concerning the beatitudes of 5:1-12, what do the first and the second parts of a beatitude describe? What values in our society today do the different beatitudes most challenge?
- Choose one of the miracles in chapters 8–9. Describe what indicates the seriousness of the situation, how the miracle is done, the response of those present and the role of faith and prayer.
- Summarize the demands of discipleship and what they reveal about the situation of Matthew's community in 8:18-22; 9:9-17; 9:35-38?
- In chapter 10, how does the disciples' mission imitate that of Jesus (see 4:23 and 9:35 for a convenient summary of Jesus' ministry).
- In chapter 13, what does Matthew's collection of parables reveal about the kingdom of heaven and our response to it? About the problems his own community might be facing?
- Matthew uses the word for assembly (Gk: *ekklēsia,* 16:18-19; 18:17-18) to describe the Christian community. Who has the power to bind and loose and what does this reveal about his understanding of the church?
- Matthew introduces much material about the traitor Judas. In 26:14-16, what reason is given for the betrayal? In 26:20-25, how do Judas' words hint at his lack of faith? Compare 27:3-10 and Acts 1:16-20. How does Judas die? What happens to the money?
- How would you use information found in Matthew's Gospel to explain

the reasons why Jesus was crucified?

- How would our Christian lives (e.g., emphasis among our beliefs about Jesus and ourselves, practices of prayer, worship, the sacraments, church organization, etc.) be different if Matthew were our only Gospel?
- What is the most important thing you have learned about the "Good News" of the kingdom of heaven from Matthew?

7. Luke"s Gospel & Acts of the Apostles

- Briefly describe the structure of Luke's Gospel.
- How would you characterize Luke's portrait of Jesus?
- How would you characterize Luke's portrait of true discipleship?
- How do these portraits challenge you to a new way of being a disciple?
- Briefly explain the most important theme for you in Luke.
- Summarize the theological message of Luke's infancy narrative.
- In chapter 4:1-30, list the passages in which Luke refers to the Old Testament either by direct quote or indirect allusion and explain how these references help to understand Jesus and his mission.
- In chapter 5:1-11, Luke synthesizes the two call stories of Mark 1:16-20. For Luke, who is prominent? How is this person depicted? What do you learn about discipleship from this call story?
- What do you think are the three most important characteristics of the new way of life as taught by Jesus in Luke 6:12–7:50.
- Luke often uses meal settings to teach lessons for his community. What do you learn from the meal stories of Luke 5:27-39 and 7:36-50 about Jesus' identity and what is expected from those whom he calls?
- Luke summarizes much of his view of Christian prayer in 11:1-13. Who is to pray the "Lord's Prayer," an individual or a community? Why ought one pray? For what? How does 11:13 differ from Matthew 7:11?
- What do the three parables of 15:3-32 teach us about the pastoral problem of reconciliation of sinners within the community?
- What does Luke's unique story of Zacchaeus (19:1-10) teach about Luke's idea of discipleship?
- What do you learn about Jesus' identity and the meaning of his passion from Luke's addition of the dialogue between Jesus and the women of Jerusalem (23:27-31) and with the criminal on the cross (23:39-43)?

SHARING THE GOOD NEWS

- In 24:4-8, what do the two men in dazzling clothes at the tomb help the women (and us!) realize and remember?
- In 24:13-35 (the journey to Emmaus), what are the different ways that we can recognize the presence of the risen Christ in our lives?
- How would our Christian lives (e.g., emphasis among our beliefs about Jesus and ourselves, practices of prayer, worship, the sacraments, church organization, etc.) be different if Luke/Acts were our only Gospel?
- What is the most important thing you have learned about the "Good News" of the kingdom of God from Luke?

Acts of the Apostles
- Briefly describe the structure of Luke's Acts of the Apostles.
- Briefly explain the most important theme for you in Acts.
- How is Luke's description of the Pentecost event in 2:1-12 influenced by the Old Testament description of Yahweh's appearance on Sinai (Ex 19:16-19) and the Tower of Babel incident (Gen 11:1-11)?
- Use the descriptions and events in chapter 4 to identify the characteristics of the early church as Luke portrays them.
- What parallels do you find between the death of Jesus and the death of Stephen in 6:8–7:60?
- How do Peter's speeches in 3:11-26 and 10:34-43 reflect the different audiences he addresses in each speech?
- Identify two passages in chapters 1–12 in which the growth and expansion of the church is under the direction of the Holy Spirit?
- Describe the pattern of Paul's missionary activity as it unfolds in chapter 13? What does this reveal about his aims and strategies?
- Summarize how Paul describes God and God's relationship to the Gentiles in the past (14:15-17; 17:22-31) and now (17:30).
- In Paul's farewell speech to the elders of Ephesus (20:17-38), what might be most relevant for Christian communities today? Why?
- In his defense speech in chapter 26, what does Paul say about the most significant difference between Jews and Christians, the origins of Christianity in Judaism and the reasons for the Gentile mission?
- What passage from chapters 13–28 encourages you to spread the Good News of Jesus in your own life? Why?

- What is the most important thing you have learned about the Good News in Acts?

8. John's Gospel

- Briefly describe the structure of John's Gospel.
- How would you characterize John's portrait of Jesus?
- How would you characterize John's portrait of true discipleship?
- How do these portraits challenge you to a new way of being a disciple?
- Briefly explain the most important theme for you in John.
- What does the prologue (1:1-18) reveal about Jesus' identity & mission?
- In what ways does the author stress the subordination of John the Baptist to Jesus?
- What do you learn about Jesus' identity and mission from the marriage at Cana (2:1-12) and the disruption of Temple business (2:13-22)?
- For one of the Jewish feasts mentioned in chapters 6–10, explain the meaning and symbolism of the feast for the Jews and how John presents Jesus as its fulfillment.
- In chapter 8, why do Jesus' "I AM" statements so bother his opponents?
- Compare the anointing at Bethany in 12:1-8 with similar incidents found in Mark 14:3-9 and Luke 7:36-50. What differences do you find? What message does each evangelist stress in his version?
- Although John does not describe the Last Supper in chapter 13 as a Passover meal, what do you learn from his account that helps us understand the meaning of our eucharistic commemoration at Mass?
- Summarize John's view of the identity and mission of the Holy Spirit (the Paraclete) in 14:16-18, 25-26; 15:26-27; 16:1-16.
- Compare and contrast the faith of the Beloved Disciple with that of Peter in 13:21-26; 18:15-27; 19:25-30; 20:1-10; 21:1-25.
- Compare the giving of the Spirit in 20:21-23 with Acts 2:1-4. What aspect(s) of the church's mission is emphasized in each account?
- In 20:31 John states the purpose for writing this Gospel. Give some examples of how you see this purpose being carried out in the Gospel.
- How would our Christian lives (e.g., emphasis among our beliefs about Jesus and ourselves, practices of prayer, worship, the sacraments, church organization, etc.) be different if John were our only Gospel?

- What is the most important thing you have learned about the "Good News" of the kingdom of God from John?

9. Shaping a Gospel Spirituality

- Think back on your life and note some significant experiences of God's presence to you. How were you changed by this experience?
- What can you recall about your "call" or invitation to follow Jesus in a more adult way? What attracted you or made you turn to Jesus?
- How has your "faith commitment" to Jesus changed over the years? What has most helped to make it stronger or weaker?
- How is God inviting you to new levels of relationship to Jesus?
- In what ways is God inviting you to new levels of holiness by prayer?
- What resistance do you experience that keeps you from following these promptings?
- In what ways is God inviting you to a new awareness of God's values?
- What resistance do you experience that keeps you from following this reordering of your values and priorities?

10. Working on God's Word

- Which Bible translation do you use (or if more than one, when and why do you prefer one version instead of the others)?
- Why is it important to learn about the social and cultural customs of Jesus' world?
- What Gospel passage seems most strange to you and reinforces the idea that Jesus was a first-century person not a twenty-first century one?
- How would you explain the difference between a book about the Gospel of Mark and a commentary on it?

"Lord, who can comprehend even one of your words? We lose more of it than we grasp, like those who drink from a living spring. For God's word offers different facets according to the capacity of the listener, and the Lord has portrayed the message in many colors, so that whoever gazes on it can see in it what is suitable. Within it God has buried manifold treasures, so that each of us might grow rich in seeking them out."

—*ST. EPHREM*
Commentary on the Diatessaron

CHAPTER TWELVE

A Brief Glossary of Terms for Gospel Study

abba (Aramaic: father) It is more familiar (like "dad" or "daddy") than the common but slightly more formal "father" and thus represents the more intimate and close relationship that Jesus has with God.

apocalyptic (Gk: to reveal) A modern, scholarly label for the Jewish and Christian attitude and writings, including sections of the Gospels like Mark 13, Luke 21 and Matthew 24–25, that eagerly anticipate and imagine God's imminent intervention into our history first to judge and then transform it.

apocrypha (Gk: hidden things) An ancient Jewish or Christian book that is not included in the community's official biblical canon of books (thus also identified as non-canonical). Such writings can be described as apocryphal.

Aramaic The Semitic language related to ancient Hebrew, widely used after about 300 BC, which was the spoken language of Judeans in the Holy Land and used by Jesus, his disciples and the apostle Paul.

baptism (Gk: to immerse in water, wash) In Judaism, there were many ceremonial washings either in preparation for celebrating a ritual or as part of a cleansing rite within a ritual. Thus "baptism" becomes a natural sign for ritual purity or holiness. But for the Christian community, baptism replaced Jewish male circumcision as the initiation ritual and sign of covenant belonging, which also meant that covenant membership was also for women and not only men.

beatitude (Lat: *beatus*, blessed or happy) Identifies a person and gives the reason why he or she is blessed. In the Old Testament, the blessed are those who receive from God an earthly fulfillment of prosperity, offspring and long life. In later Jewish writing, the blessings belong to those who will enter the final age of salvation. Jesus offers these future blessings now, for the kingdom is present in him. In his beatitudes (Matthew 5:1-2, Luke 6:20-23), Jesus reveals the characteristics of his followers who wish to enter his kingdom.

canon (Gk: a measuring ruler) The official list of books that belong to the sacred collection of a community. Such books are called canonical.

canonical criticism The scholarly study of biblical texts that focuses on the final (canonical) form of the text and not its earlier versions or sources.

codex An ancient manuscript in leaf or page form that was sewn together at the fold like books are today instead of being rolled as a scroll.

covenant (Heb: *berith*, Gk: *diathekē*, also a will, testament) A formal agreement between two persons or parties that spells out the obligations of their relationship modeled on the customs that guided relationships between persons of unequal honor, status and wealth. These relationships were voluntary and freely entered into and not required by law. The covenant bound the parties in mutual and reciprocal obligations. The "patron" (Lat: father, head of household) or more powerful person (like God) promised to provide for and protect the less powerful "clients" (Lat: dependents). In return, the clients offered public signs of honor, respect, praise, gratitude and other favors when the patron requested.

criticism (Gk: judgment) A general term to describe the scholarly study of the Bible. It includes scientific, historical and literary methods plus various other approaches for discovering the many meanings of the text.

diaspora (Gk: scattered, dispersed) A description of the many Jews who resided outside the Holy Land, for example as a result of exile, emigration or conquest.

Essenes An Israelite separatist ascetic community established to live in opposition to the Jerusalem Temple-centered political-religious establishment. These sectarians lived at Qumran, which was destroyed by the Romans in AD 68.

exegesis (Gk: draw out, hence, explanation or interpretation) The explanation of the meaning of the biblical text, in particular through the use of the historical-critical method, to understand the author's intended meaning.

form criticism The scholarly study of the origin and transmission of the biblical texts and of the sources used in their composition.

fundamentalism When used to designate a common modern approach to biblical interpretation, this term normally identifies a pre-critical approach that does not employ the historical-critical method and thus separates the Bible from its location in the Christian tradition. The result is a naïvely literalist reading of the Bible usually meant to support rigidly conservative doctrines.

Gnosticism (Gk: *gnōsis*, knowledge) A form of religion that stressed that human salvation and the right relationship with God come primarily through esoteric or mystical knowledge. It was rejected by the Christian community in the second century as heretical. In 1945–46 a cache of some 50 Gnostic texts was discovered at Nag Hammadi in Upper Egypt, which included several that scholars call "gospels" although they are very different from the four canonical Gospels.

gospel (Gk: *euangelion;* Lat: *evangelium;* Anglo-Saxon: *Godspell;* good news) A general description of the Christian message. Later it was primarily associated with the four canonical written narrative versions according to Mark, Matthew, Luke and John. Scholars today also apply it to some non-canonical texts.

heart For biblical people, heart does not just identify the physical organ but also the psychological activity associated with it: emotional changes (speeding up when we are excited) and physical life (ceasing to beat when we die). Thus heart is a general word to identify the location of the distinctively human activities of feeling, thinking and deciding. Today we might describe this as the "self."

Hebrew language The Semitic language used by the Israelites from the fourteenth to the fifth century BC, after which it was retained in their sacred written texts but was gradually replaced in everyday life by Aramaic and then by Greek for Jews in the Mediterranean *diaspora* outside of Judea.

Hebrew people Another name for the Israelites, often used by foreigners or by Israelites when speaking to foreigners.

hellenization (Gk: *Hellas,* or Greece) The domination of the Greek language, culture and thought over the whole Mediterranean world as a result of the conquests of Alexander the Great in 333–323 BC.

hermeneutics (Gk: interpretation) The scholarly study of the theory and practice of textual interpretation.

historical criticism A general term for modern critical, biblical scholarship that attempts to situate ancient texts in their specific historical circumstances in order to discover the original meaning intended by the authors.

inerrancy In the Catholic theological sense, the belief that the biblical books are without error when properly interpreted and understood. The Catholic doctrine limits the inerrancy strictly to the divinely revealed mysteries and the "truth which God wanted to put into the sacred writings for the sake of our salvation" *(Dei Verbum,* #11). Any errors of historical or scientific fact are therefore attributed to the limitations of the human authors.

inspiration In the Catholic theological sense, the belief that God somehow assisted the human authors in the composition of their biblical books so that the divinely revealed message was communicated through their human words. "Inspiration" expresses our belief *that* God helped the human authors to compose their books, but does not describe *how* it was done.

koine (Gk: common) The Greek language of everyday conversation and writing, commonly used throughout the Mediterranean world following the conquests of Alexander the Great, in which all our New Testament texts were written.

L source A scholarly designation for the verses unique to Luke's Gospel such as his infancy and resurrection narratives.

leprosy does not mean just the modern illness (Hansen's Disease) but also other skin problems, e.g., fungal infections, eczema, ringworm, psoriasis. The priest decided whether a skin eruption was leprous. If it progressed, the person was declared ritually "unclean" and could not participate in community worship.

literal sense The meaning that the author intended at the time of writing and that the written words expressed. Determining this meaning is the goal of the historical-critical method of Scripture scholarship. For Scripture scholars, to "take things literally" means to determine what the original author meant.

M source A scholarly designation for the verses unique to Matthew's Gospel such as his infancy and resurrection narratives.

Mammon (Gk: *mamōnas*) A word for earthly good, especially excessive materialism, greed, avarice and unjust worldly gain. Scholars think it comes from an Aramaic root meaning "that in which one trusts." It is also translated in Jewish writings as "resources, gain, compensation" and even "bribe."

method (Gk: a way over) A general and repeatable set of procedures used in order to explain the meaning of texts. The historical-critical method combines historical and literary procedures to determine the original historical situation and the author's originally intended meaning.

mystery In its Catholic theological sense, this identifies a divine reality that so transcends the ability of the human mind that it is impossible to fully comprehend or completely explain it, e.g., the Trinity and the Incarnation.

narrative criticism The scholarly study of biblical texts that focuses on the work as a whole "story" with characteristics that resemble those of other narratives.

New Testament The official collection (canon) of twenty-seven sacred Christian texts that are considered revealed, inspired, inerrant regarding the truths of salvation and authoritative for Christian belief and practice.

Old Testament The collection of sacred texts from the Jewish tradition that have also been included by Christians in their Bible. The number of books varies from thirty-nine (Protestant canon) to forty-six (Catholic canon) because of the inclusion of some books written in Greek for Hellenistic Jews, which were included in the ancient Greek Septuagint translation.

parable (Gk: parabolē, to "throw together" things for comparison or illustration) A short realistic story intended to encourage reflection by connecting the parable to our own life. Since one can connect the parable to various aspects of one's life or that of one's family or community, parables are always open-ended in their application. Parables were a common teaching device of the Jewish rabbis and important to Jesus in his teaching because the only way we have to talk about what is unfamiliar to us (God's ruling presence or "kingdom") is in terms that are familiar to us (our everyday life and world).

parallelism A distinctive characteristic of formal Hebrew speech rooted in their oral tradition, found especially in God's own words as reported by the prophets, poetry (the prologue of John's Gospel) and the psalms (often quoted in the Gospels). It describes the way in which balanced couplets develop a thought by variant repetition, thus leading the mind from one thought to another. Methods of variation include the second line developing the thought of the first by emphasizing either similarity (synonymous parallelism) or difference (antithetic parallelism), or by using such stylistic devices as cause/effect, statement/example, statement/reason, question/answer, if/then, "better than," etc.

Pentecost (Gk: the fiftieth day) A Jewish feast (also called Weeks or *Shavuot*) coming fifty days after Passover that celebrated the spring grain harvest and the offering to God of the firstfruits of the crop (Ex 23:14-17).

pericope (Gk: to cut around) A short section or passage of writing, such as a small division or unit of Scripture taken for reading (e.g., in the *Lectionary for Mass*) or for analysis by scripture scholars.

Pharisees A lay group, not priests, characterized by their zeal for the Jewish law. In Jesus' time, they were influential among the ordinary people because they were living examples of what every Jew was called upon to do.

prophet Those whom God calls (including John the Baptist and Jesus) to speak God's message to the Israelites and their rulers. Their intent was not to foretell the future but to recognize God's presence in current events and to identify the consequences of the ruler's or people's disregard for this presence and message.

proverb A short memorable saying that incorporates the traditional wisdom gained from careful observation of nature and human life. Proverbs were usually expressed in poetic parallelism for greater impact and easier recall.

psalm (Gk: song) A song accompanied by music. The biblical book of Psalms consists of 150 psalms divided into five parts. These songs express the whole spectrum of our human response to God in good and bad times.

Q source (German: *Quelle*, source) A scholarly designation of the collection of materials shared by both Matthew and Luke but not found in Mark.

redaction criticism The scholarly analysis of textual composition to discover how multiple sources were used in the later process of editing (redacting). This type of study is used in particular to analyze carefully the editorial process of the

A BRIEF GLOSSARY OF TERMS FOR GOSPEL STUDY

synoptic Gospels and thus to discover the unique form, content and function of each author and to appreciate each author's unique artistry and theology.

revelation (Lat: to unveil) God's free self-disclosure of the hidden mystery of God's own person and historic plan for human salvation, especially as expressed in the person and ministry of Jesus of Nazareth.

rhetorical criticism The scholarly study of biblical texts in order to understand their persuasive function, in particular how they have been shaped by their authors to bring about their effects on the audience.

sacrifice (Lat: make holy) To set apart something as a gift for God (thus making it "holy") to express one's relationship with God. To show the complete character of the gift, it would be burned (Gk: *holocautōma*, holocaust) so that the giver could not take it back. A sin-offering was a gift that would help to restore the relationship when it was threatened by unintentional rather than deliberate sins.

Sadducees A small religious faction within Judahism drawn from the priestly and higher social classes. Conservative in both politics and religion, they urged peaceful collaboration with the Romans because of their concern for the Temple as the religious and financial center for Judahism.

Sanhedrin (Gk: council) was the official group of Judahist leaders representing various Judean groups in Jerusalem that functioned both as a court to decide cases and to determine disputed points of their religious-civil Law *(Torah)*.

Septuagint (LXX) (Lat: seventy) The Greek translation of the Hebrew Bible done in Egypt beginning about 250 BC. It also included several books written in Greek. It was adopted by early Greek-speaking Christians as their Bible.

social science criticism The scholarly study of biblical texts focusing on the religious, geographical, historical, economic, social codes, and cultural values in the text by utilizing the perspectives, theories, and models of the social sciences.

source criticism The scholarly identification and analysis of the different sources that were used to shape a text, such as the two source theory (Mark and "Q," a collection of Jesus' sayings used by Luke and Matthew but not Mark) for resolving the problem of the relationships between the synoptic Gospels.

structural criticism The scholarly study of biblical texts focusing on recurring patterns of meaning or imagery common to all languages and cultures exemplified in the text itself and disregarding the original author's intended meaning or historical context.

synagogue A meeting place for community prayer and for the study and discussion of the scriptures, especially *Torah*. It was not like the Jerusalem Temple where God dwelt and worship and sacrifices took place. Thus it was not organized and run by priests but by lay people, in particular the elders of the community.

synoptic Gospels (Gk: seen with one glance) The Gospels of Matthew, Mark and Luke. Because of their literary interrelationships and their generally similar structure, they can be put into parallel columns for a closer examination of their similarities and differences.

temple (Lat: *templum*, a consecrated space) A temple was the place where heaven and earth met and served as God's house where gifts (sacrifices) were offered and God was worshipped. The Jerusalem Temple was also a market where sacrificial animals were sold and a bank for the state treasury. Since Roman and Greek coins were stamped with images of their gods and emperors, money changers exchanged these pagan coins for Jewish ones. Christians did not restrict God's presence to a temple but believed that God had come to dwell in Jesus, in Mary and in each Christian through the power of the Holy Spirit.

textual criticism The scholarly study of ancient manuscripts to ascertain the most likely original form of the text and to trace the history of its transmission through variant forms in the available manuscripts.

Torah (Heb: instruction, the Law) The first five books of the Old Testament (Genesis, Exodus, Leviticus, Numbers, Deuteronomy), also called the *Pentateuch* (Gk: five scrolls) and the *Five Books of Moses.*

typology A traditional form of biblical interpretation in which Old Testament persons or events are understood as patterns or models (types) for understanding New Testament persons or events. For example, Matthew considers Moses as the pattern or "type" that can help illuminate the person and work of Jesus as a prophet, community builder and lawgiver.

Vulgate (Lat: crowd, thus, "common") St. Jerome's Latin translation of the Bible from the Hebrew and Greek near the end of the fourth century AD. It remained the official Roman Catholic translation used both for study and for liturgical worship until the twentieth century.

wisdom literature The collection of traditional learning that deals with the mystery of our world and of everyday life. The Jewish tradition sought to merge this secular tradition with their specifically religious beliefs and guidelines *(Torah)* and the Gospels portray Jesus as a teacher of a new kind of wisdom.

Faith Alive Books publishes spiritual and religious books
in print and in eBook formats

faithalivebooks.com is a blog that reviews and recommends
Catholic and spiritual books—
"thoughtful books for thoughtful readers"

eCatechist.com is a blog that offers
ideas, information and resources
for catechists, catechetical leaders and parents

eCatechist.com also presents opportunities
for catechist certification and formation

Subscribe

To receive email notice when new items are posted,
visit and subscribe to *faithalivebooks.com* and *ecatechist.com*

Many dioceses offer catechist certification credit
to catechists who read the books
in *The Catechist's Guide Reading* Series
and complete the Catechist's Learning Page

Catechist's Learning Page

Date

Clock Hours

Signature

Notes

Title of Learning Activity

_____

Author, presenter or Facilitator

_____

Publisher, Event, Sponsor

_____

Main Idea(s)

_____

_____

_____

_____

_____

_____

_____

_____

Ideas that I can apply to my teaching

_____

_____

_____

_____

_____

_____

_____

_____

_____

_____

_____

Other Titles Available from Faith Alive Books publishing

The Catechist Reading Guides Series
by Steve Mueller
Available from Amazon

The Catechist's Guide to Reading Your Bible
A Catholic View (2014)

Who Do You Say That I Am?
The Catechist's Guide to Jesus in the Gospels (2015)

So What's the Good News?
The Catechist's Guide to Reading the Gospels (2016)

You've Got Mail!
The Catechist's Guide to Reading the New Testament Letters (projected 2017)

Reassuring Visions
The Catechist's Guide to Reading John's Book of Revelation (projected 2017)

Other Books
Available from Faith Alive Books in PDF format for download to your computer, iPad, Kindle, etc.

Enjoying God and Teaching Creatively (excerpts)
by Greg Dues

Prayer is a Hunger
by Rev. Edward J. Farrell

Working Smarter, Not Harder: A Catechist's Survival Guide
by Thomas P. Walters and Rita Tyson Walters

Reading Your Bible: The Journey that Will Change Your Life
by Steve Mueller

Discounts are available for bulk orders

For additional information and/or to place an order:
call: 616.956.5044
email: pierson.dj@gmail.com

CPSIA information can be obtained
at www.ICGtesting.com
Printed in the USA
FSOW04n0649310816
24432FS